The Imperial Dryden

The Imperial Dryden

THE POETICS

OF APPROPRIATION IN

SEVENTEENTH-CENTURY ENGLAND

David Bruce Kramer

THE UNIVERSITY OF GEORGIA PRESS

ATHENS AND LONDON

© 1994 by the University of Georgia Press
Athens, Georgia 30602
All rights reserved
Designed by Betty Palmer McDaniel
Set in 10.5 on 13 Fournier
by Tseng Information Systems, Inc.
Printed and bound by Thomson-Shore, Inc.
The paper in this book meets the guidelines for
permanence and durability of the Committee on
Production Guidelines for Book Longevity of the
Council on Library Resources.

Printed in the United States of America
98 97 96 95 94   C   5 4 3 2 1

Library of Congress Cataloging in Publication Data
Kramer, David Bruce.
The imperial Dryden : the poetics of appropriation
in seventeenth-century England / David Bruce Kramer.
p. cm.
Includes bibliographical references (p.   ) and index.
ISBN 0-8203-1543-5 (alk. paper)
1. Dryden, John, 1631–1700—Knowledge—Literature. 2. European
literature—Translations into English—History and criticism.
3. Translating and interpreting—England—History—17th century.
4. Dryden, John, 1631–1700—Knowledge—Europe. 5. European
literature—Appreciation—England. 6. Criticism—Europe—
History—17th century. 7. Influence (Literary, artistic, etc.)
8. English poetry—European influences. 9. Neoclassicism
(Literature)—England. 10. Intertextuality. I. Title.
PR3427.L5K73 1994
821'.4–dc20   92-41755

British Library Cataloging in Publication Data available

For Clara Claiborne Park

CONTENTS

ACKNOWLEDGMENTS

Many have read and commented helpfully upon sections of this work in various states; I acknowledge their aid even as I reserve all error and infelicity for my own: J. Douglas Canfield, Pierre Cintas, Lawrence Danson, Steven Fix, Marc Fumaroli, Paul Holdengraber, George and Portia Kernodle, Richard Kroll, Marie McAlister, Henry Knight Miller, Clara Claiborne Park, Julie Stone Peters, William Bowman Piper, Omar Pound, Steven Shankman, Deborah Shuger, Robert Spoo, Barbara Grace Taylor, Edwin White, John Whittier-Ferguson, James Winn, Jacob Silk, Margot Smit, who helped me begin, and Kay Yandell, who helped me finish. I also acknowledge the helpful reading given the manuscript by my colleague and friend, Brian Wilkie; the friendship and steady encouragement of Margaret Jones Bolsterli; and the aid of Robert Finlay, whose savage delight in extirpating nonsense has sometimes goaded me into doing the right thing.

The English Departments of Princeton University and the University of Arkansas afforded me time and means to conduct my research in Paris and London; Williams College provided me with office space and facilities. To these three institutions—and to their librarians—I register my gratitude.

Part of the book has appeared in different form in *Literary Transmission and Authority: Dryden and Other Authors,* ed. Earl Miner and Jennifer Brady (Cambridge: Cambridge University Press, 1993); I am grateful for permission to reprint this material.

Finally, I acknowledge extraordinary obligations, and affection and gratitude proportionable, to Margaret Anne Doody and Earl Miner.

ABBREVIATIONS

Full citations, where appropriate, will be found in the text.

ECL: Eighteenth-Century Life
Essay: Essay of Dramatick Poesy
Fables: Fables Ancient and Modern
JEGP: Journal of English and Germanic Philology
Johnson's *Life:* Johnson's *Life of Dryden*
JWCI: Journal of the Warburg and Courtauld Institute
Langbaine: Gerard Langbaine, *An Account of the English Dramatick Poets*
MLN: Modern Language Notes
Molière: Molière, *Oeuvres complètes,* ed. Georges Couton, 2 vols.
Oeuvres: Pierre Corneille, *Oeuvres complètes,* ed. Georges Couton, 3 vols.
PQ: Philological Quarterly
Poems: The Poems of John Dryden, ed. James Kinsley, 4 vols.
La Pratique: Hédelin d'Aubignac, *La Pratique du théâtre*
Rapin: René Rapin, *Réflexions sur la poétique de ce temps. . . .*
RES: Review of English Studies
RLC: Revue de littérature comparée
Scott: *The Works of John Dryden,* ed. Sir Walter Scott, 18 vols.
SEL: Studies in English Literature, 1500–1900
Sources: Ned Bliss Allen, *The Sources of John Dryden's Comedies*
Théâtre: Jean Racine, *Théâtre,* ed. Raymond Picard
Watson: John Dryden, *Of Dramatic Poesy and Other Critical Essays,* ed. George Watson, 2 vols.
Whole Art: Hédelin d'Aubignac, *The Whole Art of the Stage* [anonymous trans.]
Works: the California edition of *The Works of John Dryden,* ed. Edward N. Hooker, H. T. Swedenberg, Jr., et al., 20 vols.

INTRODUCTION

This work began in the simple observation that Dryden's criticism contains many misquotations and misstatements of fact. With a scholar's somewhat unsympathetic zeal for cataloging the errors of others, I determined to find and classify all such mythic entities as a Shakespeare who invented blank verse ("to shun the pains of continual Rhyming"), a "Tragedy of *Queen* Gorboduc," or ascriptions of opinions they never expressed to such as Aristotle or Corneille. In Dryden's criticism I reaped a rich harvest of literary-historical confusion, but as I cataloged the poet's misquotations and factual errors, I realized that to construct a typology of error was actually to reconstruct an account of Dryden's engagement with his contemporaries and predecessors. My interest shifted from what Dryden mistook to what and how he took. And, like the nobleman of Dryden's preface to *Fables* "who beginning with a Dog-kennil, never liv'd to finish the Palace he had contriv'd," this work's scope kept expanding as I followed Dryden across a writing career of more than forty years, and as I tried to look over his shoulder while he read and absorbed the works of poets and critics writing in English, French, Italian, Latin, Greek, and Spanish. Beginning in a hunt for error, I have ended with the discovery that the pattern of getting things wrong in the poet's early work bespeaks a greater and more interesting pattern of trying to get things right.

Dryden engaged with, and maintained strong views on, what to moderns seems an extraordinary number of major European writers. In the classics he ranged from Homer and Sappho through the Greek playwrights to the Roman writers of drama, epic, lyric, satire, criticism, history, and prose fiction. He read, wrote about, and often adapted or translated the works of Italians, Spaniards, and, of course, English. Dante, Boccaccio, Ariosto; Cervantes, Lope de Vega, Calderón; Chaucer, Shakespeare, Jonson, Beaumont and Fletcher, Spenser, Milton, and a host of lesser-known poets in most of the major languages of western Europe form the

I

textual ground from which Dryden's work springs. Moreover, in spite of his oft-avowed detestation of French culture and manners, Dryden's knowledge of their drama and criticism was extensive, detailed, and up-to-the-minute over a forty-year span; he read, took from, or was influenced by Pierre and Thomas Corneille, Racine, Molière, Georges and Madeleine de Scudéry, Quinault, La Calprenède, and he referred to such literary figures as St. Evremond, Boileau, Segrais, Bossu, Dacier, Rapin, l'Abbé d'Aubignac, du Bartas, Descartes, Fontenelle, Malherbe, and Perrault; toward the end of his career he even started referring to French writers with admiration. Dryden kept insisting upon his Englishness, but as we see from the list of those in whom he showed interest, his scope was decidedly European.

Accordingly, to write a history of Dryden's relations with other writers is to consider the canon of western Europe as it evolved in the late seventeenth century; it is to consider the effect of circumstance on literary consciousness, tracing the effect of dynastic shifts and national revolutions as they are reflected in poetic alliances and ruptures; it is to consider how a great poetic sensibility, the first, in W. J. Bate's view, to labor under "the burden of the past," came to define itself in concert with, and in opposition to, shifting groups of writers and schools; and it is to consider, finally, how poets' relations with predecessors can modulate from agonistic struggle into uneasy but productive truce. Tracking Dryden through this intertextual maze has led from examining the ideological content of the neo-Aristotelian unities to poetic phallicism, from imperial conquest to poetic androgyny, from examining issues of royal succession and usurpation to scrutinizing with careful eye Dryden's quotations and misquotations, his occasional plagiarisms, and his accounts of his actions as he quoted, misquoted, and stole. Dryden's relations with forebears were convoluted and complex; describing them requires a narrative of at least equal convolution and complexity.

Any account of a self's interaction with others (even in the more rarefied ontological realm of poetic self and poetic other) places the subject in a larger web of textual and personal relations, and so inevitably crosses over into biography; in the present case this is particularly so. How Dryden uses others' poetry reflects

2

His move from 'proud imperialist' to 'defeated translator'
D's early imitation of Corneille's devious ways with his forbears.
Totalitarian / monolithic 'official' line on French neoclassicism

Introduction

his own development as a poet, and the poet's evolution from
covert borrower to proud imperialist to defeated translator closely   *?*
reflects the spectacular parabolic curve described by his own fortunes, which rapidly ascended from ambitious obscurity to poetic
and social eminence as Poet Laureate—and even more suddenly
plummeted to defeat, the poet's serene misery aggravated by ad-   *?*
vancing age and declining health.

Early sections of the present work examine the circuitous
paths that the young poet, anxious and ambitious, cut for himself
through the thicket of great writers who preceded him. Dryden,
who required patterns after which to model his drama, also needed
a plausible means to deny such influence. Pierre Corneille provided both. Obtaining and carefully studying Corneille's complete
1660 edition, Dryden grasped Corneille's stratagem of reshaping
the past to revise the present, and as Dryden developed dramatic
forms peculiar to himself and to England, he employed the elder
poet's subversive technique against his own oeuvre. Hence, any
attempt to explain the Machiavellian ingenuity of Dryden's early
uses of predecessor poets and critics must begin by examining
Corneille's own use of his predecessors, for Corneille, France's
greatest playwright-critic (just as Dryden aimed to be England's),
developed to a consummate art the trick of simultaneously adher-
ing to and undercutting literary authority. Thus, my account of
Dryden's relations with other poets and critics begins in France in
the 1630s—around the time of Dryden's birth—with Pierre Corneille's dealings with poets and critics, and his coming to terms
with a system of dramatic structure that we, for short, call neoclassicism.

Neoclassicism, as it was instituted in France in the 1630s, was
the literary instrument of a state bent on centralizing and con-
solidating its authority. As we know from observing totalitarian
societies closer to us, writers whose productions are scrutinized
by the state, and for whom a too-strongly worded expression can
result in ruin, develop meticulously coded methods of writing.
Reading the work of such writers requires a knowledge of the
official systems and expectations, for it is in the slight discrepancy
between ideal form and its present enactment, in the carefully
staged moral ambiguities in works purporting to express uncriti-

3

Corneille's strategic ventriloquism — to create spurious antique authority for his own views. D's imitation of this technique

THE IMPERIAL DRYDEN

cal and total obedience, in the abstract discussions of the proper objects of imitation and the methods by which those objects will be imitated, that we discover evasion and subversion.

Corneille circumvented some of the rigidities of French neo-classical formal prescriptions by developing and refining a strategy that Dryden later used against Corneille himself, that of "misquotation." I employ the term in a wider sense than is customary, using it to denote the strategy of inventing another's words so that one's own thoughts seem to emerge from the other's mouth—a ventriloquism of voice in which language is projected backward through time, to speak as if from the past and from the dead. By this means, past literary authorities are transformed from articulating subjects into silent objects, masks from which the misquoter's own eyes peep, the misquoter's own voice sounds. By misquoting, the writer overwrites the past, causing what never happened to supplant what did. The misquoter creates fictitious histories, and claims to derive present practices from those of great predecessors who, in fact, never practiced what the misquoter ascribes to them. Such were the ways that Dryden used misquotation, creating great figures of the past from whom he claimed poetic descent, figures who, in Dryden's accounts, said and wrote whatever it was convenient for them to have said and written. This strategy he learned from and used against Pierre Corneille, who himself devised it to work free from a system that privileged the utterances of the greater dead.

Misquotation, as practiced by Dryden, is a young person's stratagem, appealing to those who lack authority but who believe in the systems that confer it, those whose present is bounded by a past exerting its power of mortmain. As Dryden grew in poetic stature and strength, he found other ways besides misquotation to come to terms with poets and critics whose work impressed him. He learned that what he needed from others, particularly French writers of secondary stature, he could simply take, in public, boldly, without apology, in acts of poetic depredation that he called "victory." Dryden also availed himself of the work of others without acknowledgment, a practice that did not escape the unfavorable notice of his contemporaries.

Misquotation, poetic imperialism (what Dryden called "vic-

4

tory"), and plagiarism are all aggressive—and, in Dryden's view, masculine—modes of acquiring the poetic or critical goods of others. After 1688, however, with Dryden's own displacement in the related realms of society, politics, poetry, and gender, came a shift in his approach to other great poets and critics, as well as a shift in the way he represented himself. He began to treat the personae and works of predecessors with far greater respect, if not trepidation, as he began to represent himself as a diminished and altered figure. Like Tiresias, his poetic persona changes from male to female and back again; rather than seeking to seize all poetry for himself, he expresses the wish to be seized, entered into, impregnated by the spirits of his great predecessors. Formerly boasting of his poetic aggressiveness, he now vaunts the degree to which he submerges his own identity as he makes of himself a conduit for the spirits of the dead. Dryden's rhetoric of defeat is, not coincidentally, the rhetoric of the great translator.

The aim of this work is to show how a great poet uses others' poetry not to copy, but to improve; not to save himself the trouble of making, but to make anew. Dryden's adaptations of foreign writing are, in his own memorable phrase, "like the Hulk of *Sir Francis Drake,* so strangely alter'd, that there scarce remain'd any Plank of the Timber which first built it," and his career culminates in a complex synthesis of personal defeat, poetic consolidation, and integration with the personae and works of past poets through the agency of translation. Learning to incorporate more and more into his poetic body, finally, at the end of a long and prolific career, he is able to look back on a whole civilization's history in poetry, and see that much of that poetry, "so strangely alter'd," now speaks in the voice of Dryden.

Apologists for the well-ordered state have always banished unruly poets, desiring them, as Socrates did, either to praise the gods and famous men, or leave. Yet a safer and surer stratagem for dealing with autonomous poets, neutralizing their propensity for subversion rather than according them the privileged status of outlaw, is to absorb them in such a way that their analyses of societal dysfunction come to be regarded as officially sanctioned. Such has been the fate of Pierre Corneille, who is now unjustly slighted for

Corneille more devious/subversive than received opinion would have it. Not simply a literary Richelieu

THE IMPERIAL DRYDEN

the same reason he was once unjustly honored—the perception that he is an apologist for an all-powerful Catholic state. By a perverse enactment of the sanitizing function Roland Barthes refers to as "inoculation,"[1] Corneille has come to be viewed in France as a kind of literary double of Cardinal Richelieu. Popularly regarded as a pious Catholic, staunch monarchist, defender of the faith and state, Corneille is viewed first and foremost as the creator of French "classics," works that are dull by virtue of their very nomenclature, works that serve power as it is constituted. By pairing the names of Corneille and Richelieu, French literary history has long suggested a partnership between the pen and the state, forming a spurious iconography neatly expressed on a recent one-hundred-franc note, from which the visages of Corneille and Richelieu glower dourly from obverse and reverse. Thus France assimilated Corneille's searching examination of the power of the state—by making him the state's official poet.

I here propose to return to an earlier Corneille, a figure untainted by government approval, the poet against whom an official campaign was instigated, the cultural critic who asked searching questions about the limits of political and literary authority. For this subtle, ingenious, and dangerous figure is the Corneille that Dryden knew almost by heart, read carefully, had by his side as he wrote the *Essay of Dramatick Poesy,* regarded, along with Shakespeare, as his greatest poetic influence, his greatest poetic threat. It is this Corneille, as Dryden so clearly saw, who can be invoked on both sides of an argument concerning the rules, and who must be taken seriously by all sides of such a debate.

Corneille early began supplying his plays with prefaces, often polemical, that concern some facet of the writing or reception of the present or a former play. Beginning in 1648 Corneille also attached prefaces to individual volumes of his collected works that attempted to bring together the main threads of his work. Finally, coinciding with the resumption of dramatic writing after an eight-year hiatus, he released his monumental edition of 1660, which contains the body of criticism for which he was then, and is today, so justly famed. Each of the twenty-three plays is prefaced by an examen, each of the three volumes is preceded by a substantial discours. This body of criticism considers his plays individually, and in defending or condemning them on particular points, tacitly im-

His 1660 collected criticism: C. now free to declare his position openly.
His asserted right to interpret his predecessors firmly.

Introduction

plicates other plays and silently responds to the positions of other critics. The criticism of 1660 attempts to synthesize what precedes it and includes many pointed rejoinders to specific points argued by the Abbé d'Aubignac's *La Pratique du théâtre,* which had appeared just three years earlier.

Corneille's criticism of 1660, composed of the three discours and the twenty-three examens, does not employ the kind of encoded refusal to submit to formal norms that such plays as *l'Illusion Comique* (1635) and *Horace* (1639) contained, for the principal reason that Corneille can now be open about what he wishes to argue. That which was hidden is now made manifest, and now that it can be manifested, it is to some degree tempered, owing to several important shifts in Corneille's position relative to the political and literary situation of 1660. Richelieu died in 1642, and Corneille was admitted into the ranks of les immortels of the Académie Française in 1647. He was universally recognized as France's greatest playwright (Racine was not to begin his career for another four years), and though Corneille's dramatic career had its failures as well as its successes, in 1660 he was acknowledged, even by his detractors, to be chief among French dramatists.[2] For this reason much of what had to be hidden earlier—his deep skepticism and resentment of literary authority, his unwillingness to follow the "rules," his arrogation of literary authority to himself—could all be declared openly, with this obvious difference: that in 1660 Corneille himself personified literary authority. No greater playwright existed; he was a member of the Académie and spoke with its authority; he was a favorite of the most powerful men in France, including Louis XIV, Mazarin, and Superintendent Fouquet.

Corneille's criticism of 1660 refers only to a restricted group of texts: Aristotle's *Poetics,* Horace's *Ad Pisos,* the ancient Greek and Roman dramatists, and Corneille's own drama.[3] Readers have remarked that Corneille's limited scope gives the *Discours* a sense of being all and only about Corneille, and to the extent to which writing is always only about its author, they are correct. By limiting the *Discours* to himself and the ancients, Corneille stages for the reader a direct relationship between himself, as creator and creative authority, and his great forebears, as creators and poetic legislators. In a kind of literary protestantism, Corneille tacitly asserts his right to read and interpret the ancients for himself, and in

7

asserting this right he eliminates the multiple layers of scholarship that clutter the space between his own endeavor and the ancients. In the direct contact between the fully engaged playwright-critic and his respected colleagues of the past, Aristotle, Horace, and Sophocles, Corneille takes control of his craft from the hands of those contemporary critics and pedants who would dictate to him. He marks out his own positions in consultation, so to speak, with his illustrious predecessors; he suggests that between himself and the ancients are neither intermediaries nor equals.

That Corneille mentions no intermediaries, however, does not mean that his staged dialogue with Aristotle does not subsume, without naming it, the intervening French neoclassical dramatic criticism. Corneille considers the major positions of his contemporaries as he speaks to Aristotle and Horace; he includes his contemporaries as an interested audience in the debate, and without explicitly identifying either critics, plays, or playwrights, he undermines, discards, and suggests replacements for many commonly held critical axioms.

Corneille's approach to Aristotle, his principal interlocutor in the *Discours,* is rhetorically complex, shaped on all sides by Corneille's several ends. He is not interested in overthrowing the name of Aristotle as an authority; on the contrary, he does all in his power to affirm the quality and permanence of Aristotle's contribution to criticism. But Corneille, whose professional training was in the law, approaches Aristotle like a lawyer approaching a contract he intends to break. Using a range of rhetorical and logical strategies, Corneille empties Aristotle of much of his content, and replaces the received Aristotle with a more congenial figure whose dicta he can affirm. This obliteration, and subsequent reconstitution, is characteristic of such a powerful reader as Corneille, trained in the law, in the theater, and in the world of literary politics; such a gesture is the literary equivalent of the most diplomatic form of usurpation: allowing the displaced figure to keep the name and attributes of power, displaying the displaced figure on ceremonial occasions with all his pomp, asserting his power and glory—and speaking in his name. Corneille's relation to Aristotle is an example of this form of "friendly" usurpation, for he exalts Aristotle while erasing him, guts and remodels the complicated edifice of neoclassical doctrine while praising the ingenuity of its

His 'dialogue' with Aristotle actually a mask for strategic 'appropriation'.

putative creator. Corneille reconstructs Aristotle, and only when Aristotle has been remade as Corneille needs him does Corneille cite him as an authority.

By first vitiating, then reconstituting, a prior authority such as Aristotle, Corneille appears to engage in dialogue with a predecessor; he purports to return to the source of all rules, to engage in a meeting of minds, which results in understandings that serve Corneille's own poetic needs. Corneille's stratagem, however, goes deeper than this seemingly generous exchange of confidences with his respected predecessor, for what appears to be dialogue is actually a monologue staged between Corneille and a fictional persona Corneille refers to as "Aristotle." Because Corneille is a dramatist, he (like Dryden soon after in *Essay of Dramatick Poesy*) does not make his victory over Aristotle too lopsided; the conversation appears to be between minds of equal strength. Theorems are proposed by one, beaten back by the other; one's tentative sallies are overcome by the other's crushing rejoinder. This battle of the minds is stirring reading and, written by the time's great dramatist, the *Discours* must be read dialogically, as drama. The voice of Corneille is a Corneille-speaker, just as the voice of Aristotle, as reconstituted by Corneille, must be read as a qualified Corneille-speaker.

Only when Corneille's larger purpose for the *Discours* is understood can all this become clear. Returning to his critical origins and usurping their power of speech, he rewrites his own literary history, providing himself with a predecessor with whom he admits tension, but to whom he accords ultimate respect and obedience. This staging of the relation between critic and forebear, poet and acknowledged authority, is perhaps Corneille's most characteristic stratagem for transforming the structures that work against him into other similar-seeming but fundamentally different structures that now work for him. By seizing control of Aristotle, by making him his own creature, Corneille creates what seems to be a dialogue with what seems to be the great authority of what seems to be the past; he can seem to generate new rules from a seeming conversation between himself and a seeming other. And by means of these newly generated rules, he can regain control of that which, ever since the *querelle du Cid* (1637), he had been ignominiously stripped: his authority to create the sort of drama he wanted.

9

Corneille's methods of appropriation are precise, logical, law-yerly. He subjects Aristotle's terms to analysis, finds them impre-cise, and replaces them with what he claims to think Aristotle must have meant. Accordingly, the first *Discours,* entitled *Discours de l'Utilité et des Parties du Poème Dramatique,* begins by arguing the necessity of clarifying commonly used critical terms:

> We agree on the name without agreeing on the thing, and we accord on the words in order to argue about their meaning. . . . The poet must treat his subject according to the probable and the necessary; Aristotle says it, and all his interpreters re-peat the same words, which to them seem so clear and intelli-gible that no one of them has deigned to inform us, any more than he did, what is meant by this probability and necessity.
>
> *(Oeuvres,* 3:117)[4]

Indeed, all through the criticism of 1660, Corneille's first gesture on approaching any large issue is to attack the imprecision of the general terms, and then to define them as he wishes.

> I can't help but say that this definition does not satisfy me at all.
>
> *(Oeuvres,* 3:123)[5]

> These terms are so general that they seem to mean nothing.
>
> *(Oeuvres,* 3:128)[6]

> These are terms that he has explained so little that he leaves us much room to question his meaning.
>
> *(Oeuvres,* 3:129)[7]

> If I may be permitted to speak my conjectures on what Aris-totle asks us by that.
>
> *(Oeuvres,* 3:129)[8]

> To embolden myself to change this term, in order to remove the difficulty.
>
> *(Oeuvres,* 3:135)[9]

> He often repeats these last words and never explains them. I shall try to supply this explanation as best I can.
>
> *(Oeuvres,* 3:161)[10]

The distinctively Cornelian notion of 'vraisemblance'

Selectively stripping Aristotle of key terms and replacing these terms with definitions constituted as Corneille wishes, he empties the name of Aristotle and refills it as a persona of Corneille. The reconstituted Aristotle, Corneille peering slyly from the eyeholes of a mask called Aristotle, is then able to work toward what is always the high ground of any dispute in neoclassical dramatic theory, the meaning and importance of probability. Besieging Aristotle's *Poetics* outside the text while usurping its power to defend itself from within, Corneille seizes this high ground to formulate and articulate a use of probability unique for the period.

In order to place the audacity of Corneille's attack on probability in perspective, we must bear in mind the primacy accorded the category of vraisemblance by Corneille's contemporaries. Here follow the views of Rapin, Chapelain, and the Abbé d'Aubignac on its importance:

The *Probable* is whatever suits with Common Opinion.

(Rapin)[11]

The one aim of probability is to take from the viewers all occasions of reflecting on what they see and of doubting its reality.

("Chapelain à Godeau," Adam, 224)[12]

There is nothing therefore but *Probability,* that can truly found a Dramatick Poem, as well as adorn and finish it.

(*Whole Art,* 1:75)[13]

These are representative opinions; from them we may infer that to attack the centrality of probability was to attack the system of poetics as it was then constituted. The radical nature of Corneille's departure from the bases of neoclassic poetics should now be evident, for he begins the *Discours de l'Utilité et des Parties du Poème Dramatique* by questioning the necessity of maintaining vraisemblance:

The great subjects that strongly stir the passions, and that oppose impetuosity to the laws of duty, or to the tendernesses of the blood, must always go beyond the probable.

(*Oeuvres,* 3:118)[14]

Corneille's devious strategies for admitting 'the improbable' as acceptable subject-matter for modern tragedy, and claiming Aristotle's support for his views!

Or, put more simply:

A beautiful tragedy's subject must never be probable.
(Examen to *Heraclius, Oeuvres,* 2:357)[15]

Corneille's reasoning, again, is orderly, logical, and plausible: the subjects of tragedies that most move, according to Aristotle, are those in which the tragic action is inflicted by family members or close friends upon one another. However, intrafamilial murder is never probable; it is not probable that Medea should slit the throats of her children, that Orestes should knife his mother. "Mais," writes Corneille, "l'histoire le dit," and Corneille appeals to the authority of history, a kind of preeminent arbiter of what is true; because whatever did happen perforce can happen, we are obliged to believe these improbable truths:[16] "The action being true, there is no need to find out whether it is probable, being certain that all truths are admissible in poetry."[17] That, Corneille argues, is why Aristotle says that the tragedians restricted themselves to writing about so few families—few families are unlucky enough to contain such events. Fortunately, Corneille finds, the intervening millennia have provided other instances of historical improbabilities from which to fashion a good tragedy, and the moderns are not so restricted as were the ancient Greeks and Romans. Corneille's strictures concerning the improbable subject, however, are firm: it must be grounded in history or fable; the poet is not licensed to invent the improbable.

Employing the Aristotelian category of the necessary, Corneille devises an "authorized" means to introduce the improbable into French neoclassic drama. In his unmediated, canny, and consummately interested reading of Aristotle, Corneille finds that Aristotle often presents an either/or dichotomy between the probable and necessary:

It is not the function of the poet to relate what has happened, but what may happen,—what is possible according to the law of probability or necessity.
(*Poetics,* 35)[18]

Corneille calls the choice between the probable and the necessary a freedom conferred upon the poet by Aristotle. And here, where it suits his purposes, Corneille elevates Aristotle to the status of

'The necessary' now posited as the principal criterion for drama. The unities of time and place used to justify 'improbability'.

Introduction

absolute lawgiver, calling on the reconstituted Aristotle for absolute justification, just as at other times he makes Aristotle "the other," and denies his authority to legislate on selected topics.[19]

Hence the new category of the necessary: Corneille claims that Aristotle grants the poet freedom to choose the necessary *instead* of the probable; the poet may show what had to happen, given the circumstances he finds in history. Corneille devises one more way for "the necessary" to decouple the drama from the probable: the dramatist may depict what had to happen for historical events to occur in one day (as occurs in *Le Cid*). Using Aristotle's terms to construct a wholly novel category of action, Corneille flatly contradicts d'Aubignac's doctrine, which was that the poet must alter history until a correct play is produced. We might imagine how d'Aubignac and the academicians writhed at Corneille's introduction of the category of the necessary, a category that preceded what (for everyone but Corneille) was the primary foundation of the drama, probability.

In a final assault on the notion of probability, Corneille turns the very terms of French neoclassic criticism against themselves; the unities of time and place are used not to support probability, as Chapelain and so many others had argued, but to evade it. Although from the beginning of his career Corneille had fought, and when he could no longer fight, had murmured, against these two rules, by the time of the three *Discours*, he found a new use for them: to justify the use of improbability in the execution of plots. By making the observance of the unities nonnegotiable, he creates for himself, using Aristotle's distinction between the necessary and the probable, the license, or in his own word, the "liberté," to do whatever necessary to make all the incidents fit into one short time and one small space. Thus Corneille barters the subsidiary rules of the unities of time and place for a means to subvert the archrule, the imperative of probability. In the following quotation from the second *Discours*, Corneille is frank about his demotion of the vraisemblable to an optional superfluity:

> This last passage shows that we are not obliged to set aside truth to give a better form to the actions of tragedy by ornaments of probability.
>
> (*Discourse on Tragedy, Dramatic Essays,* 23)[20]

C's conscripting of Aristotle into his own argument for the primacy of pleasure, and for a deterrent conception of catharsis.

THE IMPERIAL DRYDEN

Besides devaluing the hitherto sacrosanct notion of probability, Corneille also attacks the other axiom of orthodox French neo-classic theorists: that the aim of drama is to instruct, to be useful, to aid the state. Throughout his career Corneille asserts that drama has but one aim, which is to please. On this issue he recurs to the authority of the reconstituted Aristotle, observing that nowhere in the *Poetics* is the notion of the *utile* discussed.

> If I were of those who hold that the aim of poetry is to profit as well as to please . . . but for me who hold with Aristotle and Horace that our art has no end but entertainment. . . .
>
> (*Epître, Suite du Menteur, Oeuvres,* 2:95)[21]

He argues, however, that poetry cannot please except by follow-ing the rules of art and, because parts of the audience, notably old men, are not pleased by a drama unless they discern the morally useful, he concludes that pleasing with dramatic poetry includes both the rules (in some to-be-determined form) and the utile. The three kinds of poetic utility, according to Corneille, are (1) sen-tentious wisdom, (2) the correct depiction of vice and virtue (in-dependent of plot outcome, or the meting out of "poetic justice"), and (3) catharsis.

Corneille's notion of catharsis, as we might expect, is highly individual and constitutes his greatest theoretical contribution to-ward the notion of poetic utility. He holds, first, that Aristotle's ac-count of catharsis is "imaginaire," only "a beautiful idea that never worked in real life."[22] A more efficacious type of catharsis (de-rived by redefining Aristotle's terms) is that we see what befalls those who are like us, and out of fear (not pity) purge ourselves of whichever passion brought about their misfortune. Corneille finds that this deterrent mode of catharsis abounds in his own dra-mas, and his practical application of Aristotle's mysterious notion is shockingly simple: we are purged of our pride by the misfor-tune that befalls the proud Count in *Le Cid;* Cleopatra's grotesque end in *Rodogune* rids us of the desire to retain our children's birth-right.[23] Corneille makes catharsis into the mechanism of a slightly more cerebral poetic justice, but no more. Again, a reconstituted Aristotle is made to approve of the dramas of Corneille.

Corneille is wonderfully agile at transferring the demands of

Corneille's Travesty-appropriation of his predecessors, to assert his own views. Dryden's adaptation of Corneille's strategy — even against Corneille himself!

Introduction

others into secret sources of strength; authorities and forebears, ranging from Aristotle to Richelieu, are recast from antagonists into friends, from would-be tyrants to appreciative spectators. Using various permutations of the stratagem of misquotation, Corneille attains mastery over the rules and rulers of his craft and by these means transforms himself from an impotent subject in a tyranny of letters to the fashioner of his own poetics. Corneille created no school of poet-legislators; the tide was all against him. The next wave of poetic greatness was Racine's, whose glory it was to desire no slackening of the rules. The true inheritor of this curious magician's mantle was not French, but English. It was Dryden who needed techniques such as these to free himself from the demands of both contemporary and forebear. In chapter 1 I show his adaptation of these evasive, subversive, and analytical maneuvers, and detail their various uses, including the turning of these defensive, aggressive, and analytical stratagems against their very maker, Corneille.

CHAPTER ONE

Dryden and the French: Misquotation

Strong were our Syres; and as they Fought they Writ,
Conqu'ring with force of Arms, and dint of Wit;
Theirs was the Gyant Race, before the Flood.

To my Dear Friend Mr. Congreve

Strong indeed were Dryden's poetic sires, and only by dint of his own wit did he escape being crushed by the force of theirs. Yet competing with Shakespeare and Corneille, the two strong sires of Dryden's past and present age, forced him to develop a range of self-definitional, adaptive, and appropriative strategies. These strategies are often subtle and complex; though Dryden claims for himself, and other naive critics claim for him, a simple model of emulation and aversion, Dryden keeps finding different answers to the creative dilemma that has plagued every artist after God, to wit: how to make something new from something old? Dryden's response to the dilemma of creating novelties when all is old (and worse: French) is complicated by his awareness that he stands at the threshold of a new age in which new manners, language, and poetic forms separate him from the great but rude antediluvian English tradition.[1] The formal and stylistic demands of the new age, however, do not obviate the need to remain grounded (at least nominally) in the great English dramatic tradition of Shakespeare and Jonson. This tension between what is owed the past and what is demanded by the present leads Dryden to such practical and critical questions as, how write more "freely" and "politely," yet keep the vigor of the English tradition? How deal with the French, creators and legislators of the new dramatic style? How create a new and authentically English drama and criticism at a

Dryden and the French

time when all the great contemporary dramatists and critics are French? Dryden addresses these questions by creating new forms from old models, invoking the authority of example as he usurps it, borrowing secretly when he must, openly when he can, and transforming his dramatic and critical inheritance without appearing to break with the English dramatists of the last great age.

In the thirty years preceding the Restoration, during eighteen of which the English theaters were closed, the French had experienced an unprecedented flowering of the drama and dramatic criticism. At the time of the Restoration, Corneille's *Cid* and *Horace* were already twenty-five years old, Molière had just begun the Parisian career that would make him the most adapted Frenchman in England, and the great statement of French neoclassic criticism, the Abbé d'Aubignac's *La Pratique du théâtre* (1657), had recently appeared. Soon after the English Restoration, Molière, Racine, and such influential critics as Boileau, Rapin, le Bossu, and Dacier all participated in a second flowering of seventeenth-century French drama and letters. In retrospect, it is hardly surprising that with the reopening of the theaters this "new" French aesthetic should have rushed into the dramatically barren England bearing all the force with which nature abhors a vacuum.[2]

In the early years of the Restoration the relative accomplishments of the two national theaters were only too evident to English readers acquainted with the French dramatic milieu. To the finely structured and unified serious dramas of Corneille, the English could offer as competition only the spirited but rather tatty heroic drama of Davenant and Orrery; to the marvelously clever, polished, and biting comedies of Molière, the English could only offer revivals of Ben Jonson, whose comedies of humour now seemed "rude and mechanick" in this new, politer age. Dryden's pro-French disputant Lisideius, in the *Essay of Dramatick Poesy,* grounds in recent history his explanation for the disparity in quality between the two theaters: "We have been so long together bad *Englishmen,* that we had not leisure to be good Poets. . . . The Muses, who ever follow Peace, went to plant in another Countrey; it was then that the great Cardinal of *Richelieu* began to take them into his protection; and that, by his encouragement, *Corneille* and some other *Frenchmen* reform'd their Theatre (which before was

17

as much below ours as it now surpasses it and the rest of *Europe*)"
(*Works*, 17:33–34). Dryden grounds the decline in the English
stage in recent history, but the account is partial, at best. The reformation of the French theater was essentially complete by the
outbreak of the English wars, and Cardinal Richelieu (1585–1642)
had died before the English stages were closed. This historically
grounded explanation of French poetic superiority is acceptable—
or at least not a matter of dispute—to the pro-English spokes-
men Eugenius and Neander, as its basis in social unrest, however
tenuous, taxes the malignity of the Puritans without impugning
the native genius of English playwrights. The passage illustrates
the manner in which Dryden's understanding of the applications
and power of historical example is essentially rhetorical.

Readers who consider Dryden's criticism and drama out of
the context of other contemporary works cannot appreciate the
extent to which he was influenced by French developments in
poetry, drama, and criticism, for Dryden almost always denies the
French influence, even when that influence is obvious. Moreover,
his denials are often most strenuous, and his acknowledgments of
debt least forthcoming, in direct proportion to the extent of the
poetic obligation. Thus, for example, Molière is never mentioned
in *Sir Martin Mar-all* (1667), the Dryden/Newcastle adaptation of
Molière's first published play, *L'Étourdi* (1658). Corneille's presence is unremarked upon in Dryden's sole martyr play, *Tyrannick
Love* (1669), so clearly modeled on Corneille's two martyr plays,
Polyeucte (1642) and *Théodore, Vierge et Martyre* (1645).[3] Racine is
not invoked as the patron saint of *All for Love* (1677), nor as inspiration for Dryden's "correction" of the end of his adaptation
of Shakespeare's *Troilus and Cressida* (1679).[4] Molière is not mentioned in the preface to *An Evening's Love* (1668), where whole
scenes from *Le Dépit Amoureux* and *Les Précieuses Ridicules* appear
translated verbatim, nor is Madeleine de Scudéry acknowledged
to be the author of the serious plot of *Marriage A-la-Mode* (1671),
a play that ridicules the French influence on English language
and letters. Corneille is not mentioned as the model for Dryden's
early dramatic prefaces; the preface to *Secret Love* (1667) replicates
the Cornelian examen form almost exactly without mentioning
Dryden's model.[5] Corneille's examen form and critical language
are imported whole into the *Essay of Dramatick Poesy*, where they

Dryden's extensive indebtedness to French drama, as recognised by Langbaine, Buckingham, etc.

Dryden and the French

are not acknowledged to be Corneille's, and Dryden translates Corneille into the *Essay* verbatim without comment.[6] Moreover, Dryden often denies that he has been influenced even as he boasts of surpassing the very writers by whom he claims not to be influenced in the very forms they are credited with originating. The preface to the *Conquest of Granada* (1670) contains an egregious example of his dual claims to be untainted by those with whom he competes: "I shall never subject my characters to the *French* standard; where Love and Honour are to be weigh'd by drams and scruples. Yet, where I have design'd the patterns of exact vertue, such as in this Play are the Parts of *Almahide*, of *Ozmyn*, and *Benzayda*, I may safely challenge the best of theirs" (*Works*, 11:16). Especially throughout his early career, Dryden takes pains to allow the French literary tradition little or no merit as he adapts, imitates, borrows, and occasionally steals whatever he needs from French writers.

Three hundred years of source hunting has only refined our knowledge of how many of Dryden's sources, models, and inspirations are French, and many serious readers of Dryden's work have examined his relation to the French dramatic and critical tradition.[7] Beginning in Dryden's own lifetime, critics began totting up the extent of his borrowings from the French; Gerard Langbaine's stinging account of Dryden's sources in *An Account of the English Dramatick Poets* (1691) is only the best known and most extensive of the many contemporary accusations of literary theft made against Dryden, and though Langbaine was the most erudite and dogged of Dryden's seventeenth-century source detectives, others abound. Dryden's reputation as a plagiary was such that *The Rehearsal*'s ill-natured but comical jesting concerning his manner of acquiring plots and speeches, though not specifically referring to robbing the French, did not seem wholly improbable:

> *Bayes.* And I do here averr, That no man yet the Sun e'er shone upon, has parts sufficient to furnish out a Stage, except it were by the help of these my Rules.
> *Johnson.* What are those Rules, I pray?
> *Bayes.* Why, Sir, my first Rule is the Rule of Transversion, or *Regula Duplex:* changing Verse into Prose, or Prose into Verse, *alternative* as you please. . . . I take a book in my

His need to steer between apparent excessive indebtedness to (i) earlier English (ii) French drama.

THE IMPERIAL DRYDEN

hand, either at home or elsewhere, for that's all one, if there be any Wit in't, as there is no book but has some, I Transverse it; that is, if it be Prose put it into Verse, (but that takes up some time) and if it be Verse, put it into Prose.

(*The Rehearsal,* Act 1, Scene 1)[8]

In an age growing gradually aware of the limits and prerogatives of literary authorship—and hence, ownership—"transversing" and "transprosing" as appropriative strategies could no longer pass without comment, as they had in Shakespeare's day.

With the restoration of the monarchy, playwrights were again free to transverse and transprose, yet the reopening of the theaters presented a new set of problems for the aspiring playwrights it had freed to write. Though Dryden, for reasons to be discussed, could not write in the manner of his English predecessors, Jonson, Shakespeare, and Beaumont and Fletcher, neither could he admit to copy "servilely" (his favored adverb for too-close imitation) the style of the French. The demands of the past (succeeding the great age of English drama) and the present (living in the great age of French drama) constituted a kind of Scylla and Charybdis between which Dryden sailed throughout his career, now closer to one, now the other, but never out of danger.

Shakespeare, Jonson, Beaumont and Fletcher, honored as they remained on the English stage, were no longer a suitable pattern for imitation by English playwrights,[9] for so far as Dryden and many others were concerned, a new kind of history and culture had commenced with Charles II's return in 1660. It was broadly perceived in England that with the restoration of the monarchy a new kind of time had begun, bringing with it new sentiments that demanded new kinds of poetic language. Dryden specifies these new values, and their effect on the poetry of this new age, in the much-cited epilogue to *The Conquest of Granada, pt. II* (1671):

> If Love and Honour now are higher rais'd,
> 'Tis not the Poet, but the Age is prais'd.
> Wit's now ariv'd to a more high degree;
> Our native Language more refin'd and free.

(*Works,* 11:201)

Dryden and the French

Dryden attributes the new values of love, honor, freedom, and refinement in discourse to the conduct and conversation of the king
and court, and to the easy access to court notables with which
practicing poets are favored (access that, Dryden asserts, previous
poets were denied);[10] he is proud to suggest that his own writing
has been improved by hobnobbing with his social superiors. In the
*Defence of the Epilogue: or An Essay on the Dramatic Poetry of the Last
Age* (written the following year, in 1672), Dryden provides a fuller
view of the relationship between language and political authority:

> Now, if any ask me, whence it is that our conversation is
> so much refin'd? I must freely, and without flattery, ascribe
> it to the Court: and, in it, particularly to *the King; whose ex-
> ample gives a law to it.* His own mis-fortunes and the Nations,
> afforded him an opportunity, which is rarely allow'd to Sov-
> ereign Princes, I mean of travelling, and being conversant in
> the most polish'd Courts of *Europe;* and, thereby, of cultivat-
> ing a Spirit, which was form'd by Nature, to receive the im-
> pression of a gallant and generous education. At his return,
> he found a Nation lost as much in Barbarism as in Rebellion:
> and as the excellency of his Nature forgave the one, so the
> excellency of his manners reform'd the other. *The desire of imi-
> tating so great a pattern,* first waken'd the dull and heavy spirits
> of the *English,* from their natural reserv'dness: loosen'd them,
> from their stiff forms of conversation; and made them easy
> and plyant to each other in discourse (emphasis added).
>
> (*Works,* 11:216–17)

Dryden constructs a set of relationships between authority, history, and language that form a complete and coherent system
of explanation sufficient to account for why the language of the
present age is superior to the past. To Dryden, Charles II's return commences a new age in which all society acts and speaks
in a new, more refined, and easier manner.[11] This new manner,
coupled with the new set of values that emphasize Love and Honour, are attributed by Dryden directly to the king, now broadened
by his "opportunity" of traveling, principally in France where he
passed much of his exile. These imported manners, acquired in
foreign courts, form the basis of a new kind of poetic language

Dryden's spurious quotations/appropriations a way of (apparently) squaring new realities with old authority. CII's preference for French drama, and personal interest in the theatre.

THE IMPERIAL DRYDEN

fit for this new age. According to Dryden, the restoration of traditional political authority gives birth to a new age; conversely a new poetic language expressing new thoughts is created by returning to the older model of political authority.[12]

Yet a model of history looking simultaneously backward for its justification and forward to new and better truths could not but be strained when it tried to reconcile the two where they meet—in rooting the new poetic language in traditional systems of poetic and political authorization. Dryden's spurious quotations and imitations re-create in miniature the conceptual disjunction between traditional authority and new truth; the new things to be said could be said best in the new, more refined and free language of the king, whereas authority in dramatic literature, to Dryden, meant Shakespeare, Jonson, Beaumont and Fletcher, and the rest of the British worthies. In a literary re-creation of the prevailing myth of Restoration history, Dryden speaks the new truths through his use of mythic history, spurious citations, and imitations; his misquotations are a low bow of deep respect toward the diverging exigencies of past and present. Dryden justifies himself using the new model of redeemed history and reborn culture, his justification, an appeal to legitimate authority. And if there is sometimes a rift between old authority and new truth, Dryden, always the pragmatist, bridges it as best he can.

Dryden's problems of living in a new age that lacked its own vital dramatic tradition was complicated by the fact that the king, besides bringing back a new, "politer" and "freer" mode of conversation, also brought back a preference for a new kind of drama, and with that drama a new set of dramatic "rules." During the time of his exile in France, Charles II had developed a taste for the French rhymed heroic play in the style of Corneille; he returned with his taste fully formed by 1660. Charles requested that plays be written for him in the French style and, like Richelieu, took an active interest in the writing and production of plays; the king reviewed manuscripts, made detailed "suggestions" for revision, deigned to adopt at least one play as "his" (Dryden's *Secret Love,* 1667), and personally settled disputes in the theatrical company he took under his protection.[13] The stylistic and formal preferences of the king "whose example gives a law to it" became the dominant form of theater during the early part of the Restoration. Thus political

D.'s constructed genealogies of literary inheritance: but designed to disguise his true relations of enmity/paternity. big disparity betw. his real and acknowledged debts.

authority, in the less explicit form of the legislating example, came to imply a new, French-derived set of rules in the drawing rooms of a nation, and a new set of French-influenced desiderata on the stage. Dryden, as a young poet ambitious to succeed with king and court, was obliged—and was indeed well-suited—to write plays that would set the pattern for this new courtly poetic. Accordingly, Dryden studied the new French criticism with extreme care, acquired an up-to-the-minute knowledge of which plays had succeeded or failed in Paris, and read extensively in the great as well as the lesser French playwrights and critics of the time.

Concerned as Dryden was with his uneasy and shifting relationships with various poetic and critical traditions, he often took care to situate himself precisely at the end of a chain of forefathers who would account for the way he writes; his criticism, and indeed, his self-proclaimed place in English and European literary history, is framed upon a genealogy of literary inheritance. Throughout his career, Dryden displays a keen interest in the explanatory powers of literary genealogy, and from his earliest critical writings to the preface to *Fables* (1700) he fashions and refashions a family tree of poetic forebears whose "spirits" (and attendant styles) he claims have come to him by a process of legitimate descent. Great poets, observes Harold Bloom, create the means for their forebears to imitate them; they often remake their poetic sires in their own image.[14] Dryden's genealogies of literary influence are often of this constructed, or reconstructed, sort; further, their function often seems not to reveal, but to disguise Dryden's true relations of enmity and paternity.[15] Dryden's true (but undeclared) genealogy of poetic influence can be inferred only by studying what sources Dryden availed himself of, and what use he made of them. Once such a study is made, the disparity between Dryden's two poetic genealogies, that which he claimed for himself and that from which he actually descended, is often startling.

pot + kettle!

Dryden constructs genealogies that account for and authorize poetic forms and styles, as distinct from genealogies that account for individual poetic genius, such as Davenant's claim to be the illegitimate son of Shakespeare, and Dryden's own supposition on behalf of Anne Killigrew.[16] A late genealogy of the English poets, from the preface to *Fables,* spells out a few of these family lines, and illustrates how Dryden used these types of relationships:

Milton was the Poetical Son of *Spenser,* and Mr. *Waller* of *Fairfax;* for we have our Lineal Descents and Clans, as well as other Families: *Spencer* more than once insinuates, that the Soul of *Chaucer* was transfus'd into his Body; and that he was begotten by him Two hundred years after his Decease. *Milton* has acknowledg'd to me, that *Spencer* was his Original; and many besides my self have heard our famous *Waller* own, that he deriv'd the Harmony of his Numbers from the *Godfrey of Bulloign,* which was turn'd into *English* by Mr. *Fairfax.*

(*Poems,* 4:1445) [17]

Not only did Dryden explain and authorize his poetic present by means of paternal inheritance but, as he aged, he also grew interested in the next stage of the process of poetic heredity, the passing on of the mantle. Dryden uses the familiar political metaphor of interrupted monarchical lineage, a story that would have resonated still in 1693, to contextualize his relationship to Congreve, as in the following, from "To my Dear Friend Mr. Congreve":

Oh that your Brows my Lawrel had sustain'd,
Well had I been Depos'd, if You had reign'd!
The Father had descended for the Son;
For only You are lineal to the Throne.

(*Works,* 4:433)

Even *MacFlecknoe,* in a different mood, shows Dryden's fascination with the process of poetic heredity, also resorting to the metaphor, not merely of poetic paternity, but of sovereign rule ("was own'd, without dispute / Through all the realms of *Non-Sense,* absolute").[18]

Dryden knew that in the new civil, social, religious, and poetic world of the Restoration, the genealogy of useful forebears had also to be created anew—and re-created as the day-to-day events of literary politics altered what was needful. But though the exact composition of Dryden's family tree altered from time to time, its national constitution remained constant; of the three principal literatures that comprised Dryden's poetic inheritance, French, English, and antique, only two appear in this genealogy of poetic forebears, and not surprisingly, English poets figure most strongly in Dryden's constructed paternity. Ben Jonson, "Father Ben," is early invoked in Dryden's criticism, as is Shakespeare, the *"Homer, or Father of our Dramatick Poets" (Essay, Works,* 17:58). Nor was the roll of Dryden's fathers limited to the playwrights of the last great age, for Chaucer, too, is a father, the "Father of *English* poetry," and is accordingly, though belatedly (1700), given the rank of primogenitor of English poetry *(Poems,* 4:1452). His status, not only as primogenitor, but as a great poet, entitles him to a rank in some respects approaching that of Homer and Virgil, to whose *Iliad* and *Aeneid* Dryden finds the Knight's tale of Palamon and Arcite only a little inferior *(Poems,* 4:1460). Spenser, Fairfax, Waller, and Denham, as we have seen, also figure in Dryden's genealogy of English forefathers.

These "Fathers" loom large, indeed too large, across the world of poetic possibility of the mid-1660s, for, according to Dryden, these fathers' poetic achievements are so great as to render futile all striving to surpass them in their own types of writing: "We acknowledge them our Fathers in wit, but they have ruin'd their Estates themselves before they came to their childrens hands. There is scarce an Humour, a Character, or any kind of Plot, which they have not us'd. All comes sullied or wasted to us" *(Works,* 17:73). The same sentiment of being oppressed by and mildly resentful of the weight of one's ancestors' poetic accomplishment is rendered even more pungently in the epilogue to the *Conquest of Granada, pt. II:*

> Fame then was cheap, and the first commer sped;
> And they have kept it since, by being dead.
>
> *(Works,* 11:201)

Such notes of indignation often creep into Dryden's early accounts of his own sense of belatedness. The ease with which they won their fame, the wide open fields before them and, finally, the ultimate advantage they retain "by being dead" all goad Dryden to such outbursts of exasperation.

Besides deceased English poets, the great poets of antiquity are deemed both worthy and safe to serve as Dryden's poetic progenitors. As early as 1667 Dryden claims Virgil for his master;[19] he later claims both Virgil and Homer as fathers of different kinds

D's studious avoidance of confessing a French lineage. His creation of a 'polemical mythic history'

THE IMPERIAL DRYDEN

of writing, each, at different times (depending on whom Dryden is translating) sorting best with his own genius.[20]

By seeking to associate himself with the poetic lineage of Homer, Virgil, Chaucer, Jonson, Fletcher, and Shakespeare, Dryden suppresses, by genealogical exclusion, his substantial debt to the still-living writers in the French tradition, and so the French tradition comprised no part of Dryden's constructed literary genealogy.[21] Dryden admitted to no "frère Corneille"; such a familial association would have seemed monstrous, treasonous, absurd.

To accompany this "covering" genealogy of literary descent, Dryden also constructs a pendant history of literature that situates him as the *telos* of the literary chain. Perhaps the two most salient ingredients of Dryden's constructed literary history are, first, how deeply interested he is in the importance and utility of history as a shaping and justifying principle, and, second, how much of his history is demonstrably wrong. Most examples of Drydenian mythic history, that is, fictitious accounts of literary events designed to mask other literary events whose truths are unassimilable, occur at polemical moments;[22] polemical exigencies stress the past into what is needful, although Dryden often errs in his accounts of literary history in ways possible only to someone generally uninterested in the concordance of statement with fact, signifier with signified.[23] Because so many of his literary "facts" are imaginary, we can regard Dryden's critical project as an extended historical fiction—at some points, as with many fictions, close to a verifiable historical actuality, at other points, imaginary. It is a polemical fiction, now true, now false, that justifies him to the ancients, to the moderns, to the English of the last great age, and to the French. Only by knowing how the assertions of the criticism differ from the literary events they purport to describe can we fairly evaluate Dryden's critical project, for only when the range of error is known can wish be separated from fact, polemic from poetry. Along these lines, though referring to a different topic, Steven Zwicker remarks, "to assume throughout that Dryden is a truth-teller is to narrow our understanding of the character of his achievement both as poet and polemicist."[24] Dryden's use of polemical mythic history diminishes during the more than four

Dryden and the French

decades of his publishing career; his need to dominate the poetic past decreases as he grows more comfortable in his poetic present. Dryden's literary mythic history chronicles his literary anxieties; where he is uncomfortable, there he invents. For example, refusing to credit the French with the development of the rhymed drama then in fashion in England, Dryden against all evidence claims it as a native development, insisting (wrongly) that pre-Shakespearean comedies were once written in rhyming alexandrines;[25] in the same connection he holds up as a pattern "the Tragedy of *Queen* Gorboduc in *English* Verse [that is, rhymed couplets]"—a work that a glance would have told him concerned *King* Gorboduc, and that, save the stanzaic choruses, is all in blank verse.[26] Determined that Shakespeare should be the father of English poetic form as well as the "*Homer,* or Father of our Dramatick Poets," Dryden credits him with the invention of blank verse, being "the first, who to shun the pains of continual Rhyming, invented that kind of Writing, which we call Blanck Verse" (*Works,* 8:99). Eager to prove that the English can be as regular as the French, he claims that Jonson's *Silent Woman* observes the liaison des scènes, which it does not (*Essay, Works,* 17:59). Reversing the flow of Anglo-Gallic literary influence, Dryden asserts that Molière, who appears not ever to have read anything by any Englishman, was copying the "quick turns and graces of the *English* Stage."[27] Along these same lines, years later he claims to have heard that Madeleine de Scudéry ("who is as old as *Sibyl,* and inspir'd like her by the same God of Poetry") is translating Chaucer into modern French, a most unlikely proposition considering the complete lack of French interest in, and utter ignorance of, English poetry at this time (*Poems,* 4:1459). Citing Sidney's *Apology for Poetry,* Dryden confuses Sidney's argument for the superiority of poetry over prose for one of rhyme over blank verse (*Works,* 8:100). The *Essay of Dramatick Poesy*'s Neander, a most accomplished mythic historian, claims the liaison des scènes in *Le Cid* is broken only once; actually it is broken constantly.[28] Neander also claims that there are "many scenes of rhyme together" in Jonson's tragedies *Sejanus* and *Catiline,* either unaware or unconcerned that *Catiline* contains no scene in rhyme. Seeking to show that the English have outgrown the use of alexandrines, Dryden cites Chapman's Homer as an early example, not knowing, perhaps, that Chapman's *Iliad* is in heptameters, his *Odyssey* in pentameters (Preface to *Annus Mirabilis, Works,* 1:51). Wishing to find at least one regular comedy by Shakespeare, Dryden so declares *The Merry Wives of Windsor,* possibly unaware that it is not.[29] Dryden cites Spenser as his "legislating example" for the use of the triplet and alexandrine, and Chapman's Homer after him; taken together they are the "Magna Charta" of English heroic poetry. But Spenser does not use the triplet, and Chapman does not use the alexandrine.[30] Puffing his and Lee's version by proving that *Oedipus* is the greatest play of all time, Dryden claims that Horace and Lucullus mention it—though nowhere do Horace and Lucullus mention it (Preface to *Oedipus, Works,* 13:115).

Aristotle in particular undergoes some interesting mutations in Dryden's criticism. Seeking to justify the heroic drama, Dryden asserts that Aristotle esteemed epic "the greatest work of human nature," a position Aristotle did not hold, claiming, on the contrary, that tragedy "is a higher art."[31] Dryden provides names for the four parts of a play and falsely ascribes the terms to Aristotle (*Essay, Works,* 17:23). Dryden also informs us that "the end of Tragedies or serious Playes, sayes *Aristotle,* is to beget admiration, compassion, or concernment," whereas "admiration" is not mentioned in the *Poetics* (*Essay, Works,* 17:35). When Dryden finds an opinion of Aristotle insupportably in conflict with his own, he rewrites Aristotle. "They who would justify the madness of Poetry from the Authority of *Aristotle,* have mistaken the text, & consequently the Interpretation: I imagine it to be false read, where he says of Poetry, that it is Εὐφυοῦς ἢ μανικοῦ, that it had always somewhat in it either of a genius, or of a madman. 'Tis more probable that the Original ran thus, that Poetry was Εὐφυοῦς οὐ μανικοῦ, That it belongs to a Witty man, but not to a madman" (*The Grounds of Criticism in Tragedy, Works,* 13:241–42). Dryden rewrites Aristotle's judgments of Sophocles and Euripides and invents a preference between their styles of representation that Aristotle did not state.[32] As he becomes increasingly concerned with epic, Dryden claims that Aristotle derives his rules for the theater, first, from the epic, and only then from observation of the drama—a statement for which there is no authority in the *Poetics*.

As Dryden misrepresents the works of his forebears, so he sometimes misrepresents himself. Adept at employing the products of the past to buttress his own positions, Dryden is equally adept at conforming his own literary persona to the same mythically historical scheme of plausible fiction, spurious ancestor, and invented history. In 1670 Dryden disowns his obvious debt to French criticism, now claiming that the writing of prefaces to plays was invented "Perhaps by some Ape of the *French* Eloquence, who uses to make a business of a Letter of gallantry, an examen of a Farce" (*Works,* 10:3).

Not only does Dryden cover his tracks when convenient (as in the above example), but he sometimes asserts propositions concerning his own work that are patently false, such as the claim that *Secret Love* (1667), a tragicomedy with a serious and comic plot only passably tacked together, is "regular, according to the strictest of Dramatick Laws" (Preface, *Works,* 9:115), or that, in a play full of verbatim translations from Molière, he "seldome use[s] the wit and language of any Romance or Play which [he] undertake[s] to alter" (Preface to *An Evening's Love, Works,* 10:211).

Dryden, in order to fit himself into a literary milieu that seemed inhospitable to a young and ambitious poet, begot his own fathers and recorded their literary exploits as he needed fathers and exploits; it did not matter whether any of the lineage or history was untrue in any verifiable sense, for it was true in the way Dryden required it to be true—it justified his own poetic and critical project. Nor was this work of historical and genealogical revision necessarily disrespectful toward those whose lives and accomplishments were modified, for in modifying the past, Dryden asserted his belief in its primacy; in usurping for himself the past's power to form the present, he reasserted his belief in the power of the past to make us what we are. In this he followed in the footsteps of the one master he could not acknowledge, the greatest living playwright and critic in France, Pierre Corneille—for whom, ironically, there was no room in any of Dryden's justifying autobiographies of lineage or literary exploit.

Just as the scope of Corneille's critical project cannot be appreciated without considering the literary politics of his time, ap-

Corneille as D's most obvious predecessor in drama and criticism. Dryden a more conscious manipulator of predecessors than Bloom's 'anxiety' theory would allow.

THE IMPERIAL DRYDEN

preciating the scope of Dryden's criticism requires a knowledge of Corneille, the major French playwright and critic with whom Dryden was obliged to come to terms. Both Corneille and Dryden were well-connected poets from middle-class backgrounds, professional playwrights, scholars, and critics. Moreover, both formulated critical systems intended to culminate in dramatic renaissances in which their own dramas would take pride of place. Yet similarities of background, temperament, genius, and aims could only have aggravated for Dryden the fact that he was very much the latecomer. Corneille was writing plays before Dryden was born;[33] he was still writing plays and criticism at the time of the Restoration; and he was to continue writing plays until 1674. He had developed the pattern of the rhymed heroic play and had authored its greatest examples, *Le Cid, Horace, Cinna,* and *La Mort de Pompée,* all of which were known and referred to by Dryden.[34] At least as important for Dryden, Corneille was author of the single greatest body of French criticism of the time, the examens and *Trois Discours* of the 1660 edition, which were to define the terms for much of Dryden's critical discourse during the ensuing decade. Corneille's shoes were large, and impossible to fill since Corneille was still in them.[35]

To use the term Harold Bloom so beautifully coins, we might say that Corneille and Shakespeare—and later Racine—were Dryden's "anxieties of influence," a term whose use raises the issue of my own work's relationship to Bloom's critical project. My account of Dryden's relationship to Corneille, Molière, and Racine touches Bloom's grand scheme at several points, but such contact is accidental, and is neither welcomed nor avoided by me. Although some of the general outline may apply, the axioms and grammar of Bloom's larger project do not apply to Dryden's relationships with his contemporaries and predecessors; what I describe herein are not the "misreadings" of a "strong" poet, but the misspeakings of a cagey one. Dryden exhibits greater intentionality in manipulating his predecessors than Bloom admits into his system, a system based on so much of the creative process remaining a secret from the poet. Dryden's struggles with his "anxieties of influence" are on the surface, both in the subterfuges of the criticism and their attempts to conceal the ori-

D's strategic point-scoring of Corneillian drama, (while admiring its 'marmoreal beauty').

Dryden and the French

gins of the drama; they could only reflect conscious activity on Dryden's part. Moreover, Bloom is primarily concerned with the *agon* of one great, or "strong," living figure with one other great elder figure. Dryden was amazingly well integrated into his literary milieu; if he had had to wrestle each of his phalanx of distinguished "fathers" (Homer, Virgil, Chaucer, Jonson, Shakespeare, Corneille, Racine) he would have been too bruised by oedipal struggle to grasp the pen.

Though Dryden did not have to wrestle each of his predecessors, he still had to come to terms with the chief of them, and the movement he represented. That Corneille was France's greatest living playwright and critic, as well as a favorite of the English court set, obliged Dryden to take an interest in his work;[36] however, Dryden found reasons to resist, at least overtly, the pressure to write in Corneille's style. Since Dryden was determined to create a drama written by the English for the peculiar English character ("weav'd in English Loomes," as Neander remarks in the *Essay of Dramatick Poesy*), he found numerous reasons to dislike the kinds of plays Corneille wrote: their plots were too narrow; they contained neither good humours nor sufficient tonal variety ("the Feast is too dull and solemn without the Fiddles" [Preface to *Spanish Fryar, Works*, 14:103]); the unities of time, place, and action were unnecessary, and were such as only servile imitators of the bygone glories of the ancients would think to bind themselves.[37] Their portrayals of human nature, too, were stiff and artificial and, consequently, the plots were stiff and lacking the kind of action pleasing to the English taste. Neander says, "those beauties of the *French*-poesie are such as will raise perfection higher where it is, but are not sufficient to give it where it is not: they are indeed the Beauties of a Statue, but not of a Man, because not animated with the Soul of Poesie" (*Essay, Works*, 17:44). Dryden, ever eager to score a point for the English (and thus for himself) at the expense of the French, associates the Cornelian drama with a mode of representation that implies essentially undramatic qualities: marmoreal perfection exists only at the expense of the ability to move (that is, the ability to fulfill Aristotle's basic prescription for tragedy—that it be the imitation of an *action*). Making the undeniable but inimitable beauties of Corneille's drama "the Beauties of a Statue" allowed Dryden to affirm Corneille's achievement while deprecating its dramatic qualities. Such still and silent beauties, perfect as they might be, were not for the English stage.

Because Corneille was foreign, established, and unquestionably great, because his works together constituted a kind of poetic law to Dryden, Corneille was the one member of Dryden's poetic "family" who was practically unassimilable. Accordingly, as Dryden sought a modern-day equivalent to the *gloria inimicatarum,* the fame and honor young Roman nobles sought by mounting an attack on an older, prominent politician, he targeted the greatest of the French playwright-critics as the object of his earnest resentment.[38] Obliged by the pressures of history, custom, the desire for fame and success—and a share of the gloria inimicatarum— Dryden adopted Shakespeare as a father, Corneille as a foe. But to Dryden's actual dramatic practice, especially in the earlier phases, Shakespeare was more of a foe—an unassimilable greatness— than Corneille, between Dryden and whom subsisted what might be called a sibling rivalry.

Though Dryden could not borrow much from Shakespeare, his formal debt to Corneille is extensive, and has been well, if somewhat superficially, chronicled over the years. But a class of debt that remains unexamined concerns the rhetorical strategies by which poets appropriate either the authority or the material of their poetic forebears, strategies developed by Corneille to a high art whose purpose was to win the power to determine a poetic system that suited him. To this end Corneille developed the three evasive/subversive techniques alluded to in the introduction: (1) the formal bravade, which used a mandated form to score a point directly contrary to the aim for which it was originally created; (2) the feigned submission, which involved seeming resignation either to an authority or such tokens as rules and formal precepts; and (3) the strategy that, judging by his use of it, Dryden found most sympathetic—misquotation. Of these three strategies of evasion, the feigned submission and the bravade are the most dependent on a rigidly prescribed set of codes, both formal and preceptual, against which such formal ironies may be telling. Indeed, the more sharply defined the demands of the authority, the more precisely delineated may be the covert means of

J. attacking Corneille for the very neo-Aristotelianism which he (C) deplored. His strategic "misquotation" of C in EDP

Dryden and the French

analysis or subversion. But as authority diffuses, becomes a generalized weight rather than a specific set of demands, these means lose their point; such was Dryden's situation.

In the Restoration climate of diffused literary authority, where several dramatic styles flourished simultaneously even as the king made known his preference for the style of Corneille, Dryden turned the subversive techniques he had learned from Corneille against Corneille himself, emptying out the Corneille of the *Trois Discours* and examens and reconstituting him as a Corneille-speaker more amenable to the aims of Dryden's critical project. Reading the *Trois Discours* and examens acontextually and unsympathetically, Dryden took Corneille, France's greatest dramatist and anti-neo-Aristotelian, as an advocate for the rigid neo-Aristotelianism both Corneille and Dryden deplored. Using Corneille to represent Corneille's less-famous legislating enemies, Dryden reconstructed Corneille in a counterimage to himself. Execrating Corneille's name and inventing his substance, Dryden attacked him for legislating an academic version of French neoclassicism, a charge of which he was innocent.

Dryden was determined to take Corneille's place in the mind of the English theatergoing set by creating works that would displace those of his predecessor, and few works of the period seek to topple a rival from his niche so aggressively as the *Essay of Dramatick Poesy*.[39] That the *Essay* uses against Corneille Corneille's own methods for supplanting his rivals merely compounds the irony, for Dryden did not miss Corneille's trick of misquoting the past in order to win control of a disputed present; the use of misquotation's usurping function is perhaps the most telling of Dryden's "quotations" from Corneille's *Discours,* even more important, though not nearly so evident, as Dryden's use of Corneille's critical terms.

In the face of the recent French dramatic and critical vogue, the *Essay* takes on "the Universe" and all previous literature to prove that English plays are the greatest and that English playwrights, aside from the English king, alone possess the power and right to legislate the form of what will be represented on the English stage. The avowed purpose of the *Essay* is to take control of the English stage from the partisans of the ancients and the French, "to vindi-

Corneille's aesthetic subsumed/extended within an English scheme.

cate the honour of our *English* Writers, from the censure of those who unjustly prefer the *French* before them" (*Works,* 17:7).[40] Yet the debate with all of literature occurs, curiously, not on English ground, but on Corneille's. A preponderance of the critical vocabulary in the *Essay* is borrowed or adapted from Corneille's *examens* and the *Trois Discours,* and all four interlocutors show familiarity with Corneille and his works, as each refers to him.[41]

A key strategy in Dryden's war against the French is his trick of quoting Corneille (or French practice—they are often used interchangeably) only to illustrate the myriad ways in which English drama, and specifically Dryden's own, subsumes the Franco-Cornelian aesthetic in a more varied and comprehensive system. This technique, often coupled with misquotation, subsumes the (often misrepresented) Franco-Cornelian position within a larger Anglo-Drydenian scheme.

The *Essay* commences with an instance of its most typical movement, in which Dryden misquotes the French, then subsumes that misquotation in a larger English effect. The *Essay*'s first five words ("It was that memorable day") tacitly refer to the supposed advantage, mentioned by Corneille and amplified upon by Dryden, of locating the action on a momentous, destiny-deciding, long-awaited day. The object was to situate the dramatic action on a day that held the accumulated potential energies of a substantial body of history, a day that would both sum up all that had preceded and determine all that would follow, as those stored up energies were released in dramatic action.[42] Neander (whom I, with critical tradition, regard as a spokesperson for Dryden),[43] in his *examen* of Ben Jonson's *Silent Woman,* states Dryden's own case, judging from his frequent use of the strategy: "One of these advantages [given by Jonson to *The Silent Woman*] is that which *Corneille* has laid down as *the greatest which can arrive to any Poem,* and which he himself could never compass above thrice in all this [sic] Playes, *viz.* the making choice of some signal and long-expected day, whereon the action of the Play is to depend" (emphasis added) (*Works,* 17:62). As does so much of Dryden's commentary on Corneille, the passage tells us more of Dryden's anxiety regarding Corneille than of Corneille himself, for the passage contains the traces of a complicated system of evasion, subterfuge, misquotation, and misstatement.

For all Neander's bravado, his "quotation" of Corneille reveals Corneille's true place in Dryden's critical scheme, for Dryden cites him as the legislator of a play's "greatest advantages"; Dryden refers to him both as solon (whose views must be considered) and tyrant (whose rule must be overthrown). Dryden carefully frames the section so that Corneille's own dramatic abilities are made to seem limited in the face of this superlative ("greatest") desideratum; the French master himself, Dryden proudly informs us, only managed it thrice.

This passage also proves that Dryden's claim to have written the *Essay* "without the help of Books"[44] is false, and we learn, not only that he had the complete Corneille by his side, but precisely which edition; from Dryden's mistranslation of an ambiguous passage in the 1660 edition, which Corneille corrected in the 1663 edition, we learn that Dryden possessed the edition of 1660, from which he translates liberally—sometimes with acknowledgment—throughout the *Essay*. [45]

This passage also illustrates the length to which Dryden would go to misrepresent the opinions of a distinguished antagonist, as this statement of the "greatest advantage" is nowhere to be found in the works of Corneille. Neander vastly exaggerates the importance Corneille allowed to this temporal disposition ("the greatest which can arrive to any Poem"); this "greatest" ornament is mentioned only once in all Corneille's criticism,[46] in the following language: "The choice of an illustrious and long-awaited day is a great ornament to a poem. Occasions do not always present themselves, and in all that I have done until now, you will find only four of this nature" (*Discours des Trois Unités, Oeuvres,* 3:186).[47] Dryden employs Corneille's misrepresented desideratum as an absolute criterion by which to laud Jonson's play and, by extension, Dryden's own plays and, by yet further extension, the very work—the *Essay*—in which the issue is raised ("It was that memorable day"); like so much of the ostensibly outward-directed discussion in the *Essay of Dramatick Poesy,* this brief observation subtly reflects upon the conditions of the *Essay*'s creation and of Dryden's mingled pride and uncertainty regarding its standing, when compared to the works of Corneille.

Following the *Essay*'s beginning reference to itself as a fiction fulfilling the Cornelian precept, the anonymous narrator prepares us for a simulated debate between four friends, concerned principally with fixing on a model for English playwriting (and retrospectively justifying the dramatic principles of the *Essay*'s author). The first part of the debate pits the ancients against the moderns and, that battle carried by the moderns, the second half of the *Essay* weighs the relative merits of the French and English dramatic styles. After an examination of principles, Neander, champion of the English style, selects a play of Ben Jonson's and examines it according to French rules in a section entitled "Examen of *The Silent Woman.*" The examen is the sole extended examination of a play in the *Essay,* and as such shows how Dryden uses French principles and analytical methods to assert English superiority in the drama.[48]

The examen, the yardstick with which Dryden takes the measure of *The Silent Woman,* was hardly a neutral means of scrutinizing the quiddities and qualities of a play, for the form came to England from France already charged with the various uses to which it had been put. Although the word itself is ancient (the Latin examen was a means of weighing, the tongue of a balance), the examen in France achieved its first institutionalized prominence as the Académie Française's official form for examining literary works.[49] Members of the Académie would submit their works to a panel of their peers, which presented its findings in this official form; like so many critical formulations, the academic examen's application to a given work tended tautologously to confirm those principles that underlay it.

The examen was used outside the Académie as well. L'Abbé d'Aubignac wrote an examen of Sophocles's *Ajax* as an illustration of the principles propounded in his *Pratique du théâtre.*[50] In d'Aubignac's hands the examen applies the mechanical yardsticks of the unities of subject, time, and place; ascertains that the scenes are well tied together; checks for the equity of act-breaks; and verifies that the time elapsed between acts is of equal duration. D'Aubignac treats the principles of propriety and probability as cardinal, and not surprisingly, given his unwavering admiration for the ancients, he finds that the action of *Ajax* is both probable and decorous.

The examens that Dryden had in mind and at hand as he wrote

the *Essay of Dramatick Poesy,* however, were Corneille's, which, appearing in the great 1660 edition, constituted the largest body of practical dramatic criticism in French up until that time and as such were bound to weigh heavily in any English assessment of the French tradition.[51] The succinct examen form,[52] as Corneille developed it, served a wide range of uses. It defended the eccentricities and license of a twenty-three-year-old play (*Le Cid*); it argued for Corneille's own notion of drama's right to alter received history (*Heraclius*); it explained characters' motivations from the author's privileged position; and it evaluated how well a given work observed the unities of time, place, and action, sometimes justifying, sometimes condemning, when the play did not.

Corneille's examen usually begins with several pages of analysis of the play's observance of the unities, followed by brief character analyses that consider the characters' observance of decorum. Next comes a consideration of the plot's adherence to the rules of probability, and Corneille frequently concludes by briefly summing up his general opinion of the play. The examen often lists the play's sources and describes the finished play's relation to them. Sometimes, as in the examen to *Le Menteur,* Corneille justifies his "pillage" of his sources;[53] in others, Corneille wonders whether he might have gone too far in his adaptation. The examen often describes the play's reception, and if the play failed, Corneille attempts to explain why. Corneille's examens of his own plays, written concurrently to evaluate a body of work that spanned three decades, generally defend the plays against critics, although by 1660 Corneille could afford to sacrifice a few early plays to his mature critical wisdom.

Besides defending his drama, Corneille's other principal aim for his examens was to apply and justify his critical principles, specifically those expounded in the *Trois Discours,* written concurrently with the examens. By turning against d'Aubignac and the academic theorists the very examen form they had used to impose rules on him, Corneille began the motion we now see continued by Dryden—turned, however, against Corneille. Dryden, contextualizing Corneille in the world of English letters, read him not as a fellow playwright struggling against the dogma of a too-rigid poetic aesthetic, but as a representative of that very aesthetic, another d'Aubignac. Hence, Corneille's examen, for Corneille himself a subtly potent instrument for liberating himself from the toils of neoclassical doctrine, in Dryden's eyes reverted to a repressive agent of just that constricting neoclassicism from which Corneille had tried to free himself.

As Dryden appropriated the form of Corneille's examen, just as Corneille had d'Aubignac's and the Académie's, he duplicated Corneille's revisionary use of the examen almost exactly. Taking what Dryden regarded as an instrument of poetic repression in the hands of the unwelcome "father," a critical cudgel used to beat unruly dramatic material into submission, Dryden misquotes it (the result of his unsympathetic reading—and how could he have read Corneille otherwise?) against the poet he regarded as the champion of all for which the form stood. The examen in the *Essay of Dramatick Poesy* is a peculiarly elaborate example of misquotation; an "official" form adapted by Corneille to free him from the academics is misread by Dryden back to its original "official" status, and readapted to free him from Corneille. The transmission from Corneille to Dryden is not, as others have claimed, one of the reception of rules, but of a means to evade the rules, the senior poet's evasion congealing into the junior poet's formal limits, then to be evaded by methods supplied by the elder poet in his evasions of his own would-be legislators.

In the final link in this chain of misreading, Dryden, who struggled constantly, vigorously, ingeniously, to rid himself of the French neoclassical "burden," is now often anthologized under the rubric "neoclassic poet and critic," as if he had inherited the mantle intact from Corneille. In my view the term "neoclassical" can be applied to Dryden only if we define neoclassicism as a systematic practice of misquotation that overtly accepts and covertly refuses some portion of a precisely defined "classical" heritage; a doctrine relying on the authority of a largely imaginary or reconstructed forebear to justify what one has one's self to say; a poetic system that stresses not the poet's inheritance, but his or her evasion of the prescriptiveness of the past. Using such a definition, Dryden is indeed a neoclassical poet, for he consistently misuses the classical in order to formulate utterances of the modern. His figure for himself is, after all, Neander: the "new man," named in an ancient language.

Dryden and the French

Once we understand the importance of the examen (in Dryden's hands a new form named in an ancient language) to seventeenth-century critical practice, we see why Dryden accorded the "Examen of *The Silent Woman*" such a prominent place in the *Essay of Dramatick Poesy*. The speeches of Crites, Eugenius, and Lisideius increase in seriousness and rhetorical intensity; in Neander's speech the pro-English spokesperson delineates a set of general principles that prove the English drama superior to the French. After invoking the great names of the English fathers, Shakespeare, Jonson, Beaumont, and Fletcher, Neander executes a formal analysis of Jonson's play that, both by position and content, serves to key in the arch of debate stretching from the carpings of the anti-Modernist Crites to the Francophile Lisideius's sniffing at some of the excesses of the English stage.

On first reading Dryden's examen, most modern readers are struck by the apparent inanity of Neander's criteria and the superficiality of his method of analysis. Dryden makes *The Silent Woman* lie down on the Procrustean bed of the unities (which it is found she fits), after which follows some strikingly unpenetrating commentary on the characters and plot of the play. The examen concludes with a chauvinistic assertion that the English pen is at least as mighty, in relation to the rest of the universe, as the English sword, and one finishes the examen with, at best, little more understanding of the Silent Woman than that with which one began. As Robert Hume says, "any undergraduate ought to be able to produce a better examen than Dryden's on *The Silent Woman*."[54]

Yet, I shall argue, what readers experience as critical obtusity is only apparent, for the examen successfully yet subtly resolves a dilemma arising from Dryden's delicate position facing the new wave of French criticism. Corneille's popularity at court and in literary circles meant that Dryden could not reject his criticism outright; he had to show, not that the French dramatic criteria were bad, but that the English were better ("the Beauties of a Statue . . . not of a Man"). Like Dryden, Neander, himself a modern English playwright, is concerned "to vindicate the honour of our *English* Writers, from the censure of those who unjustly prefer the *French* before them" (*Works*, 17:7). The examen of *The Silent Woman,* as it vindicates the English writers, applies and extends Neander's critical principles, and itself implies a pseudodebate (similar to Corneille's with Aristotle in the *Discours*) between what purport to be the two national modes of playwriting. When read as a debate between opposing aesthetics (the larger structure of the *Essay* recapitulated in small), Neander's digressive method, so apparently slapdash, reveals its centrality to the controversy. These digressive excurses include his lengthy disquisition on "humour," his historical review of the modes of comedy, and the apparently discontinuous conclusion in which he leaps from a discussion of the plot mechanics of a nearly sixty-year-old play to asserting that contemporary English playwrights "have far surpass'd all the Ancients, and the Modern Writers of other Countreys" (*Works,* 17:64).

Neander begins his examen of *The Silent Woman* as Corneille did his examens: by measuring how closely the play observes the unities. Dryden spends proportionately less time than Corneille shoehorning the play into regularity, but in so doing, Dryden typically re-creates *The Silent Woman,* not as it was written, but as he appears to wish it had been written. Just as Dryden misquoted poets and critics, so he misquotes the shape of formal structures when it suits his purposes, finding *The Silent Woman* as regular as anything by the French only by misdescribing the larger structure of the play. He correctly observes that the play maintains the unity of time, but errs in claiming that the action occupies three and a half hours; as Herford and Simpson observe, the action "occupies some twelve hours, from morning till nightfall."[55] Neander errs again in finding the unity of place maintained, for he claims the action occurs in only two houses, "and after the first Act, in one";[56] the action actually occurs in five places, and it is not until act 3, scene 4 that the action moves permanently to Morose's house. As a corollary to this supposed unity of place, Neander claims the liaisons des scènes are generally maintained, "not [being] broken above twice or thrice at most in the whole Comedy" (*Works,* 17:59); however, as George Watson observes, "there is not a single instance of *liaison des scènes* between any of the ten scenes that comprise [the play]" (Watson, 1:71).

After "proving" that *The Silent Woman* is as regular as any French play, Neander undertakes an extended historical review of humour that searches more theoretical means to subsume the Franco-Cornelian rules. He begins by discussing the genesis and qualities of Morose's peculiarities. "Some who would be thought Criticks," he says, "say this humour of his is forc'd" (*Works,* 17:59). Neander then offers several explanations for how Morose's hearing might have attained its morbid sensitivity, expending substantial analytical energy to establish the verisimilitude of Morose's affliction, which he effects by claiming that Jonson actually knew such a man. Neander's tack here exactly replicates Corneille's pioneering argument, formulated to break the grip of the neo-Aristotelian doctrine of probability over the often more interesting, but less probable historical event; in the *Discours de la Tragédie* Corneille uses particular incident to license representation of an improbable (but historical) occurrence.[57] Dryden takes Corneille's argument in the nutshell: what is historical, by definition, is credible, since we must believe that whatever did happen, could happen (to paraphrase Aristotle). Morose's humour is not improbable because Jonson actually knew such a man.[58]

Neander, however, pushes Corneille's argument even further, deriving a definition of humour from the notion of singularity (improbable but historical particularity) that will in turn serve as the theoretical basis for an entire English genre. "Others say," claims Neander, "it is not enough to find one man of such an humour; it must be common to more, and the more common the more natural."[59] But Neander soon establishes that "others'" objection to Morose's uniqueness is grounded in the French aesthetic, an aesthetic in turn derived, says Neander, from the ridiculum of Aristophanic Old Comedy, in which what matters most is the "odd conceit"—not imitating the peculiarities of men. Neander anticipates the neo-Aristotelian critique of humoural uniqueness by defining humour so that singularity signifies the essence of humours comedy: "Humour is the ridiculous extravagance of conversation, wherein one man differs from all others. If then it be common, or communicated to many, how differs it from other mens? or what indeed causes it to be ridiculous as much as the singularity of it?" (*Works,* 17:59). Once having proven that humour is not what people share, but what individuates them, Neander explores the uses of humour by quickly reviewing the development of comedy. Beginning with Aristophanic Old Comedy, in which what was comic "was not so much to imitate a man, as to make the people

41

laugh at some odd conceit, which had commonly somewhat of unnatural or obscene in it," Neander stresses the Old Comedy's intellectual, nonmimetic qualities (*Works,* 17:60). These are embodied conceits, he argues, not a "just and lively Image of Humane Nature, representing its Passions and Humours," as Lisideius's earlier definition of a play prescribes (*Works,* 17:15). Old Comedy was followed by New Comedy, whose poets tried to express the ethos. "But," Neander objects, "this ἦθος contain'd onely the general Characters of men and manners; as old men, Lovers, Servingmen . . . all which they made alike" (*Works,* 17:60). The ethos too fails to imitate individuals, but depicts only broad comic types, both far from the humours' essence and the drama's aim as the *Essay* defines them. Neander then places the French comic spirit in the balance, and finds it wanting: "As for the *French,* though they have the word *humeur* among them, yet they have small use of it in their Comedies, or Farces; they being but ill imitations of the *ridiculum,* or that which stirr'd up laughter in the old Comedy" (*Works,* 17:60). According to Neander, the Old Comedy did not imitate people, New Comedy only imitated types, and what is comic in French Comedy is but an "ill imitation" of what was comic in the Old Comedy. Neander triumphantly concludes that it is the humour comedy of the English that "most frequently begets that malicious pleasure in the Audience which is testified by laughter . . . though by the way this laughter is onely accidental, as the person represented is Fantastick or Bizarre; but pleasure is essential to it, as the imitation of what is natural" (*Works,* 17:61). Here again the qualities of the fantastic or bizarre in character (English humour's "singularity," neither New nor Old Comedic) are associated with laughter, and the imitation of the natural (not Old Comedic, hence not French), associated with pleasure. In Dryden's scheme only the English fulfill both halves of the prescription—their humours are both fantastic and bizarre (producing laughter) and imitations of human nature (producing pleasure). The improbable singularity of Morose's humour is found to triumph over both the Old Comic spirit (a spirit not of imitation but of conceit) and the New Comic spirit of nondifferentiated character. Ascribing centrality to humour renders French comedy only partially satisfying; its ridiculum of conceit is not rejected, but subsumed into a larger and better-integrated whole.

Dryden and the French

Humours characters, however, delightful as they may be in and of themselves, comprise only the basic unit of Neander's next class of comparison. From the distinctive traits of humour Neander extrapolates the genre of Jonsonian humours comedy, a genre he in turn offers as vindication of the English style. As he draws out into an entire genre the principles that underlie the individual humour character, he also introduces the first strand of what will be his master argument "to vindicate the honor of our English Writers." ". . . Besides *Morose,* there are at least 9 or 10 different Characters and humours in the *Silent Woman,* all which persons have several concernments of their own, yet are all us'd by the Poet, to the conducting of the main design to perfection" (*Works,* 17:61). The thread is picked up again to praise the "contrivance," that is, the secret of Epicoene's sex: "But I dare not take upon me to commend the Fabrick of it, because it is altogether so full of Art, that I must unravel every Scene in it to commend it as I ought" (*Works,* 17:61). Here Neander suggests more fully that if the artifact that best embodies the French aesthetic is a statue, that which most resembles the English humours play is tapestry; we are to imagine each humours character a strand, woven to form a dramatic artifact of suppleness and textural complexity. Dryden, repeating his technique throughout the examen, continues to counterpose the English "tapestry" against the French "Beauties of a Statue" and glories in the English drama's difference from the "conceit" of Old Comedy, the generalized ethos of the New. Neander delineates a genre of comedy he believes unique, a cunningly contrived knot tied from "at least 9 or 10 different Characters and humours" woven together into a "Fabrick . . . altogether . . . full of Art." Tapestry, an artificial metaphor for complex English plots, subsumes the French drama, for in its fulfillment of the French requirements for regularity and in its capacity to contain figural representations of the French "Beauties of a Statue" it surpasses the French in another dimension—that of multiplicity of character and attendant complication of plot (or to use the English word, variety). These plots, as Neander remarks elsewhere, are "weav'd in *English* Loomes."

Neander's woven emblem sums up the strengths of the English tradition as Dryden argues it in the *Essay.* Complication of character and complexity of plot harmonize more pleasingly with the temporal extension of drama than does the marmoreal but extensionless beauty of the perfectly proportioned, perfectly still French tableau. Variety, the key desideratum of the English style, is better served by "weaving" a plot from multiple elements than by reducing the dramatic event into a singly unified "block."[60] The emblem of tapestry shows the rich "texture" of the English drama, its ability to take up unrelated elements and incorporate them into a tightly integrated artifact whose origins in multiplicity are retained, but made secondary to a new, higher, distinctively English kind of unity.

Neander's final exposition of the virtues of *The Silent Woman* also contains Dryden's most telling demonstration of the inherent vitality of the English stage tradition, as compared to the French. Generally scornful of the academic rulemongers, poring over the remnants of vanished civilizations only to discover ever-more-binding precepts with which to regulate ("servilely," Dryden says again and again) their productions for the stage, Neander finds that English writers of the last age, and by implication English writers of the present, and by further implication, Dryden himself, may generate *their own* rules, rules based not on literary authority, but on the typically English basis of what is found to work. The following passage illustrates the English dramatic and critical tradition's final supersession of the French, reflected in the play between the French and English languages as well as in the concept itself: "There is another artifice of the Poet [Jonson], which I cannot here omit, because by the frequent practice of it in his Comedies, he has left it to us almost as a Rule, that is, when he has any Character or humour wherein he would show a *Coup de Maistre*. . . ." (*Works,* 17:62). Neander adopts a practice used so frequently that it has become an English "rule." The practice introduces the playwright's "Coup de Maistre," but this is an English "Coup," a "Coup" impossible to realize in a French comedy. English drama proves its vitality and autonomy by generating *its own* rules, its own, distinctively English, "Coups de Maistre," beyond the reach of French "art." With Dryden's own "Coup de Maistre" he subjugates his version of Corneille, for in the ability of the English to rule themselves, to make their own rules for the stage, to see what works and institute it as if Greece and Rome (or

No clear connection betw. the 'demonstration' of Jonson's excellence and the claim for the pre-eminence of post-1660 Eng. lit. drama.

Dryden and the French

France) had never existed or legislated, Dryden finds the means both to assimilate and to transcend what the French have to offer, appropriating their very language ("Coup de Maistre") to describe an English development.[61]

With this assertion of the English capacity to invent superior rules and forms, the examen per se concludes. Bearing in mind, however, that the examen demonstrates Neander's larger point—identical with Dryden's avowed aim of vindicating the honor of the English writers—it is of interest to note how Dryden integrates Neander's practical demonstration into his larger argument. Eschewing standard French critical practice, he does not derive a set of binding rules from Jonson's technique, nor does he present *The Silent Woman* as a model for present poets to follow. He uses the excellence of the play as only one instance of the superiority of English wit. "But we need not call our Hero's to our ayde; Be it spoken to the honour of the *English,* our Nation can never want in any Age such who are able to dispute the Empire of Wit with any people in the Universe" (*Works,* 17:63). Apparently transported by his own enthusiasm, Neander provides no basis for his leap from the proven excellence of this one "hero" of the last age to his ringing declaration of the general superiority of contemporary English poets to any on earth; nor does he justify his final leap over the shoulders of the "Hero's" of the last age to his final assertion that "as it is no less'ning to us to yield to some Playes, and those not many of our own Nation in the last Age, so can it be no addition to pronounce of our present Poets that they have far surpass'd all the Ancients, and the Modern Writers of other Countreys" (*Works,* 17:64). Neander breaks out of the extended and closely argued examen to come to the point of the *Essay:* "our present Poets"—chief among them, Dryden—are the greatest in history, the greatest in the world.

Although Neander has shown no specific reason why the excellencies of *The Silent Woman* are only some of the many treasures of the English stage, and those not necessarily the most precious, Dryden, in his inimitably subtle fashion, has provided a vocabulary and grammar with which to discuss the varying merits of the two national dramas. He has proven that the English drama, first of all, can meet the French on its own ground of the rules, and that the English drama—unlike the French—can generate its own rules, based on what actually pleases an audience. Though one must not always expect humours drama from the English, one can expect that English drama, while preserving the unity of action (easily managed since the term remains generally undefined), will present a greater variety of character and plot, with its wealth of subplot and byplay, than will French drama. Though Neander does not dwell much on Restoration drama, for the stated reason that "Vivorum, ut magnat admiratio ita censura difficilis" ("betwixt the extreams of admiration and malice, 'tis hard to judge uprightly of the living") and for the implicit difficulty of having the character evaluate the work of his creator, Dryden does provide the reader with a means to assess contemporary drama, placing it in an English tradition, within a framework both based upon and transcendent of the "authority" of the Franco-Cornelian dramatic and critical tradition.

There is something strange and a little terrible in the figure of the ambitious young poet making a name for himself at the expense of his elder, using weapons of the elder's creation to vitiate other works of their very inventor. But perhaps the most singular part of the story is that the battle was conducted by only one of the two parties; Corneille's distance from Dryden both in space and stature kept Corneille unaware of what would to him have seemed a very small affair. That Dryden could actually engage Corneille himself in any controversy seems to have been absent from his thoughts, as we glimpse at the end of the *Essay of Dramatick Poesy* when, following the verbal battle for the domination of the English stage (recapitulating in miniature the battle for domination of the seas occurring not far distant), the disputants land and pass "up through a crowd of *French* people who were merrily dancing in the open air, and nothing concern'd for the noise of Guns which had allarm'd the Town that afternoon"[62] (*Works,* 17:80–81). The French, "nothing concerned," were not the object of Dryden's objections to their theater; it was the English, Dryden's contemporaries and audience, whom he sought to provide with a new set of terms with which to judge the merits of the two different dramas. As far as Dryden was concerned, the French might dance as merrily as they pleased.[63]

Dryden wrote the *Essay of Dramatick Poesy* at the apogee of

Corneille's reputation in Restoration England. By the mid-1670s, however, Corneille's stock in the English marketplace of literary reputation had plummeted, to be replaced by the French stage's new darling, Racine. Accordingly, it is Dryden's relationship with Racine, and that relationship's finest and best-known product, *All for Love,* to which we now turn.

Teachers dutifully assign *All for Love,* and students dutifully read it, as if it were a telescope through which modern readers might view seventeenth-century attitudes toward the works of Shakespeare. By analyzing the changes Dryden wrought in *Antony and Cleopatra,* the argument runs, we can see where Elizabethan and "neoclassic" aesthetics differ. (Dryden is in this case always referred to as a neoclassical poet). Nor is this standard view unreasonable; Dryden, after all, suggests that we make such connections by including prefatory remarks such as the following: "*All for Love: or, the World Well Lost.* A Tragedy, as it is Acted at the Theatre-Royal; And Written in Imitation of *Shakespeare's* Stile" (title page of the first edition of *All for Love,* 1678, *Works,* 13:2). "By imitating him [Shakespeare], I have excell'd my self throughout the Play" (Preface to *All for Love, Works,* 13:18–19). By claiming to imitate Shakespeare's style and boasting that he has excelled himself in doing so, Dryden invites us to consider his play alongside Shakespeare's, and from its 1677 premiere until the present, critics have accepted Dryden's invitation by including somewhere in their remarks on *All for Love* a comparison of Dryden's and Shakespeare's plays.[64]

If we remove *All for Love* from Dryden's avowed system of Shakespearean "imitation," however, and place it (where I shall argue it properly belongs) in Dryden's covert matrix of misquotation, that is, reading *All for Love* not "in Imitation of *Shakespeare's* Stile" but as a work written in silent opposition to that style, we find that Dryden's insistence upon the play's spurious connection to Shakespeare serves to distract the reader from remarking upon the play's genuine connection to Racine, France's most successful tragedian of the period and the playwright from whose work Dryden borrowed principles of formal organization, elements of plot, inspiration for characters, much of the tone, and some of the language of *All for Love.*

When critics consider *All for Love* apart from *Antony and Cleo-*

The 'symmetry', 'taste' (etc.) of *All for Love* quite an Shakespearian.

THE IMPERIAL DRYDEN

patra, their observations tend to suggest not similarities to, but differences from, Shakespeare's work. Robert Gould, in *The Play-house, A Satyr* (1709), holds *All for Love* to be the "most Correct of all" Dryden's plays.[65] Johnson, in his *Life of Dryden,* damns *All for Love* with this faint praise: "[It] is by universal consent accounted the work in which he [Dryden] has admitted the fewest impro-prieties of style or character" (133). Scott mentions "the general good taste evinced throughout the . . . piece" (5:291). F. R. Leavis writes that Dryden "aims at symmetry, a neat and obvious design, a balanced arrangement . . . a ballet-like completeness of pattern, and an elegantly stylized decorum."[66] Norman Suckling judges *All for Love* to be "the greatest—perhaps the only great—classical tragedy in English."[67] Correct, few improprieties, tasteful, sym-metrical, neat, balanced, decorous, classical—these terms, which most readers would agree are descriptive of *All for Love,* are also, readers would agree, most undescriptive of Shakespeare (though they do describe the dramas of Racine). Moreover, since even Shakespeare's champions in the seventeenth century considered him a cornucopia of splendidly erratic productions unregulated by the rules of art, the genius both of English poetry and of English impropriety, it becomes apparent that we have, in essence, two different accounts of Dryden's play. The first, Dryden's claim to imitate Shakespeare, seems countered by the remarks of Gould, Johnson, Scott, Leavis, and Suckling, which, taken together, imply that if Dryden imitated Shakespeare, he succeeded only in produc-ing a fundamentally un-Shakespearean work. Before attempting to reconcile these two accounts of the play, let us bear in mind the inadvisability of permitting Dryden's own commentary to guide us, remarking of him in particular what Northrop Frye remarks of poets in general—their writings on their own poetry have "a peculiar interest, but not a peculiar authority."[68]

By professing "to imitate the Divine *Shakespeare,*" Dryden is considered by some recent commentators to mean that he has imi-tated Shakespeare's rhetorical and poetic style.[69] Dryden does in-deed use "style" to denote such narrowly rhetorical and prosodic traits, as in such comments as "the style is easy and naturall,"[70] "he neither studied the sublime stile, nor affected the flowry" (*Life of Plutarch, Works,* 17:278), and "as for his style, 'tis rather *Ciceronian*"

Dryden and the French

(Postscript to *History of the League,* 18:415). But Dryden also uses "style" to signify more general phenomena; the term may denote the aggregate of an individual's particularities, the sum of those qualities that constitute his or her individual identity. Dryden uses the term in this broadly comprehensive sense in the dedication to *Plutarchs Lives* (1683): "The difference is as plainly seen, betwixt Sophistry and truth, as it is betwixt the stile of a Gentleman, and the clumsy stifness of a Pedant" (*Works,* 17:235). When Dryden writes of imitating the "style" of other writers, he rarely employs the term to denote its narrow, rhetorical sense; on the contrary, when speaking of imitating other writers, Dryden uses the term in its larger sense, to denote the sum of the writer's distinctive traits. We see this in the following advice from "To Mr. Southern; On His Comedy, Called *The Wives Excuse*":

> But if thou wou'dst be seen, as well as read;
> Copy one living Author, and one dead;
> The Standard of thy Style, let *Etherege* be:
> For Wit, th'Immortal Spring of *Wycherly.*
> Learn after both, to draw some just Design,
> And the next Age will learn to Copy thine.
>
> (*Works,* 3:227–28)

In Dryden's friendly consolation on the tepid success of his play, the younger poet is urged to imitate Etherege's total style as a writer and as a man ("let *Etherege* be"), and the more restricted category of Wycherley's "wit." Dryden draws a clear distinction between a limited component of comic writing ("wit") and the larger category that is equated with the whole person.

Another indication that Dryden, when referring to Shakespeare's "stile," refers more to general than to specifically poetic or rhetorical qualities, is that when Dryden limits himself to discussing only Shakespeare's poetic style, he refers to it with contempt. In the *Defence of the Epilogue* (1672) he says: "[Shakespeare] writes in many places, below the dullest Writer of ours, or of any precedent Age. Never did any Author precipitate himself from such heights of thought to so low expressions, as he often does. He is the very *Janus* of Poets; he wears, almost every where two faces: and you have scarce begun to admire the one,

I just merely attempting to imitate Sh's local manners.

e're you despise the other" (*Works,* 11:212–13). And only a year after *All for Love*'s publication, in the preface to *Troilus and Cressida,* Dryden confesses that there is much in Shakespeare's *poetic* style not worthy of imitation: "[Shakespeare's] whole stile is so pester'd with Figurative expressions, that it is as affected as it is obscure" (*Works,* 13:225). Though Dryden expresses many such reservations regarding Shakespeare's poetic style, his admiration for Shakespeare's larger accomplishment is practically without reserve. "He was the man who of all Modern, and perhaps Ancient Poets, had the largest and most comprehensive soul," Dryden begins in the *Essay of Dramatick Poesy,* and he goes on to attribute almost godlike omniscience to Shakespeare—he was "naturally learn'd," and "needed not the spectacles of Books to read Nature; he look'd inwards, and found her there" (*Works,* 17:55). Because Dryden consistently damns the particulars of Shakespeare's poetic "stile," and as consistently praises Shakespeare's general accomplishment, it would seem that in claiming to imitate Shakespeare's style Dryden could only have been referring to Shakespeare's comprehensiveness of soul, his near-omniscient "divinity," his large poetic and dramatic effects. That Dryden meant to say that in *All for Love* he was imitating a poetic style he elsewhere labels "affected" and "obscure," "below the dullest Writer" of his or any age, while conceivable, seems vastly unlikely.

Having established the probability that Dryden laid mimetic claim to more than the particulars of Shakespeare's poetic style, we may now disprove his claim entirely by examining how *All for Love* differs from its putative model and closest Shakespearean analogue, *Antony and Cleopatra.* As commentators have observed, the scope of the action is greatly reduced: *All for Love* begins at the eleventh scene of *Antony and Cleopatra*'s third act, after the battle of Actium—almost two-thirds through Shakespeare's play. The dramatis personae of *Antony and Cleopatra* lists thirty-four characters; *All for Love* lists ten, excluding Antony's daughters who together speak one word. The scenes of *Antony and Cleopatra* range over continents; *All for Love* remains in Alexandria. If Dryden is indeed imitating Shakespeare, he has selected about a third of *Antony and Cleopatra*'s events and scenes, only a minute fraction of its duration, and just a bit of its spatial extension.

Dryden and the French

Although the scene and action might seem fractionally to derive from Shakespeare, the characters of *All for Love* appear not to be drawn from *Antony and Cleopatra* at all. Dryden's Antony is a beaten man; whining and indecisive, he is convinced by the last person to speak to him, whoever that might be. His passion for Cleopatra is humorless, self-immolatory, obsessional; he seems more a feckless playboy than a great military leader in defeat—a type that the later *Cleomenes* (1692) was to explore so searchingly. *All for Love*'s Antony, in Dryden's own words,

> Bates of his mettle; and scarce rants at all:
> He's somewhat lewd; but a well-meaning mind;
> Weeps much; fights little; but is wond'rous kind:
> In short, a Pattern, and Companion fit,
> For all the keeping *Tonyes* of the Pit.
>
> (Prologue, *Works,* 13:20)

Though Dryden's poetic self-assessments must always be approached skeptically, in this case we need not dispute Dryden's summation of his hero as kind, tearful, well-meaning, the fight gone out of him—close in nature to his contemporary namesakes, the "Tonyes," the mistress-keepers of the pit.

Dryden's Cleopatra, most readers agree, is well suited to Dryden's Antony. Closer in character to Shakespeare's Octavia than to his Cleopatra, she is intended by nature to be, as she is made to say,

> A Wife, a silly harmless houshold Dove,
> Fond without art; and kind without deceit.
>
> (*Works,* 13:75)

Dryden's Cleopatra is a compelling portrait of an obsessive love, of a woman thrust by circumstances into a role she lacks quite the bite to play. This Cleopatra lacks not only infinite, but any variety, striking only the note of amorous desperation throughout the play; there is nothing in her of Shakespeare's *monstre sacrée,* the vibrant creature whom priests bless when riggish.

Dryden's "Tony" and Cleopatra partake in none of the rough grandeur of Shakespeare's characters and, but for a number of merely verbal echoes, seem only nominally related to them. Dryden's principals lack the splendor, the *public* quality of Shake-

D's introspective despairers closer to Racine's chaos. than Sh.'s.
His blank verse not like Sh.'s

speare's, although they live a more intense, and perhaps a more precisely visualized *inner* life.[71] Although Dryden's Antony and Cleopatra are related to Shakespeare's by name and general function, the reader will search in vain for any more than a nominal connection between Dryden's Ventidius and Alexas—and not even that for Dolabella—and the characters of *Antony and Cleopatra.*

The note of the pathétique that characters strike throughout the play recalls the closeted despair of Antonio and the Duchess of Malfi, or the roughly contemporary domestic despair of Otway's Jaffeir and Belvidera—sympathetic characters simply not up to what fate demands of them. The vividly articulated desperation of Dryden's Antony and Cleopatra, their capacity for self-analysis, the intrigues of characters driven more by passion than by events, as well as the specific plot functions of such subsidiary characters as Dolabella and Ventidius, are all closer, as we shall see, to the dramas of Racine than to those of Shakespeare.

If Dryden's Antony and Cleopatra seem only nominally related to Shakespeare's, neither do they speak in Shakespeare's "stile." Released from the fetters of rhyme—such as Sedley's *Antony and Cleopatra* of the same year employed—Dryden can experiment with a new kind of poetic diction, but it is not the blank verse of Shakespeare. T. S. Eliot called Dryden's achievement "a miracle of revivification," and then proceeded to argue, and in this I feel he is right, that Dryden reappropriates the blank verse line for himself. What is great about the verse of *All for Love,* argues Eliot, is that it is *not* like Shakespeare's.[72] Dryden's line, for all its metrical virtuosity, shares none of Shakespeare's baroquely imagistic splendor. The lament of the eunuch Alexas will serve as an example:

> Pleasure forsook my early'st Infancy,
> The luxury of others robb'd my Cradle,
> And ravish'd thence the promise of a Man:
> Cast out from Nature, disinherited
> Of what her meanest Children claim by kind;
> Yet, greatness kept me from contempt: that's gone.
> Had *Cleopatra* follow'd my advice,
> Then he had been betray'd, who now forsakes.

> She dies for love; but she has known its joys:
> Gods, is this just, that I, who know no joys,
> Must die, because she loves?
>
> (*Works,* 13:67–68)

It is fine verse; metrically sure, informed by the effects of the couplet (the inversion of "love" and "joys" in the last three lines) without being dominated by it, spare and simple in expression, powerfully conceived. But no one who read these lines would imagine them Shakespeare's, or written in imitation of Shakespeare. Indeed, for all the fine writing in *All for Love,* at no moment in the play (with the possible exception of the barge speech, to which we shall return) do most readers feel that they are reading work written in imitation of Shakespeare, although we do come across occasional Shakespearean lines quoted more or less verbatim. Dryden's blank verse, though it does not belong to the Dryden of the heroic dramas, is nonetheless the blank verse of Dryden, not Shakespeare.

Because *All for Love* employs only a fraction of Shakespeare's duration and spatial extension and virtually none of Shakespeare's characters or diction, and because most readers experience no tonal instances that remind them of Shakespeare, I believe it fair to conclude that if Dryden truly imitated Shakespeare's style, he chose a very reduced bit to imitate, and failed to imitate even that bit. But rather than take Dryden at his word (thus admitting that he imitates Shakespeare badly), it is more just to Dryden, and to a play that virtually all readers have felt to be of lasting value (if not quite, as Saintsbury puts it, "gigantic in the manner of the good giants"),[73] to propose that Dryden does not imitate Shakespeare in any of the senses of style hitherto defined.

To explain why, and the mechanism whereby, Dryden would have claimed to imitate a poet he did not actually imitate, requires a summation of the scattered points of this chapter, an overview of the means by which Dryden assimilated the productions of other poets and critics. An avid and wide-ranging reader, Dryden took what he could use from all the literary traditions available to him, the antique, sacred, continental, and English. But depending both on the occasion and the stature of the poet or critic, Dryden employed one of four means to incorporate their works into his own.

Dryden greatly favored the acknowledged verbatim insertion of the words or opinions of others into his own works—quotation. He quoted almost as widely as he read, which was widely indeed. Quotations ground Dryden's work in a fabric of textuality, in which what is written is woven from what has already been written and is thus grounded in the authority of the literary traditions available to him.

The mode of assimilation Dryden used least, though that which most interested his contemporaries, is a process whereby the writer inserts material originating in the works of another poet more or less verbatim into the writer's own work, without acknowledgment. This unacknowledged borrowing from the works of other poets—plagiarism—occurred often enough to elicit unfavorable comment during Dryden's lifetime. Gerard Langbaine's scathing account of Dryden's sources in *An Account of the English Dramatick Poets* (1691) is only the best known and most extensive of the many accusations of unacknowledged borrowings made against Dryden during and after his lifetime. The author(s) of the *Censure of the Rota* claim that Dryden's descriptions are "borrewed from *Statius,* and *Montaigns* Essays, the Reason and Politicall Ornaments from Mr *Hobs,* and the Astrologicall (and if need be, the Language too) from *Ibrahim,* or the *Illustrious Bassa.*"[74] The anonymous author of *The Tory-Poets: A Satyr* (1682), exhorts:

> Read *Dry*——*ns* plays, and read *Corneille*'s too,
> You'l swear the *Frenchman* speaks good *English* now.[75]

Of Dryden's pillagings Matthew Prior writes in "A Satyr on the Modern Translators" (1685):

> But when not satisfy'd with Spoils at home,
> The Pyrate wou'd to foreign Borders roam.[76]

The vitriolic Martin Clifford begins his *Notes upon Mr. Dryden's Poems in Four Letters* (1687) by threatening: "And next I will detect your Thefts, letting the World know how great a Plagiary you are."[77] Goaded by such criticisms as this, Dryden mounted a magnificent defense in the preface to *An Evening's Love* (1668). His extended rebuttal begins with a brief recension of his critics'

D's 'literary imperialism' (appropriation of lesser writers)
His appropriation of professors' authority via misquotation.

Dryden and the French

charges: "I am tax'd with stealing all my Playes" (*Works,* 10:210).

Another method by which Dryden assimilated material from other poets might be referred to as the imperial mode. Literary imperialism, the poetic equivalent of forcibly seizing weak foreign realms and diverting their resources back to the conquering capital, occurs when the poet openly and without apology commits his or her depredations upon the literary works of others. Dryden articulates this mode in characteristic fashion by ascribing it to another. Of Ben Jonson he writes:

> But *Ben* made nobly his, what he did mould,
> What was anothere's Lead, becomes his Gold;
> Like an unrighteous Conquerer he raigns,
> Yet rules that well, which he unjustly gains.
>   (Prologue to Tomkis's *Albumazar* [1668], *Works,* 1:141)

Literary imperialism, as the term implies, is always practiced upon foreign poets and usually those deemed of lesser stature, or upon writers in lesser genres. Poets of undisputed stature, such as Shakespeare, Jonson, Corneille, or Racine, could not be assimilated in this manner; for poets such as these, a more subtle mode of appropriation was called for.

This fourth form of appropriation is misquotation. By claiming one's own writing for another's, misquotation appropriates literary authority, not literary material; the procedure spuriously grounds the misquoter's own opinions or work in established literary culture. Whereas plagiarism steals the other's work, misquotation steals the other tout entier, calling the other master while making him a slave. Misquotation shows respect for the name as signifier of an established structure of literary power and contempt for the structure itself. In the act of misquotation appears a radical fracturing of the identity we customarily assume between an author and her "work," an authority and his "law." Hence, misquoting is the most efficient procedure with which to treat a figure whose fame one must celebrate, but whose poetic authority one finds oppressive. Misquotation wrests all prescriptive power from the very authority it pretends to affirm; it is a quiet, subtle, near-invisible palace revolt, a coup d'état behind the wall of words.

As Dryden affirms previous literary authority by the act of

Various types of misquotation in D.. D. evoking Sh.'s
authority in _All for Love_ to endorse quite un-Shakespearian practice

THE IMPERIAL DRYDEN

quotation, he vitiates it by altering the transmitted matter; in
the case of Dryden's claim that Shakespeare originated blank
verse,[78] Dryden's legislating simulacrum (he who "originated"
blank verse) is upheld as the hero of English poets, while the
bones of Shakespeare (he who did not originate blank verse) are
plowed under to make way for Dryden's mythic figure, who then
legislates as Dryden would have him. Shakespeare's authority is
thus usurped by Dryden, who makes of him, and makes him to
say, whatever Dryden wishes.

Dryden uses this technique on four related levels, ranging from
other writers' words themselves through their styles. When Dryden misquotes a line of Ovid in order to justify a poetic turn of his
own, we might call this a verbatim misquotation.[79] Besides being
the simplest and most direct form of misquotation, it is also the
easiest to prove, since the verbatim quotation presumes an absolute identity with that which it purports to quote. Abstracted from
the level of verbatim misquotation to the level of complete utterance, when Dryden writes that Aristotle thought epic a higher
form than tragedy, we might call this a misquotation of position or thought.[80] A somewhat more complex form of misquotation occurs when Dryden credits Shakespeare with having originated blank verse. In this case, Dryden mistransmits, not words
or thoughts, but actions; by doing so he formulates an alternative
literary history that in turn authorizes certain of his formal proce-
dures and critical positions. Finally, when Dryden claims that he
is going to imitate Shakespeare's style, but then imitates the style
of another, or writes as it pleases him, we might call the claim to
imitate Shakespeare a misquotation of style.

Stylistic misquotation is difficult to prove, for we must show,
first, that the misquoter lays claim to another's style, and second,
that the misquoter substitutes another style for that which he or
she claims to imitate. In the case of *All for Love,* we can show that
Dryden claims to imitate, or quote, the style of Shakespeare, because he tells us so. "In my Stile I have profess'd to imitate the
Divine *Shakespeare,*" Dryden writes in the preface to *All for Love*
(*Works,* 13:18), but the ambiguity of "profess'd" is revealing; as
always, Dryden finds it difficult to keep his own secrets. We have

seen how little Dryden actually imitated Shakespeare; it now remains to show *All for Love*'s stylistic connection to Racine.

Dryden would have had the opportunity to read most of
Racine's dramas before writing *All for Love,* for ten of Racine's
twelve plays were already in print in 1678, including the sequence
for which we principally know him: *Andromaque* (1668), *Britannicus*
(1670), *Bérénice* (1671), *Bajazet* (1672), *Mithridate* (1673), *Iphigénie*
(1675), and *Phèdre* (1677).[81] Not only do we know that Dryden had
the opportunity to read Racine, we know that he did. We learn that
Racine was on Dryden's mind at about the time of *All for Love*'s
composition from its preface, which contains a substantial polemic
against "their Hippolitus." From the precision of Dryden's satire
on the manners of *Phèdre* we learn that he read it with care, just
as, ten years earlier, the exactness of Dryden's arguments against
Corneille prove that the *Essay* was written with the Corneille edition of 1660 at his side, despite Dryden's claim that the *Essay* was
written "without the help of Books" (*Works,* 17:7).

Dryden finds the same faults with *Phèdre* that he finds with
Racine elsewhere—to Dryden, the Racinian hero is effete, too
civil, and too well bred. Dryden charges that the author "has
chosen to give him [Hippolitus] the turn of Gallantry, sent him
to travel from *Athens* to *Paris,* taught him to make love, and trans-
form'd the *Hippolitus* of *Euripides* into Monsieur *Hippolite*" (*Works,*
13:13). A charge, one might observe, that might have been leveled
at Dryden's Antony as well. A year later, in the preface to *Troilus
and Cressida,* Dryden similarly observes: "*Racine's Bajazet* is bred
at *Constantinople;* but his civilities are convey'd to him by some
secret passage, from *Versailles* into the *Seraglio*" (*Works,* 13:238).
From such hostile notice it would seem that Dryden deplored the
Racinian style, but as we have seen, negative notice in Dryden's
criticism, such as Corneille's drama received in the 1660s, and
such as Racine receives in the 1670s, often seems to indicate posi-
tive interest, envy, an intent to emulate, or even the apparent wish
to conceal such emulation.[82]

Besides the full, albeit negative attention Racine receives in
the preface, the many structural and tonal parallels between *All
for Love* and the nine serious dramas of Racine published before

1677 suggest that Dryden admired more in the new French dramatic style than he was willing to admit.[83] Three plays, *Britannicus, Bérénice,* and *Phèdre,* seem particularly to have influenced him. In *Britannicus* (1669) the Emperor Nero has fallen violently in love with Junie, the betrothed of his deposed stepbrother, Britannicus. Agrippine, Nero's mother, threatens to foment revolution, and uses the young and trusting Britannicus as her pawn. Nero's tutor, Burrhus, argues for restraint.

Dryden's interest in *Britannicus* was evidently aroused by the scenes between Nero and his tutor, Burrhus, who, like Ventidius, is a plainspoken military man. And, like Ventidius, he tries to dissuade his master from an illicit and potentially catastrophic passion, a passion that, like Antony's for Cleopatra, threatens to foment a civil war, with the opposing side led by a family member. Burrhus, while urging Nero to cease his attempts on Junie's virtue, also tries to persuade the emperor back to his marital obligations with his empress, named, like Antony's wife, Octavia:

> [If you] deigned, my lord, a little to remember
> Octavia's virtues, which deserve better than this,
> And her chaste love, still strong though you despise her;
> If, above all, you avoided Junia,
> Condemning your eyes to some days of absence:
> Believe me, however love seems to charm you,
> One does not love, my lord, unless one wants to.[84]

Burrhus's sturdy and indefatigable eloquence employed in favor of Roman duty, custom, and will ("on n'aime point, si l'on ne veut aimer"), and in favor of avoiding war by reuniting with an empress named Octavia, seems to have provided the inspiration for the first scene of *All for Love,* in which Ventidius cajoles and argues Antony back into a martial—Roman—state of mind.

In a passage of characteristically Drydenian tracks-covering in the preface to *All for Love,* Dryden comments on this scene between Antony and Ventidius. He first asserts that he has excelled himself by imitating Shakespeare, then that the Antony/Ventidius scene (certainly more like the analogous scene in Racine than the one in Shakespeare) is his favorite scene of this type: "Yet I hope I may affirm, and without vanity, that by imitating him [Shakespeare], I have excell'd my self throughout the Play; and particularly, that I prefer the Scene betwixt *Antony* and *Ventidius* in the first Act, to any thing which I have written in this kind" (*Works*, 13:18–19). Because there is no discernible connection between the Antony/Ventidius scene and the works of Shakespeare and because Dryden appears to wish to suppress his debt to Racine, we may conclude that Dryden stresses his debt to Shakespeare in such strongly self-congratulatory terms precisely because there is little, if any, such debt.

Racine's next play after *Britannicus*, *Bérénice* (printed 1671), seems closer in tone, and, at points, in structure, to *All for Love* than anything in *Antony and Cleopatra*. [85] Racine's play concerns the separation of the emperor Titus from his beloved oriental queen, Bérénice. Roman law forbids his marrying a queen, and the emperor, distraught but determined to appease the senate and people, finally brings himself to separate from his lifelong beloved, whom he orders back to Syria. With its plot of Roman emperor forced from a near-eastern queen, its turns and counterturns dependent solely on changes of heart, its elegiac tone of fin d'amour, its many scenes of weeping and romantic lamentation, *Bérénice* seems to have provided Dryden with inspiration for the tone—and for some plot elements—of *All for Love*. [86]

Antony's frustrating indecision is much like that of the emperor Titus, who has decided to separate from Bérénice, but cannot bring himself to inform her. The reverberations of emotion, each participant in the drama reacting to others' changes of heart, go far, but not all the way, toward disguising the fact that this is a drama in which nothing happens, a drama (or *pièce folle*, as Madame de Sévigné called it) that hangs fire until the last scene. In the preface Racine is unabashed in his rejection of the Cornelian (or to the English, "heroic") drama of vulgar action. "Only the probable touches us in tragedy. And how probable is it that a multitude of things should occur in one day that could hardly occur in several weeks? Some think that this simplicity marks a lack of invention. They do not dream that, on the contrary, *all the invention consists in making something out of nothing*" (my translation and emphasis) (*Théâtre*, 466). [87] The Racinian aesthetic of dramatic invention consists, godlike, of making something of nothing, a

The Dolabella / Cleopatra subplot based on R's Antiochus / Bérénice subplot. Plot //s p. other R. plays.

THE IMPERIAL DRYDEN

principle that Dryden seems to have taken to heart as he made an entire drama out of the duration of what had been only the conclusion of another.

In addition to *Bérénice*'s general tone and the masterful achievement of the suspended action—the making of something from nothing—the Antiochus/Bérénice subplot seems certainly to have inspired Dryden with the Dolabella/Cleopatra subplot in *All for Love*. Antiochus, bosom friend to the emperor, has long loved Bérénice in secret. Although in deference to his friend he has refrained from declaring himself, his passion eventually erupts in a confession to Bérénice, and they agree to avoid each other. Antiochus next finds himself in the peculiar position of having to inform her, at the emperor's command, that Titus intends to end the relationship. This Antiochus/Bérénice subplot is precisely reflected in *All for Love,* where Dolabella is sent to inform the queen he secretly loves of Antony's return to Octavia. Although the two queens' reactions differ (Cleopatra feigns romantic interest in Dolabella; Bérénice, made of sterner stuff, refuses to believe Antiochus), common to both plays is the piquant dilemma of using one's best male friend (secret lover of one's beloved) to sever the relationship with that beloved.

Others of Racine's plays also seem to have provided Dryden with ideas for *All for Love*. In *Mithridate* and *Bajazet* a trusted friend, left alone with the love-object to work the protagonist's romantic designs, works his own. A scene of multiple naming in *Iphigénie* (1674) might well be the source for the infamous "Emperor! Friend! Husband! Father!" scene in *All for Love*.[88] In *Phèdre,* the work of Racine closest in time to *All for Love,* the scheming of Phèdre's maid to bring about the consummation of her mistress's illicit love parallels the scheming of Cleopatra's much less clever eunuch, Alexas; Cleopatra's final blaming of Alexas for disturbing their love through his machinations seems closely related to Phèdre's final, and much more terrible, condemnation of her Machiavellian maid.

Besides the plot parallels, the change in Dryden's poetic diction from the rhymed verse of the heroic plays seems more determined by Racine than by Shakespeare. Compared to Shakespeare's much grander effects and the swollen rhetoric of Dryden's pre-

Dryden and the French

vious heroic plays, the diction of *All for Love* at moments attains a kind of simple dignity unheard before in English. Though not, like Racine's language, almost bare of metaphor, the poetry of *All for Love* is considerably more spare than that of Shakespeare or the heroic drama; one need only compare the barge speeches from *All for Love* and *Antony and Cleopatra* to see the degree to which Dryden streamlines.[89] This simplicity of diction, as we see from Dryden's comments on Shakespeare's poetic style quoted above, was not a simplicity he associated with Shakespeare.

Apparently aware that his play did not fulfill the promise of its title page or the repeated protestations in the preface, Dryden made certain that readers would be prepared for a play that did not resemble Shakespeare's. Adept at shaping his audience's response to his works, Dryden excuses *All for Love*'s failure to resemble *Antony and Cleopatra* in the following words: "I hope I need not to explain my self, that I have not Copy'd my Author servilely: Words and Phrases must of necessity receive a change in succeeding Ages" (*Works*, 13:18). Besides this disclaimer, Dryden sprinkled *All for Love* with snippets of quotation from several of Shakespeare's plays, the longest of these being, of course, Dolabella's barge speech.[90] However, when we read *All for Love* not as an imitation of Shakespeare, but as an extended misquotation of style, then those elements in *All for Love* that evoke or are borrowed from Shakespeare's play appear in a different light. Dolabella's much-discussed barge speech is neither an imitation nor tribute, but a red herring—a signpost pointing exactly the wrong way, suggesting quotation as the play itself leads away from it toward an unacknowledged experiment in imitation of the age's dramatic idol, Jean Racine.

Dryden early acquired a knack for establishing his poetic bona fides in borrowed personae, imitating Corneille as he wore, in the person of Neander, the sword of the English chauvinist; imitating Racine cloaked in the mantle of Shakespeare. The oblique manner in which he approached the works and reputations of Corneille, Racine, and Shakespeare shows that he shared, with many subsequent writers in the English tradition, the sense of coming after "the giant race before the flood." Yet Dryden (in Bate's view the first great English poet to experience this chastening belatedness) approached this new, typically modern anxiety with all the energy and dash of someone approaching a problem for the first time. If, because there had already been one, he could not be a Shakespeare, "the Homer, or father of English poetry," he could indeed fashion himself the "Homer, or father of English belatedness," and the passion and ingenuity with which he approached his own dilemma indicates how large, persistent, and potentially crippling a problem he found it.

Dryden's anxiety regarding his predecessors struck at the very root of his poetic identity, and it was through the assumption of other identities that he chose to combat it. When it came to approaching the works of those whose poetic or critical reputations he regarded with respect, the question of identity became fluid; borders softened, terms permuted, quotation marks became masks for what he wished to say in a form of ventriloquistic projection. Yet assuming from afar the identities of others, animating with his own voice the hollow figures of Corneille, Shakespeare, or Aristotle, was by no means Dryden's sole means of approaching the works and reputations of his contemporaries and predecessors— not all poets had to be controlled through this projection of voice. Those whom Dryden had little reason to fear could be assaulted in broad daylight, robbed of their poetic treasures on the open road, and sent on their way. This bold-faced highway robbery, what I call literary imperialism, is the focus of chapter 2.

CHAPTER TWO

Onely Victory in Him:
The Imperial Dryden

> He invades Authours like a Monarch, and what would
> be theft in other Poets, is onely victory in him.
>
> *Essay of Dramatick Poesy, Works,* 17:57

In chapter 1 I grounded the discussion of literary misquotation
in the terms of political usurpation, as the usurper, like the misquoter, requires a familial, or quasi-familial, proximity to the loci
of power. The usurper attains power by claiming kinship and asserting a right of legitimate ownership or descent; he or she claims
to interpret the wishes of a still-reigning power unable to speak for
itself. That one usurps—or misquotes—suggests a need to operate in the name, according to the rules, of the literary or political
authority, and the misquoter, by claiming to operate according to
the rules of power-conferring structures, implies a remnant respect
for the very structures he or she subverts. Dryden, as we have
seen, uses this technique against those whose poetic achievement
weighs heavily upon him, those he names fathers (Shakespeare
and Jonson), and the de facto legislators of poetic form and critical vocabulary, Corneille and Racine.

Yet besides misquoting—and quoting—Dryden uses a more
direct means of appropriating and assimilating the work and traditions of others. The appropriative strategy this chapter treats
might be described, using another analogy borrowed from systems of political power, by the term literary imperialism. Literary imperialism—in practical terms, the appropriation of others'
writing openly and without apology—resembles plagiarism in its
rough outlines, yet fundamentally differs from it in its essence
and implications. The imperial poet, by claiming greater poetic
strength, asserts the right to seize upon and appropriate the work

63

... on the grounds that it will yield better results in the seizer's hands.   widespread imperialism in the period.

THE IMPERIAL DRYDEN

of other poets; the imperial poet claims not only that other poets' works are worth taking, but that other poets are weak. Imperial poets claim that they deserve what they take more than the artifact's present possessor because they can do more with it; poetic strength licenses the taking, since the appropriated material will yield better results in more capable hands. The very act of imperially taking comments on the status of the predecessor poet, whereas the act of plagiarism speaks only of the value of the work. Though both take what does not belong to them, the poetic imperialist differs from the plagiarist as much as Cortez, marching to the valley of Mexico, differs from a cat burglar entering a second-story window.

Dryden's interest in the forcible seizure of others' wealth was not peculiar to himself; the appetitive traits of literary imperialism precisely reflect larger political concerns of Dryden's age. As Margaret Anne Doody demonstrates in *The Daring Muse,* imperialism is a theme running through Restoration and early eighteenth-century poetry;[1] the shining vision of London that concludes *Annus Mirabilis* (1667) is but one of many visions of a world-dominating England:

> Now, like a Maiden Queen, she will behold,
>   From her high Turrets, hourly Sutors come:
> The East with Incense, and the West with Gold,
>   Will stand, like Suppliants, to receive her doom.
>   (*Works,* 1:104)

In this luminous vision, not only of a rebuilt London, but of a post-conquest empire, the mother city commands the wealth and will of the world, no longer by force, but by the power of its own beauty.[2] The poetry itself shows an unusual amount of metrical fragmentation, as if to reflect the constructed quality of the new city; each line is elaborated of two or three short clauses, bits of verbal brick and marble themselves reflecting the beautifully re-created quality of the architectural reconstruction the stanza anticipates.

Sweet as the ultimate fruits of imperialism may be for the victor, the sine qua non of imperial ambition is military might; accordingly, Dryden often invokes, restates, and reworks the myth of English invincibility, both poetic and military. For example, in the *Essay of Dramatick Poesy* pens and swords, evoking one another,

64

conflate into a statement by Eugenius of England's poetic and military invincibility: "I am at all times ready to defend the honour of my Countrey against the *French,* and to maintain, we are as well able to vanquish them with our Pens as our Ancestors have been with their swords" (*Works,* 17:33). In this passage, as in many others, Dryden measures the strength of the English tradition and of individual English poets against that of other countries and poets ("able to vanquish them with our Pens"). Aware of the relative strengths of both countries and writers, Dryden is also acutely conscious of the means and forms by which countries— and poets—measure their strength. We see Dryden's concern with intercultural strife most clearly in his drama, in which fifteen of the twenty-eight plays contain competitions between nations or cultures. Throughout the drama, from the earliest works of the 1660s through the final masterpieces of the 1690s, this measuring of strength, expressed in the conquering of one culture by another, is explored in substantial detail from myriad points of view.

Dryden's representations of the contests between rival cultures, interesting as the struggles of generals and armies might be, is examined with the ulterior aim of understanding Dryden's own relations with foreign contemporaries and predecessors. His views of national and poetic destiny mirror one another, and he uses similar language to describe both national and poetic events. For example, of Ben Jonson's use of the work of predecessors, Dryden writes:

> But *Ben* made nobly his, what he did mould,
> What was anothere's Lead, becomes his Gold;
> Like an unrighteous Conquerer he raigns,
> Yet rules that well, which he unjustly gains.
> (Prologue to *Albumazar* [1668], *Works,* 1:141)

Dryden uses the same imperial language as above (conquering, ruling territory unjustly appropriated, and improving the seized material beyond its original quality) when referring to his own depredations upon the work of others. Of obtaining plot material for *An Evening's Love,* he says of himself:

> [The Poet] us'd the *French* like Enemies,
> And did not steal their Plots, but made 'em prize.
> (Epilogue, *Works,* 10:313–14)

Plots, in the imperial scheme, are lawful booty, the rightful possession of whoever has the poetic strength to take them. To the imperial poet the works of others are to be made war upon, "made prize" (taken), and "ruled well" (reworked). This pattern recurs often in Dryden's mythologies of poetic origin, inheritance, and strength.

Emblems of the struggle between cultures and poets often bridge the shifting boundaries separating the political from the poetic; naval cannon fire begins the *Essay of Dramatick Poesy, The Indian Emperour,* and *Annus Mirabilis,* all works dealing with the hegemony of one culture over another, either Spanish over Indian, English over Dutch, or Dryden's own rule (as the soon-to-be laureate) over "all the Ancients, and the Modern Writers of other Countreys."

Dryden's representations of the clash of cultures may be read not only as a way of discussing his views of gaining power over others, but as a means of considering the mixed virtues of the losing side and in what consists the loser's wealth. Such heterocultural plays as *The Indian Emperour* dramatize a view of what classes of wealth might lawfully be taken from other cultures, by what means, the price one pays for such conquest, the special kinds of knowledge other cultures might possess that can be transferred, and what cannot be transferred. As Dryden considers what types of knowledge might be peculiar to other cultures, he often represents pagan religions not as fraudulent shams with which to blind and bind a too-crediting populace (such criticism, at least during his early career, he reserves for Catholicism), but as a valid but lesser means of knowing. In *The Indian Emperour* (1665), *All for Love* (1677), and *King Arthur* (1691), to name just three plays spread throughout his career, priests, by their supernatural manipulations, obtain knowledge that would otherwise be unknowable. In *The Indian Emperour* the native religion is valid and true (unlike, it is made clear, the claims of the avaricious Catholic priest), but is simply not strong enough to withstand the advent of the Christians' deity. A chthonic spirit explains his predicament to the priest and Montezuma:

> *Spirit.* In vain, O mortal men your Prayers implore
> The aid of powers below, which want it more:

66

Dsirable (and much-afford) qualities in foreign cultures.

> A God more strong, who all the gods commands,
> Drives us to exile from our Native Lands;
> The Air swarms thick with wandring Deities,
> Which drowsily like humming Beetles rise
> From their lov'd Earth.
>
> *(Works,* 9:46)

The ability of the priest to call such a spirit from the vasty deep (and have him come) demonstrates a supernatural knowledge—and attendant power—of a high order. Although the spirit replicates in the spirit world the cultural displacements of our own, the important point is that there *are* spirits, and that Mexicans can command them. In such scenes as this throughout the drama, Dryden creates fables that operate on the premise that foreign cultures possess classes of knowledge that Europeans or the English lack. Moreover, Dryden's fables of foreign wealth show that these cultures may produce individuals who possess virtues their conquerors lack, such as Montezuma's unrivaled personal nobility or, in another key, St. Catherine's sanctity in *Tyrannick Love* (1669). These virtues, found in lesser cultures, are also found in lesser poets.

Dryden represents the various permutations of imperial struggle by casting all such conflicts in one of three oppositions: himself versus certain foreign poets, England versus countries of the European continent, and Europe versus the pagan cultures (often associated with the Orient). Each pair of oppositions can be ordered with respect to their distance from the actual conditions of creation of Dryden's poetry, as follows:

self		*other*
Dryden	versus	foreign poets
England	versus	European continent
Europe	versus	pagans

Dryden often uses terms from the same side of the scheme to signify each other; "England" can signify "Dryden," and "Europe" can betoken "England." Because he employs a range of roughly equivalent terms, we may often read his attitude toward the works of foreign poets in representations of cultural alterity that deal with neither Englishmen nor poets. The differences are to be read in the border of exchange between what is familiar and power-ful (Europe-England-himself), and what is rich and strange (the Orient-Europe-the Americas-foreign poets).

Representations of cultural alterity in the drama, dramatized always in a state of opposition to that which constitutes home to Dryden (Europe-England-himself), are usually of a piece: before 1688 Dryden's side consistently triumphs. After 1688 the side with which Dryden associates himself (Europeans-English-himself) is always vanquished and exiled in a strange land (or one's own land made strange, as in *Amphitryon*). That the balance between the two clashing cultures should shift so absolutely with the reversal in Dryden's own fortunes suggests a close connection between the plots of these heterocultural plays and the events of Dryden's own life. Hence, when the English best the Spaniards in Madrid, as occurs in *An Evening's Love,* we might read the play at least in part as a dramatization of Dryden's getting the better of Thomas Corneille, from whom he seized the play. When Don Sebastian, guilty of a crime he unknowingly committed, buries himself for-ever in a monastery in a strange land, we might read that too as a reflection of Dryden's status in the new order—defeated, stripped of his official titles, and exiled from the center of official power.

The most frequently occurring, widest ranging, and most gen-eral of Dryden's imperial meetings between cultures occur when an imaginatively reconstituted Europe clashes with an imagi-natively reconstituted Oriental power. Such East-West struggles occur in *The Indian Emperour* (1665), *Tyrannick Love* (1669), *The Conquest of Granada, pts. I & II* (1670–71), *All for Love* (1677), *Troilus and Cressida* (1679), *Don Sebastian* (1690), and *Cleomenes* (1692)—nearly a third of his plays. Moors (three plays), Egyptians (three plays), and Aztecs and Trojans (one apiece) constitute the ad-versarial other that Europeans (Spaniards, three; Romans, two; Greeks, two; Portuguese, one) encounter and defeat.

Dryden's next most common form of representing the imperial urge is the depiction of England struggling with another coun-try, either in the comic or heroic mode. Such encounters occur in *Annus Mirabilis* (1666), the *Essay of Dramatick Poesy* (1668), *An Evening's Love* (1668), *Marriage A-la-Mode* (1671), *Amboyna* (1673), and *King Arthur* (1691).[3] Five of the six dramas depicting

Onely Victory in Him

the English fighting with other nations were written during the two Anglo-Dutch wars (1665–67, 1672–74), and the English encounter Dutch in three of these six works. In the remaining three, the English encounter Spaniards, French (specifically their customs and language in *Marriage*), and heathen Saxons. Dramatic in nature (though not a drama per se), the *Essay of Dramatick Poesy* has an especially contentious setting; a sea battle against the Dutch frames three verbal battles fought between four disputants for the terms of contemporary dramatic writing, pitting the English against the French, Spanish, Italians, Ancient Greeks, and Romans. Reflecting the eventual outcome of the sea battle that frames the debate, the English are found to win every battle. Replete as it is with so many different types of interrelated conflict, the *Essay of Dramatick Poesy* contains a key articulation of Dryden's doctrine of the seizure of poetic property by force. Neander (the speaker for Dryden's position) says of Ben Jonson: "He was deeply conversant in the Ancients, both *Greek* and *Latine,* and he borrow'd boldly from them: there is scarce a Poet or Historian among the *Roman* Authours of those times whom he has not translated in *Sejanus* and *Catiline.* But he has done his Robberies so openly, that one may see he fears not to be taxed by any Law. He invades Authours like a Monarch, and what would be theft in other Poets, is onely victory in him" (*Works,* 17:57). Bold borrowing, disregard for the conventions of poetic property, regal invasion of others—all describe the imperial mode of taking from other poets, in which theft (plagiarism) is transcended—at least so the commentator claims—for a more public form of appropriation in which sources are acknowledged and poetic originators named as their poetic material itself is seized upon and refashioned. Though Dryden uses misquotation to appropriate the voices of poets he regards as superiors, he takes Jonson's route of the conquering monarch as he approaches the work of those he regards as poetic equals or inferiors, of those whose fame or greatness does not threaten to define the way he wishes to write. Just as Almanzor conquered all "because he dared," so Dryden often follows Jonson down the high road of imperial conquest, doing "his Robberies so openly, that one may see he fears not to be taxed by any Law."

Dryden treats the work of his forebears and contemporaries

with varying degrees of esteem, ranging from the most respect-
ful quotation down to the contemptuous light-fingered swipe. His
oft-stated cavils aside, Dryden treats the work of his English
fathers, Shakespeare and Jonson, with considerable respect. His
adaptation of Shakespeare's *Troilus and Cressida* (1679), the one
Shakespearean adaptation Dryden performed unassisted, is exe-
cuted with a reverence for his source that we do not see again
until such translations of the 1690s as the Juvenal, Persius, and
Virgil and the *Fables*.[4] Nor could Dryden borrow contemptu-
ously from Corneille, because of the great status Corneille enjoyed. But from Molière (to Dryden, merely a prodigious far-
ceur), Quinault, Thomas Corneille (Pierre's younger brother),
Madeleine and George de Scudéry, La Calprenède, and a host of
others, Dryden felt licensed by his nationality and poetic status
to take what he needed without apology. That these writers were
French merely served to justify Dryden's imperial attitude. Such
invasion, mounted in daylight, is not an ignominious theft, but a
patriotic "victory."

As he depicts either aggressively imperial or nobly defeated
nations or cultures, Dryden often grounds his representations in
terms of other, better-known empires, and their subjects. Throughout *Annus Mirabilis,* England is cast and recast as a modern type of
Rome, Holland as a richer but weaker type of Carthage. Holland's
association with Carthage extends down to the repeated mention
of Dutch riches as exotic luxuries that evoke an oriental magnificence:

> For them alone the Heav'ns had kindly heat,
>   In Eastern Quarries ripening precious Dew:
> For them the *Idumæan* Balm did sweat,
>   And in hot *Ceilon* Spicy Forrests grew.
> (Works, 1:60)

> And now approach'd their Fleet from *India,* fraught
>   With all the riches of the rising Sun. . . .
> By the rich scent we found our perfum'd prey
> (Works, 1:63)

> Amidst whole heaps of Spices lights a Ball,
>   And now their Odours arm'd against them flie:

Onely Victory in Him

> Some preciously by shatter'd Porc'lain fall,
>   And some by Aromatick splinters die.
>
> (*Works*, 1:64)

Not only is Holland associated with Oriental extravagance, but Dryden implies that such luxuries have weakened the Dutch into a state of near-helpless voluptuousness. The weight and quality of this eastern magnificence weakens, then destroys, its possessor; the Dutch ships (the "perfum'd prey") are found by their "rich scent," their inflammable spices fire the ships, turning the very spicy smell against them; porcelain shatters into shrapnel, precious wood, to sharpened spears.

By linking Holland with Carthage, Dryden conducts argument on both an associational and discursive plane; an event may occur, or may be justified, by its resemblance to another event with which a similarity may be found. For example, as spoken of in *Annus Mirabilis,* war with and the defeat of Holland is as inevitable as was the destruction of Carthage:

> Thus mighty in her Ships, stood *Carthage* long,
>   And swept the riches of the world from far;
> Yet stoop'd to *Rome,* less wealthy, but more strong:
>   And this may prove our second Punick War.
>
> What peace can be where both to one pretend?
>   (But they more diligent, and we more strong)
> Or if a peace, it soon must have an end
>   For they would grow too pow'rful were it long.
>
> (*Works*, 1:60)

The argument that finds war (concluding in victory) inevitable is conducted twice in the preceding stanzas, in the first by means of association with Rome, in the second by means of deduction from general principles. The first stanza contains the first of *Annus Mirabilis*'s many linkages between England and imperial Rome: first England/Rome is seen struggling against a richer but weaker neighbor, Holland/Carthage; Holland's eventual defeat (though in the future) is as ineluctable as Carthage's. The second stanza transposes the same argument to another mode, arguing ex post facto that war was inevitable since peace cannot exist between two powers who seek the same goal. Both arguments, of course, are specious; association with a vanished great power does not license imperial conquest any more than does the abstract truism that nations must always fight when they seek the same end. But what is of interest is Dryden's method of pursuing the justification by these two means; in *Annus Mirabilis* one method is rarely used without the support of the other, creating a rich fabric of discursive and emblematic association which magnifies a local trade war into an event of near-cosmic significance.

Leaping from this dual mode of justificatory argument to a final prophecy, the poem concludes with a shining vision of metropolitan London gathering in the riches of empire. Throughout *Annus Mirabilis* Dryden shows a deep awareness of a restored England's imperial aspirations, and in a final prophetic vision combining association with both Rome and Jerusalem, Dryden shows the rightness of England's rule of the world, its management of other cultures, and its absorption of their riches.

These large associational claims to empire are buttressed by many subassociations: in *Annus Mirabilis* Holmes is likened to Achates, the Duke of York to Scipio, Charles to Caesar, and London to Rome. London is the metropolis (literally "the mother city"), the city from which other cities spring, the city by which, presumably, the universe will be ruled when the following prediction is fulfilled:

> Instructed ships shall sail to quick Commerce;
> > By which remotest Regions are alli'd:
> Which makes one City of the Universe,
> > Where some may gain, and all may be suppli'd.
> > > (*Works,* 1:84)

For the purposes of the present discussion, however, Dryden's most important subanalogy between England and Rome concerns himself; throughout the text and preface to *Annus Mirabilis* Dryden associates himself with Latin poets, playwrights, and historians, chief among them, Virgil.[5]

Dryden makes several kinds of connections between his own poetic language and persona and Virgil's. The preface to *Annus Mirabilis* contains a fine appreciation of Virgil, as incisive, though not so extended, as the more famous appreciation of Shakespeare

Roman imperial authority being deployed to English ends.

in the *Essay of Dramatick Poesy*. Directly following this appreciation comes a passage in which Dryden associates himself as closely as possible with Virgil's style and language: "He has been my Master in this Poem: I have followed him every where, I know not with what success, but I am sure with diligence enough: my Images are many of them copied from him, and the rest are imitations of him. My expressions also are as near as the Idioms of the two Languages would admit of in translation" (*Works,* 1:55). Dryden's entire output contains no stronger statement of desire for poetic association with a great predecessor, and the association is borne out throughout *Annus Mirabilis,* where the original Latin of Virgil, Horace, Ovid, et al. is placed in the margin, in order, Dryden says, that he "might not seem a Plagiary" (*Works,* 1:56). But there are further reasons for marginalizing the poets of Latinity. Dryden's association with Virgil, the great epic poet of Rome's Augustan age, lends his larger associational argument the richness and authority of yet another connection between England and Rome.[6] Such a connection also shines some of Virgil's light, albeit reflected, upon Dryden himself.[7] Dryden transmutes the poetry of another empire into the fabric of the poem itself; the original, marginalized, Dryden transforms to authority-conferring gloss.

Annus Mirabilis's system of typological relations magnifies Dryden among the larger nation of poets as it magnifies England's position among the larger world of nations. Dryden casts himself as the modern type of Virgil, great epic poet and type of the great poet of empire; England becomes a type of Rome, itself a type of great empire. Casting himself in the same relation to Charles II as Virgil to Augustus Caesar, Dryden suggests that he too will write (writes, has written) great poetry of this modern empire. Yet the very borrowing of Virgil's language, the authority-conferring association Dryden makes between the great dead (Virgil) and the great living (himself), the taking of Virgil's language and name to further Dryden's own power of utterance, all suggest a personal imperialism toward the past and the other of a piece with the larger imperialism depicted in the poem itself. Though Dryden claims Virgil as a model and master, he appropriates him as a slave, taking from Virgil what is needed to increase Dryden's own poetic power. Dryden takes care not to seem a plagiary (what, elsewhere, he is all too content to be) because the public quality of these plunderings from the past is seen to increase Dryden's own poetic capital.

For the imperialist to prevail, the other's powers must be inferior to his own, and just as the imperialist devises myths and language to express his supposed military and cultural superiority, so he devises complementary myths and language to express the other's supposed cultural and military—and in Dryden's case, poetic—inferiority. Articulations of the other's weakness are repeated, in political and symbolic terms, throughout the Dryden corpus, not only in *Annus Mirabilis* ("[Carthage] . . . stoop'd to Rome, less wealthy, but more strong" l. 19; "they more diligent, and we more strong" l. 22), but throughout *The Indian Emperour,* where the technological superiority of the Spaniards, experienced by the Aztecs as language, renders them invincible:

> *Monteʒuma.* What Divine Monsters, O ye gods, are these
>   That float in air and flye upon the Seas!
>   Came they alive or dead upon the shore?
> *Guyomar.* Alas, they liv'd too sure, I heard them roar:
>   All turn'd their sides, and to each other spoke,
>   I saw their words break out in fire and smoke.
>   Sure 'tis their voice that Thunders from on high,
>   Or these the younger brothers of the Skie.
>
> (Works, 9:36)

Dryden represents the overwhelming force of the Spaniards as translation into a kind of speech, a language of heaven transposed. The other, as Dryden represents him, perceives technological superiority as an untranslatable idiom, a discourse of the skies whose thunderous locutions mark these interlopers as creatures of an irresistibly higher status.[8]

Besides the military weakness of the other, Dryden explores the other's supposed cultural inferiority; representing the defeated as culturally inferior may justify the imperialist in his administration of the colonial culture. Imperial powers, poetic as well as national, often seek not only to remove wealth from the conquered province, but to impose a language and culture upon the other, who is perceived to lack essential moral or cultural traits that are, naturally, possessed in abundance by the conqueror.

Onely Victory in Him

Although Dryden, before 1688, appears to be an apostle of English and personal imperialism, he rarely shows himself incapable of sympathy for the other, whoever that might be.[9] The Aztecs in *The Indian Emperour,* the Egyptians of *All for Love,* even *Annus Mirabilis*'s Dutch sailors (with whom the English were at war), are treated with respect and imaginative sympathy:

> The Son, who, twice three month's on th' Ocean tost,
>> Prepar'd to tell what he had pass'd before,
> Now sees, in *English* Ships the *Holland* Coast,
>> And Parents arms in vain stretch'd from the shore.
>
> This carefull Husband had been long away,
>> Whom his chast wife and little children mourn;
> Who on their fingers learn'd to tell the day
>> On which their Father promis'd to return.
>
>> *(Works,* 1:64)

Dryden's almost unfailing sympathy with the weaker culture is one of the constant pleasures of the drama; simple conquest over a merely brutish other is never lauded. There is always sorrow, imaginatively expressed, at the necessity to conquer and destroy one's noble adversary. Dryden's imaginative sympathy with the defeated culture, constant throughout his pre-1688 career, increases manyfold to form the focus of the heterocultural dramas after the Revolution of 1688. *[cp. Virgil]*

Dryden's fourth play, *The Indian Emperour* (1665), is wholly concerned with the conquering of the New World by the Old. In it, he explores the complex relationship between imperialist and other, examining as well the contrasting virtues of each civilization (as pictured by Dryden), the nature of the New World riches that were assimilable into the Old, and the nature of those that were not. Although *The Indian Emperour* contains many scenes that explore the dilemma of the conquered Indians facing their new rulers (and cultural legislators), Dryden's drama contains no more graphic depiction of the dilemma of both conqueror and conquered than the scene in which Montezuma is racked, as the wicked priest attempts to convert him by force.

The racking scene is one of Dryden's most complex, not to say baroque, representations of imperial appetite, native resistance, personal honor, and impersonal cruelty. In this scene, perhaps more than anywhere else in his drama, he explores the pressure to which the language of imperial desire is subjected, twisting each locution (be it moral or martial, religious or overtly rapacious) into an instrument whose sole intent is to extract wealth from the other. In this scene Dryden shows his awareness of the kinds of wealth that are and are not exportable from the richer and weaker subject, and he shows us, finally, the terrible cost the imperialist must pay for his appetite, the realization of which pitches the proud conqueror, weeping, to the feet of the weaker, but in some higher sense, stronger, other.[10]

Montezuma, the Indian emperor of the title, is a precursor of the Almanzorian "noble savage" (Dryden's coinage, from *The Conquest of Granada*), of whose savagery we learn almost immediately—to celebrate his birthday with greater pomp he plans to sacrifice five hundred captives. Yet we soon learn that Montezuma also possesses all the virtues of the seventeenth-century hero such as he was understood in Restoration England's assumption of the Cornelian heroic drama. Montezuma is a heroic lover in the classic mode: "Love rules my heart, and is your Monarchs King (*Works*, 9:46); a tireless warrior:

> Charge, charge, their ground the faint *Taxallans* yield,
> Bold in close Ambush, base in open Field . . .
> Thus Fought, thus Conquer'd I when I was young.
> (*Works*, 9:53)

and willing to sacrifice all, even the well-being of his nation, to maintain his own personal glory:

> If either Death or Bondage I must chuse,
> I'll keep my Freedom, though my life I lose.
> (*Works*, 9:79)

In *The Indian Emperour*, Cortes, leader of the Spaniards, is not the cruel monster he is often portrayed as. He, like Montezuma, incarnates the heroic virtues, and is capable of complete self-sacrifice for king, love, and his own honor. That the Spanish contact with the Aztecs degenerates from friendly near-worship to efforts at peaceful coercion, to war, to slaughter, to disgrace of the defeated

His torture as a stimulus to Cortes's self-questioning.

Aztecs, is not Cortes's doing; he struggles to avert each down-
ward step and deeply feels the consequences of the disastrous turn
in relations between them:

> On pain of death kill none but those who fight;
> I much repent me of this bloody night:
> Slaughter grows murder when it goes too far,
> And makes a Massacre what was a War:
> Sheath all your weapons and in silence move.
>
> (*Works,* 9:101)

Just at the moment Cortes voices his growing realization of the disaster wrought upon the Aztecs, he discovers his worthy adversary,
Montezuma, ignobly stretched upon the rack. Learning the consequences of his—and his army's—actions proves too much for
Cortes; the torture of Montezuma serves as anagnorisis to Cortes,
who recognizes not only the moral falsity of the imperial position, but that imperial appetite will have harmed his own country
(just as befell the Dutch in *Annus Mirabilis*). By the end of the
racking scene the physical positions of imperialist and subject are
reversed; where Montezuma was bound and impotent at the feet
of the Spaniards, Cortes lies weeping at the feet of Montezuma.

The racking scene, comprising the first 150 lines of act 5, scene
2, occurs after the Aztec forces are unequivocally defeated. Cortes's lieutenant, Pizarro, the Christian priest, and a group of armed
soldiers have brought Montezuma and his priest into the prison
in Montezuma's palace. Pizarro, whose one avowed aim throughout the play is to enrich himself, calls on Montezuma to reveal the
location of the remainder of the Aztec gold; Montezuma refuses.
At his refusal, the Christian priest who, like Pizarro, seems the
incarnation of avarice and cruelty, calls on the soldiers to kill the
heroic warrior:

> How wickedly he has refus'd his wealth,
> And hid his Gold, from Christian hands, by stealth:
> Down with him, Kill him, merit Heaven thereby.
>
> (*Works,* 9:98)

But Pizarro is craftier than the priest and orders that Montezuma
and his Indian priest be tortured, rather than immediately killed,
whereupon they are tied to the machine already present in the

The attempted 'unlocking' of Montezuma's gold/mind.
Stronger leaner forces warring on the flourishing weak.

THE IMPERIAL DRYDEN

prison, and the racking commences. In spite of his pain, Montezuma taunts his torturers:

> The gods, who made me once a King, shall know
> I still am worthy to continue so:
> Though now the subject of your Tyrrany,
> I'le Plague you worse then you can punish me.
> Know I have Gold, which you shall never find,
> No Pains, no Tortures shall unlock my Mind.
>
> (*Works,* 9:98)

To which the Christian priest replies: "Pull harder yet; he does
not feel the rack" (*Works,* 9:98). As we see in this and every interchange in the racking scene, the pressures of Spanish avarice and
Indian resistance stress the accepted meanings of language until
every metaphor, every train of thought, every exchange of argument, has to do either with the extraction or retention of native
riches. The unlocking of Montezuma's mind is synonymous with
the surrender of the Aztec treasure, and the Christian priest's
notion of conversion is another way to speak of unlocking Montezuma's mind to extract the gold.[11] In the racking scene every
use of such abstract terms as "God," "gods," "integrity," "pride,"
"reason," "honor," is a sign, each further from the concrete, for
the surrender of native wealth or the refusal to surrender.

The tableau itself uses characteristically Drydenian representations of imperialist confrontation. The representatives of the
non-English-European-Drydenian culture, the others, are captured and bound, reenacting the recurring pattern of Dryden's
representations of alterity; others are weak (evidenced first by
their having been defeated and captured, but most graphically,
by the pain being inflicted on their very bodies as we watch),
but others are also rich. Dryden's representations of the imperialist and subject seem always to evoke these comparisons of the
stronger, leaner force warring upon the flourishing weak; the successful prosecution of the war of a small band of Spaniards against
a nation of Indians exemplifies the pattern of representation of
imperialism that seems to have come naturally to Dryden, other
notable examples being the Spaniards' war against the Moors in
The Conquest of Granada, the gods' sortie against men in *Amphitryon,*
and the Romans' campaign against the Egyptians in *All for Love.*

Onely Victory in Him

The minds and aims of imperialist and subject are, at this stage in Dryden's drama, depicted not only differently from each other, but with differing degrees of artistic and imaginative success. Dryden almost always depicts the expansionist urge of the imperialist in terms of the characteristically male vocabulary of energy, vigor, glory, heroism, and poetic splendor,[12] and even when a manifestation of this urge is unequivocally despicable, as in the racking scene, Dryden's poetic and dramatic representations of imperial activity flicker with a light that chills as it illuminates. But when we examine these representations of the interrelations between powerful avarice and innocent wealth, we find a less successful realization of the rich and helpless other—a wellmeaning failure of imagination that does not become success until Dryden's own defeat in the larger battles of 1688 bring him to understand the motivations and inner complexities of rich others in a land no longer their own. Although Dryden is sympathetic to the cause of the Indians, he seems to understand the Spaniards better; they are full of desires, noble and ignoble: Cortes wishes to extend the reign of Charles V; Pizarro and the Christian priest want gold (and tangentially, souls); Vasquez wants a woman. But Montezuma, poetic and disputational hero as he is, wants nothing but a vanished past. He possesses kingly glory but no outward-directed will, no inner life but the nostalgia for the forever-destroyed status quo. His noble recalcitrance in the racking scene signifies Dryden's failure to make him real, and fully to recreate an "other" culture. Montezuma's affect is static; his power, when he had it, was conservative. Victorious, Montezuma could have only what he had; defeated, he can but resist. For all his poetic splendor, no light of character illuminates him, not even the borrowed light of his father the sun; in his greatest moment his sole aim is to preserve the self inviolate as his body is violated. Not until the post-1688 dramas do defeated heroes such as Montezuma have the freedom of motion, the full range of desires, and the dignity usually accorded to male heroes.

The very subjection of Montezuma's body seems to free his mind to an inspired flight of skeptical disputation with the Christian priest, an argument that conflates Montezuma's wished-for conversion with the surrendering of his gold. As before in the play, the Indian culture demonstrates considerable poetic, if not

79

Montezuma : rich, weak, defeated, 'other', poetically gorgeous.
His religious scepticism.

THE IMPERIAL DRYDEN

martial, resilience in the face of the threat from outside. To the
Christian priest's threats of damnation, Montezuma counterposes
his own, poetically richer (yet characteristically frail) vision of a
postmortem existence:

> *Chr. Pr.* Those Pains, O Prince, thou sufferest now are light
> Compar'd to those, which when thy Soul takes flight,
> Immortal, endless, thou must then endure:
> Which Death begins, and Time can never cure.
> *Montezuma.* Thou art deceiv'd: for whensoe're I Dye,
> The Sun my Father bears my Soul on high:
> He lets me down a Beam, and mounted there,
> He draws it back, and pulls me through the Air:
> I in the Eastern parts, and rising Sky,
> You in Heaven's downfal, and the West must lye.
>
> (*Works,* 9:99)

Montezuma, the rich, weak, defeated other, poetically resituates
himself back to his true spiritual location in the syntax of representing others: the East (although the East is the invaders' place
of origin, not Montezuma's).[13] The poetic gorgeousness of Montezuma's language parallels the richness of the golden treasure he
refuses to reveal; rendered impotent by a greater force, his secular
and poetic treasures remain superior to those of his captors. Here,
as at every turn in *The Indian Emperour,* the fictionalized other en-
joys an existence at a higher and richer mythic and poetic (and accordingly less concrete) plane than the more ambitious and wilier
invaders. Through depictions of the Aztecs' religious rites and
through the figurative splendor of their language, Dryden shows
them capable of a naively elevated life poetically and morally superior to the mere efficient brutality of the Spaniards. In *The Indian
Emperour* the Spaniards may have cannon and swords of steel, but
the Aztecs have the desirable women, the richly worked gold, and
all the good lines. Even the religious imagery of the Spaniards is
poor and cold compared with that of the Indians.

Montezuma takes a skeptical line regarding religion that stands
in contrast to the pleas and arguments of both Indian and Christian priests; he argues for a light of reason that animates a middle
way of common knowledge, to be preferred over the extravagant bypaths of revelation. As in the exchange of visions of post-

mortem existence, Montezuma also gets the better arguments, and the arguments of the Christian priest are made to look self-serving and weak. Montezuma's facility at rhymed disputation while being torn asunder is indeed impressive:

> *Chr. Pr.* But we do by Martyrdom our Faith avow.
> *Montezuma.* You do no more then I for ours do now.
>   To prove Religion true———
>   If either Wit or Suff'rings would suffice,
>   All Faiths afford the Constant and the Wise:
>   And yet ev'n they, by Education sway'd,
>   In Age defend what Infancy obey'd.
> *Chr. Pr.* Since Age by erring Child-hood is misled,
>   Refer your self to our Un-erring Head.
> *Montezuma.* Man and not erre! what reason can you give?
> *Chr. Pr.* Renounce that carnal reason, and believe.
> *Montezuma.* The Light of Nature should I thus betray,
>   'Twere to wink hard that I might see the day.
>
> (*Works,* 9:100)

The Christian priest never does make a passable argument, and Montezuma remains unconvinced.

The actual racking ends upon Cortes's victorious arrival. Entering the stage expressing his horror at the bloody massacre of the defeated Aztecs, he is further shocked to see his worthy enemy thus reduced; releasing him immediately, Cortes first rages at the priest, then curses gold, to which he attributes the evil just committed, as well as future evils. To the priest he fulminates:

> And you,—
> Who sawcily, teach Monarchs to obey,
> And the wide World in narrow Cloysters sway;
> Set up by Kings as humble aids of power,
> You that which bred you, Viper-like devour,
> You Enemies of Crowns—
>
> (*Works,* 9:102)

And he apostrophizes to gold:

> Accursed Gold, 'tis thou hast caus'd these crimes;
> Thou turn'st our Steel against thy Parent Climes!

And into *Spain* wilt fatally be brought,
Since with the price of Blood thou here art bought.

(Works, 9:102)

Cortes's indictment of the church seems curiously limited; his strictures are restricted to monastic orders, and are further restricted only to those who usurp a monarch's power. While the six lines of his tirade are full of sound and fury, they signify little concerning the church, and certainly do not set Cortes off as a freethinker, as Montezuma appears to be during the racking scene.[14]

Cortes's curse upon gold is of particular interest. He blames the immediate crimes on it (a transference of culpability typical of Dryden's excuses for imperialism, such as those in *Annus Mirabilis,* where he excuses the Anglo-Dutch war on the specious grounds that Rome fought Carthage and that two nations who desire the same aim must fight), yet he ascribes a peculiar power to this ill-gotten booty. In an oracular flight unique to this moment, Cortes predicts that this gold will be fatal to Spain, since it is here bought with blood, and that the blows struck with Spanish steel in the New World will be turned against their "Parent Climes." He realizes with horror that the imperial urges that have led him to the victory of that night, the subjection of his enemy, the ensuing massacre, and the present scene of the bondage of his admired adversary, will next lead to the destruction of his own land, as if he had fought against instead of for it. Upon realizing the limits of imperial ambition, he makes literal the moral geography of the scene, kneels at Montezuma's feet, and weeps; the scene concludes with Cortes in tears at the feet of the king he had taken such pains to conquer. The rich other has achieved a kind of victory over his devastated conqueror, for the gold that will pour from treasuries and mines is not only tainted with blood, but cursed.

Mexican gold can and will be removed from the Mexicans, but other sorts of wealth, perhaps of greater value, cannot be exported. Although the Spaniards find the Aztec culture attractive and admirable, what the Spaniards can export from the New World is limited to gold and mineral riches, that which in Cortes's mind is cursed. The greater richness that Montezuma displays on the rack, the riches of poetic splendor, philosophical clarity, personal hero-

D. on fruitful and destructive literary 'imperialism'
Defence of an Essay : Montezuma bowing before the English Princess Anne.

Onely Victory in Him

ism—these are not so easily taken from one culture into another, and the realization of this is one element of what leads Cortes to weep at the feet of his prisoner.

Although equating foreign gold and foreign plays here would be simple and wrong, we may legitimately observe, in connection with the racking scene, that Dryden does not merely take what is simple from the riches of other cultures; he tends to appropriate complex forms, rich in themselves, yet capable of further enrichment. Surveying the wealth of other cultures, Dryden is keenly sensitive to what he might use. The moral, and in a sense, poetic defeat of Cortes is one Dryden seeks to avoid; he shows his awareness of the proper manner to extract poetic riches from others by making characters of, and plots about, those who take well, and those who take badly. Those who take well enrich their native land, as Dryden says of Jonson in the preface to *An Evening's Love:* "no man has borrow'd so much from the Ancients as he has done: And he did well in it, for he has thereby beautifi'd our language" (*Works,* 10:212). Those who take badly do themselves and their native land no good, as Cortes realizes to his dismay.

When *The Indian Emperour* was printed in 1667, two years after its composition and production, it contained, besides the soon-suppressed *Defence of an Essay of Dramatique Poesie,* a dedication to Princess Anne, daughter-in-law to the king, who had championed the play at court. The dedication to Princess Anne contains the figure of Montezuma, though represented as indomitable of spirit in the play, kneeling in submission before her: "Under your Patronage *Montezuma* hopes he is more safe than in his Native *Indies:* and therefore comes to throw himself at your Graces feet; paying that homage to your Beauty, which he refus'd to the violence of his Conquerours. He begs only that when he shall relate his sufferings, you will consider he is an *Indian* Prince, and not expect any other Eloquence from his simplicity, then that, with which his griefs have furnished him" (*Works,* 9:25). Here we have the first imaginative representation of English (as opposed to foreign) imperialism in the plays of Dryden; a foreign king bows at the feet of an English duchess. Although Montezuma is but a character in a play, and in this place a sign for the play itself, he also serves as a sign of foreign culture that will receive better treat-

princess ?

ment under the care of an English monarch than under the Spanish. This dedicatory scene in which a representative of an exotic culture crosses oceans to offer homage to English beauty (the beauty of a dominatrix) recalls the final vision of a rebuilt London in *Annus Mirabilis:*

> Now, like a Maiden Queen, she will behold,
>> From her high Turrets, hourly Sutors come:
> The East with Incense, and the West with Gold,
>> Will stand, like Suppliants, to receive her doom.
>> *(Works,* 1:104)

In the dedicatory vision, Montezuma ("the West with Gold") is wrested away (along with his gold) from the brutal rule of the Spaniards; Dryden represents him as a willing participant in a vision of higher harmony where riches need not be extracted from the world by blood, but are attracted to England by its virtue. Montezuma comes, as Dryden writes to Princess Anne, to pay "homage to your Beauty."

The relation of foreign riches to foreign plays is a complex and open one, especially as depicted in *The Indian Emperour.* Tempting as it is to schematize a relationship between plays and gold, Cortes and Dryden, rather than subject such a rich and evocative scene to my own interpretational imperialism, I turn to a discussion of *An Evening's Love,* where the relationships between foreign riches and foreign plays are explicit and carefully worked out.

Dryden's interest in the imaginative representation and conquest of other cultures finds one of its fullest expressions in *An Evening's Love, or the Mock Astrologer* (1668, published 1671), a play less often read than its merits deserve. Written in the year of the *Essay of Dramatick Poesy*'s publication (also the year of Dryden's accession to the laureateship), *An Evening's Love* succeeded on the stage and was revived at irregular intervals until its last recorded performance in 1717 (see *Works,* 10:434).

Although much scholarly ink has been spilled in ascertaining the sources of individual sections of *An Evening's Love,* the origins of the main plot and the most salient scenes have long been known.[15] The main plot is adapted directly from Thomas Corneille's *Le Feint Astrologue* (1650), which in turn is adapted from

Calderón's *El Astrologo Fingido* (1648). Dryden made no secret of
his debt to Corneille, admitting it in the epilogue to the play. An
English Monsieur is made to say:

> I am a rogue
> But he has quite spoil'd the *feint Astrologue*. . . .
> [The Poet] *neither swore nor storm'd as Poets do,*
> *But, most unlike an Author, vow'd 'twas true.*
>
> (*Works*, 10:313)

Dryden here admits the larger borrowing from Thomas Corneille,
but other important—though unacknowledged—scenes are translated from Molière's *Le Dépit Amoureux* (1658) and that rich mine
of Restoration and eighteenth-century English comedy, *Les Précieuses Ridicules* (1659). Dryden's sources were remarked upon at
the time; Mrs. Pepys observed his debt to Madeleine de Scudéry
(*Works*, 10:433), and Gerard Langbaine retailed a list of sources—
many certain, others dubious.[16]

Thomas Corneille's *Le Feint Astrologue* takes place entirely
within the city of Madrid (thus observing the unity of place as
defined by Thomas's older brother, Pierre).[17] The comedy opens
with the playboy Don Fernand complaining of Lucrèce's indifference. His servant, Phillipin, soon learns through Lucrèce's maid,
Beatrix, that Lucrèce loves the impoverished aristocrat Don Juan,
who, though pretending to have gone to Flanders, actually hides
at the house of his friend Don Lope, suitor to Lucrèce's cousin,
Léonor. Don Juan visits Lucrèce's garden nightly, but has also
courted Léonor (who believes him en route to Flanders).

When Don Fernand hints to Lucrèce that he knows of her
lover, she rightly suspects her servant Beatrix of betraying her.
To save Beatrix's job, Phillipin wildly asserts that his master
learned of Don Juan's nightly visits through astrology, and soon
all Madrid knows of Don Fernand's powers. Léonor, desiring the
spiritual body of Don Juan to appear to her, consults the now great
astrologer, who dictates a letter to Don Juan's spirit, requesting a
rendezvous. Phillipin then delivers the letter to the horrified Don
Juan, who believes Léonor has discovered the ruse of his self-
concealment. The scene changes (in the middle of the act, thus
breaking the liaison des scènes) to Léonor and her suivante await-

ing the apparition of Don Juan's spirit. Calm as they await him, at his appearance Léonor hides in a closet, Jacinte under the table. Don Juan, understandably confused, leaves to keep his previous appointment with Lucrèce.

The dénouement occurs at night in the garden of Leonard, Lucrèce's father. Leonard and Don Fernand arrive, Léonor accuses Lucrèce of loving Don Juan, and of meeting with and concealing him in the garden. Her father commands a search, Don Juan reveals himself, admits his love, and asks Leonard for his daughter. "The stars decree," says Don Fernand to Leonard, "that Lucrèce must marry Don Juan," and Leonard dutifully orders the nuptials.

As one might gather from the preceding summary, Corneille's *Feint Astrologue* is not a piece for the ages. The characters are flat and lack the bold delineation of such early comedies of Pierre Corneille as *La Suivante* (1633), *Clitandre* (1630), or the greatest and strangest of them all, *La Place Royale, ou l'Amoureux Extravagant* (1633). Indeed, the general uniformity of the characters in *Le Feint Astrologue* lends credence to Dryden's (Neander's) judgment of French drama, appearing in the same year as *An Evening's Love:* "Those beauties of the *French*-poesie . . . are indeed the Beauties of a Statue, but not of a Man, because not animated with the Soul of Poesie, which is imitation of humour and passions. . . . He who will look upon theirs which have been written till these last ten years or thereabouts, will find it an hard matter to pick out two or three passable humours amongst them. . . . In the rest of *Corneilles* Comedies you have little humour" (*Works,* 17:44–45). And in the preface to *An Evening's Love,* Dryden hones his appraisal of French playwrights' characters: "Their Poets wanting judgement to make, or to maintain true characters, strive to cover their defects with ridiculous Figures and Grimaces" (*Works,* 10:204). The observation that French poets lack "judgement to make, or to maintain true characters," while absurdly biased, is fairly close to the mark when applied to Corneille's *Le Feint Astrologue,* for the play's characters are notably thin. No trace of individuality differentiates Lucrèce from Léonor. The two-timing Don Juan is neither admirably clever nor more than mildly repugnant (and why this flawed and unattractive character is rewarded with Lucrèce and her father's money is not clear); Juan's friend Don Lope is only

'Imperialist' interest of D's version : ① wholesale
appropriation of TC's plot ② Transformation into a Spain/England
conflict.

Onely Victory in Him

mildly faithful; and the mock astrologer, Don Fernand, is only
mildly resourceful. The wily servant Phillipin is not above robbing
and humiliating an old man, the industrious Beatrix not above betraying her mistress. The rather sour conclusion does not much
please or displease, and one is relieved, not that the couples are
paired off, but that the play is over.

Seventeenth-century formalist critics would have seen that *Le
Feint Astrologue* contains serious structural flaws. The play observes
neither the unity of time nor the liaison des scènes, for the action
takes place over a period of two days and two nights, and the third,
fourth, and fifth acts break into three, two, and two scenes. More
seriously, unity of character is not maintained; Don Fernand, who
throughout the play expresses only odium and scorn for Lucrèce,
inexplicably helps her to marry the man she wants. Leonard, ada-
mant that his daughter marry a rich man, consents without a mur-
mur to her marrying a poor one. Don Juan, in hiding for days,
appears for no reason in the street. The sense of poetic justice is
wounded by the playwright's allowing Don Juan to triumph.

We do not know what brought this lackluster product of a
second-tier talent to Dryden's attention (perhaps it was the English translation that appeared in 1668), but the changes Dryden
wrought in the play show, in a myriad of ways, his interest in
entering into the discourse of imperialism, both as an active imperialist in the realm of poetry, and as a representor of the larger
struggle for wealth between England and other cultures.

Dryden's version of Corneille's play shows interest in the drama
of imperialism in two complementary ways. First, the stuff of the
drama itself—characters, main plot outline, title—are all taken
from Thomas Corneille in an act of poetic appropriation whose
magnitude is not uncommon in Dryden's work.[18] Second, what
was in the hands both of Thomas Corneille and Calderón a local
love intrigue played out only between Spaniards, becomes in
Dryden's play a battle for women, money, and national glory
waged between Spaniards and Englishmen. Moreover, as his interest in imperialism is shown on two planes so his defense of this
type of struggle is also dual; regarding the appropriation of the
play itself, he mounts his most complete defense of poetic appropriation in the preface, which appeared in 1671, three years after

the writing of the play. Dryden's justification for international struggle per se is contained within the play itself.

Turning first to Dryden's staging of international struggle in the body of the play, we again note the most salient alteration from Corneille's original: Corneille's Spanish characters act and speak like Frenchmen, and Corneille incorporates no Spanish element into the scenery or language. Dryden, on the other hand, recasts the plot as a struggle between Spaniards and Englishmen, and he attempts to suggest (if not actually to depict in detail) characteristic mores of each. Although Corneille's Madrid, for all its situational vagueness, might have been Paris or London, Dryden's Madrid is truly exotic, and brims with Gypsies, Moors, Spanish food, Catholicism, street names, serenaders, and many words from the Spanish language itself (Corneille's play contains none).

The principal love affairs have increased from two to three; two Englishmen named Wildblood and Bellamy, attached to the English ambassador's entourage in Madrid, fall in love with two sisters, Jacinta and Theodosia. The two-timer of Corneille's play, now named Don Melchor, makes love to both Theodosia and the sisters' cousin, Aurelia. The wily servant Phillipin is replaced by the much wilier servant Maskall, who is brilliantly inventive and unwaveringly cowardly. Characters have recognizable humours; Jacinta is bold and quick, forming half of one of the first Restoration "gay couples." The father, Don Alonzo, can let no one finish speaking, interjecting "I know what you would say," then miscompleting his interlocutor's intended statement. Aurelia, whose humour of affected speech is discussed further on, imports words from the French language, and uses "furious" and "furiously" at every opportunity.

The act of appropriating *Le Feint Astrologue* from Corneille is reinscribed in the plot itself, in which English men defeat Spanish men in the battle for women, money, and national honor. This battle between nations (conducted on the very border between Englishness and Alterity) is waged on a number of fronts. English language, religion, dramatic form, food, wit, swordsmanship, music, and especially standards of masculinity are all measured against their Spanish counterparts; in every case the Spanish counterpart is found inferior.

The theme of international war is carried into the plot and language of the love intrigue itself; each contact between Englishman and Spaniard comes to signify a competition between two nations for a limited number of resources. In determining to apprise Theodosia of Don Melchor's duplicity, Bellamy says: " 'Tis but trying my fortune to tell her of his Infidelity, and my love. If she yields she makes me happy; if not, I shall be sure *Don Melchor* has not planted the Armes of *Spain* in the Fort before me" (*Works,* 10:279). Women are fortresses to be taken (as are the plays of others); conquest gives the victor the right to fly the national flag over the conquered object, be it fort, woman, or play.

The languages of love and international strife conflate in a scene that is itself the result of international poetic strife. Whereas the scene depicts a joint lovers' quarrel in which master and man fall out with mistress and maid—couched in terms of international war—the scene itself is lifted without acknowledgment from Molière's *Le Dépit Amoureux* (see *Sources,* 156–57, and *Works,* 10:438–39). The very terms of Dryden's imperial appropriation from Molière are reinscribed in the language of the scene:

Maskall. —Courage, Sir; how goes the battel on your wing?
Wildblood. Just drawing off on both sides. Adieu *Spain.*
Jacinta. Farewel old *England.*
Beatrix. Come away in Triumph; the day's your own Madam.
Maskall. I'll bear you off upon my shoulders, Sir; we have broke their hearts.
Wildblood. Let her go first then; I'll stay, and keep the honor of the Field.
Jacinta. I'll not retreat, if you stay till midnight.

                      (*Works,* 10:292)

And as the couples begin to mend the quarrel, they modulate from the language of warfare to that of diplomacy:

Maskall. Do you hear this, *Beatrix?* they are just upon the point of accommodation; we must make haste or they'll make a peace by themselves; and exclude us from the Treaty. . . .
Jacinta. The prime Articles between *Spain* and *England* are

national characteristics revealed in love intrigues

> seal'd; for the rest concerning a more strict alliance, if you please we'll dispute them in the Garden.
>
> *Wildblood.* But in the first place let us agree on the Article of Navigation, I beseech you.
>
> *Beatrix.* These Leagues offensive and defensive will be too strict for us, *Maskall:* a Treaty of commerce will serve our turn.
>
> (Works, 10:293)

Structuring amorous interchange along the lines of international discourse permits Dryden to mingle national (and martial) qualities with romantic conversation. There is much banter, and actual disagreement, conducted in the terms of English and Spanish characteristics, as perceived by the characters themselves. For example, the following interchange (occurring in a Catholic church) takes place between the two pairs of future lovers:

> *Bellamy.* As for their wit, you may judge it by their breeding, which is commonly in a Nunnerie; where the want of mankind while they are there, makes them value the blessing ever after.
>
> *Theodosia.* Prethee dear *Jacinta* tell me, what kind of creatures were those we saw yesterday at the Audience? Those I mean that look'd so like *Frenchmen* in their habits, but only became their Apishness so much worse.
>
> *Jacinta. Englishmen* I think they call'd 'em.
>
> *Theodosia.* Crie you mercy; they were of your wild *English* indeed, that is a kind of Northern Beast, that is taught its feats of activity in *Monsieurland,* and for doing 'em too lubberly, is laugh'd at all the world over.
>
> (Works, 10:227)

Even the banter between characters recapitulates English borrowing from the residents of *Monsieurland.* The dialogue throughout is suffused with spirited references to all sorts of relations between nations and races; indeed, the word "racy," used to denote "a distinctive quality of character or intellect; lively, spirited, full of 'go'" (*OED*) receives its first recorded use in this play. Wildblood, as he invites his intended to England, drops the new word while describing the stodginess of the English: "Faith, we live in a good honest Country, where we are content with our old vices, partly because we want wit to invent more new. A Colonie of *Spaniards,* or spiritual *Italians* planted among us would make us much more racy" (*Works,* 10:232). Unlike Corneille's *Feint Astrologue,* Dryden's *An Evening's Love* is itself *racy,* that is, it incorporates the attributes of an imagined other by its inclusion of Spanish language, place names, and customs. *Alguazil, juego de cannas, Calle Major, St. Jago, inamorado, borachos, Sennor Ingles, albricias, corigidore,* are some of the Spanish words Dryden introduces into the play, vocabulary that reminds us that these Englishmen face a foreign world that is truly different, where whatever they obtain will be by their wits.

Nearly every measure of comparison between cultures in *An Evening's Love* can be seen to have a corollary in the production, staging, and reception of English plays. For example, Spanish food is found wanting in exactly the same terms that foreign drama is found wanting in the contemporaneous *Essay of Dramatick Poesy,* wherein Neander remarks on the differences between English and French dramatic writing: "the barrenness of the *French* Plots . . . the variety and copiousness of the *English* . . . [English] variety, if well order'd, will afford a greater pleasure to the audience . . . our own [plots] are fuller of variety" (*Works,* 17:46–47, 53). Foreign poetic productions, Dryden emphasizes again and again, are dull, uniform, restrained, similar each to other. So, says one Englishman to the other in *An Evening's Love,* is Spanish food:

Bellamy. I hope we had variety enough.
Wildblood. I, it look'd like variety, till we came to taste it; there were twenty several dishes to the eye, but in the pallat nothing but Spices. I had a mind to eat of a Pheasant, and as soon as I got it into my mouth, I found I was chawing a limb of Cinnamon; then I went to cut a piece of Kid, and no sooner it had touch'd my lips, but it turn'd to red Pepper: at last I began to think my self another kind of *Midas,* that everything I touch'd should be turn'd to Spice.

Bellamy. And for my part, I imagin'd his Catholick Majesty
had invited us to eat his *Indies.*

(*Works,* 10:218)

The vocabulary is the same: variety, that prime English desideratum of both drama and cuisine, is absent from foreign productions
of stage and kitchen. Not only are Bellamy and Wildblood forced
to eat dish after dish that seem different but turn out to be the
same, but Wildblood's speech indicates his awareness of a kind of
copious but undifferentiated material wealth, similar, down to the
eastern exoticism, to the language describing Holland/Carthage in
Annus Mirabilis. Food and spices abound, as do foreign plays; what
all lack, each in its own sphere, is variety. And variety—even in
this discussion of Spanish food—is precisely what Dryden introduces into Corneille's version of Calderón's play. This discussion
of Spanish food occurs in the first scene and is the first of many
instances in which plot and speech comment both on the play's
origins in foreign alterity and on the process of the play's transformation from one more boring item of foreign wealth to a various,
rich, and full product ready to please the English dramatic palate
with its variety.

Even the quality of personal honor, an overabundance of which
is often ascribed to the Spanish constitution during this period,
is introduced into this English drama only to find it inefficient,
as well as morally defective. When the two-timing Don Melchor
threatens to inform the father of Jacinta and Theodosia as they
elope with Bellamy and Wildblood, he invokes his (deeply compromised) honor:

Melchor. No Sir, 'tis not for my honor, to be assisting to you:
I'll to *Don Alonzo,* and help to revenge the injury you are
doing him.
Bellamy. Then we are lost, I can do nothing.
Wildblood. Nay, and you talk of honor, by your leave Sir.
[*Falls upon him & throws him down.*]
I hate your *Spanish* honor ever since it spoyl'd our *English*
Playes, with faces about and t'other side.

(*Works,* 10:299)

Spanish honor spoils English plays, just as Spanish honor is about to spoil the "plot" of the Englishmen within this play. As Wildblood cavalierly dismisses Spanish honor ("I hate your *Spanish honor*"), entire ethical categories are dismissed out of hand because they do not suit the English taste: honor, fidelity, the bonds of friendship—all are cracked by the Englishmen in *An Evening's Love* as they strive to gain their ends. And the cracking of these bonds, in the interest of the entrepreneurial spirit, is applauded as a kind of national virtue within the frame of the play itself:

> *Don Lopez.* But I have engag'd my promise to that friend to serve him in his passion to my Mistress.
> *Bellamy.* We *English* seldom make such scruples; Women are not compris'd in our Laws of friendship: they are *feræ naturæ;* our common game, like Hare and Patridge: every man has equal right to them, as he has to the Sun and Elements.
> *Don Lopez.* Must I then betray my friend?
> *Bellamy.* In that case my friend is a *Turk* to me.
>
> (*Works,* 10:282)

Women, like imperial goods (or foreign plays), are to be taken as one can, from whoever possesses them. Further intermingling the language of nations with the discourse of love, Bellamy distances a friend from whom he hopes to take a woman by temporarily ascribing to him yet another nationality, one to whom no Christian owes faith or honorable treatment—"a *Turk.*"

In *An Evening's Love* sex is treated as an event of multiple import, connoting pleasure indeed but, perhaps more importantly, serving as an emblem for artistic and political concerns. Both in the prologue and epilogue to *An Evening's Love,* Dryden explicitly likens writing and reading poetry to the male aspect of sexual union; he conflates physical and poetic begetting into a vision of the poet, a newly wedded groom, writing poetry with the pen of the body:

> When first our Poet set himself to write,
> Like a young Bridegroom on his Wedding-night
> He layd about him, and did so bestir him,
> His Muse could never lye in quiet for him.
>
> (Prologue, *Works,* 10:214)

93

Dryden develops this equating of sex with poetry throughout the play; the irresistible Englishmen seize Spanish women sexually, as Dryden seizes foreign plays with his pen. Here at the imaginatively reconstituted border of England's relations with the foreign world (literally—the protagonists are attached to the ambassador), the front line of imperial penetration consists of these three men, who seek with ingenuity and ardor to possess the objects of their sexual desires; in Dryden, the imperial urge is always gendered, always male. Writing, reading, and a peculiarly appropriative and masculine version of sex, rendered interchangeable by the prologue and epilogue, are the means to represent and understand the actions depicted in the play, and signs for one another. Winning women from foreigners, Dryden implies, is like taking plays from foreign poets. The martial vocabulary of forts and sieges, applied to foreign women, by extension applies equally well to foreign plays. For Englishmen, Dryden suggests, the wealth of the world is for the taking, be it in another country's ships (*Annus Mirabilis*), another country's women (the plot of *An Evening's Love*), or another country's plays (the actual appropriation of *An Evening's Love*).

Dryden's gendered notion of imperial power is enacted on yet another plane as these three voracious Englishmen seek to appropriate the sexual and monetary goods of Spain. As portrayed in *An Evening's Love,* there is a natural rightness in the Englishman's spirit that makes his appetites charming, his lusts justified. Dashing and likable, he is all but irresistible to the sex-starved women of Spain, and Spanish women leap to his arms as if no Spanish male had ever existed. Elopement with English men is made to seem liberating in a sexual modulation of a myth that often accompanies the act of imperialism: that to be conquered and subjugated by the imperial power represents an enlargement from the slavery and misery of living outside imperial rule and is thus instinctively welcomed by the new subjects of the empire. Since Dryden uses relations between English men and Spanish women as a way to talk about English and foreign poetry, we might read the Spanish women's eagerness to be taken by the English as Dryden's imperial recognition that foreign plays require appropriation, use, and improvement at the hands of a capable, wily, and ardent English poet. In yet another way the plot of *An Eve-ning's Love* recapitulates its origins in gendered literary rapture.

An Evening's Love's metaphorical equation of writing with sex invites us to accord the play's use of sex other significations than that of mere sensual gratification. But on the level of plot, brute sexual desire drives the events of the play; Wildblood in particular provides much of the comedy as he attempts to seduce Jacinta, principal object of his affections, each time she reappears disguised as another woman. Seeking indiscriminately to possess whatever woman is near him, Wildblood swears undying love to whoever wears a mask and skirts, be she even a servant or a Moor. As he turns from England outward toward female alterity, his omnivorous appetite makes him a sympathetic parody of the imperial urge. Dryden renders explicit the connection between seizing women and countries in the disguised Jacinta's bemused reprimand: "Heyday, You dispatch your Mistresses as fast, as if you meant to o're-run all Woman-kind: sure you aime at the Universal-Monarchy" (*Works,* 10:272). In this parody of insatiable desire for the foreign, the indefatigable sexual urge of the likable young Englishman takes upon itself the desire to possess all of foreign womankind—an analogue, implied in the play's motif of literature as sex, of the poet's literary satyriasis toward the works of Molière, Quinault, Corneille, and the de Scudérys.

Certain classes of alterations effected by Dryden in Thomas Corneille's *Feint Astrologue* justify his poetic imperialism by dem-onstrating that the appropriated material is better ruled under the governance of its new master. A self-designated conqueror vis-à-vis the appropriation of *An Evening's Love* from Corneille ("[the Poet] us'd the *French* like Enemies, / And did not steal their Plots, but made 'em prize" [Epilogue, ll. 28–29]), Dryden demonstrates his determination that the poetic realms he rules, though "unright-eously conquered," be "ruled well"—like Jonson's poetic appro-priations before him. To that end Dryden improves his conquered material, and from the nature of these improvements we learn something of his aims and anxieties regarding the French.

One such improvement is the compression of the incidents. The French theoretical ideal for dramatic extension in time was that the action represented in a play ought ideally to occur in the time taken to represent it. The complete coincidence of stage time with real time remained an infrequently attained absolute to the French; few plays actually achieved it, and few playwrights seem to have tried. As Thomas Corneille adapted Calderón's *El Astrologo Fingido,* he reduced the duration from three days to two. Dryden, however, in a tour de force of dramatic compression, shortened the time from two days to an evening, and in case the public might have overlooked either the fact itself or the importance of this dramatic nicety, he called attention to this improvement by naming the play after the play's duration, relegating its former title to subtitle. And if, in spite of the title, the audience remained unaware of or unimpressed by his improvements, he mocked their lack of concern in the person of a fop who mingles oaths with a brutish insensitivity to the fine points of seventeenth-century dramatic rules and decorums:

> Pox, *says another;* here's so great a stir
> With a son of a whore Farce that's regular,
> A rule where nothing must decorum shock!
> Dam' me 'ts as dull as dining by the clock.
> An Evening! why the devil should we be vext
> Whither he gets the Wench this night, or next?
> (Epilogue, *Works,* 10:313)

Dryden underscores the importance he gives his own improvements by ascribing indifference to them to a contemptible fool seated among us. By means of the fool's dramatized insensitivity, Dryden indicates precisely to what he wishes us to be sensitive.

Another improvement of Dryden's (like the play's duration, drawn attention to throughout) was also based on a French prescription (or what was perceived to be one)—that the play occur on a special or long-awaited day. Neander describes the prescription thus in the *Essay of Dramatick Poesy:* "One of these advantages is that which *Corneille* has laid down as the greatest which can arrive to any Poem, and which he himself could never compass above thrice in all this Playes, *viz.* the making choice of some signal and long-expected day, whereon the action of the Play is to depend" (*Works,* 17:62).[19] In *An Evening's Love,* the special day is the last day of Carnival, the day before the advent of Lent, when

Increased speed of D's action. The play brisker in the hands of its new 'ruler'.

Onely Victory in Him

all merriment and jollity will cease and a climate of mournful self-denial will commence.[20] Most importantly, at least as far as stage conventions are concerned, marriage is prohibited until Lent expires; the prohibition exerts considerable pressure on the lovers to marry and bed before Lent's arrival the next morning, after which time the marriage (and pendant consummation) must be postponed an unendurable forty days. Hence Dryden's characters frequently express concern over the shortness of time: "this being the last Evening of the Carnival" (*Works,* 10:244), Wildblood reminds as he serenades; "in one half-hour I have learnt to Cant with an indifferent good grace" (*Works,* 10:248) says Bellamy, accounting for his sudden acquisition of the language of astrology. Maskall bounds the frame of the entire drama thus: "If the business had gone on till to morrow, when *Lent* begins, you would have grown so peevish (as all good Catholicks are with fasting) that the quarrel would never have been ended" (*Works,* 10:288). The extreme compression of events occurring all on a Cornelian special day yields a play of amazing bustle; the three Englishmen spot, woo, win, and marry their women—with all the attendant sub- and byplots, including the astrologer- and Jacinta-masquerades, swordfights, gaming, masques, songs, and dances—in the space of a single evening. No other drama of Dryden's moves with this rapidity. Perhaps Dryden, working on an inferior play by the lesser Corneille, wished to enter into competition with a great play of the greater elder, for in a curious way the speed of action in *An Evening's Love* echoes the same note of glorious inverisimilitude struck by Pierre Corneille in *Le Cid,* in which Rodrigo avenges his father by killing Chimène's, fights and vanquishes the Moors, overcomes Chimène's anger at him, and betroths her, all in less than twenty-four hours.

By means of such ingenious improvements, Dryden demonstrates that French material prospers better under English than Gallic rule, for a French prescription is used to improve a French play beyond what the French themselves could manage—one more proof, if proof were needed, that this dramatic property is in better hands under the care of its new ruler, the "unrighteous conqueror."

Marvelously crafted as a comparison with Corneille's *Feint Astro-*

D's defence against charge of plagiarism : ① his plays
have pleased the king ② 'wit' and 'fancy' more imp. to a play than plot.

THE IMPERIAL DRYDEN

logue shows *An Evening's Love* to be, many of Dryden's contemporaries were disturbed by what appeared to be, without more careful consideration, simple theft. In a reply to these critics, Dryden
makes no bones about having taken the story, or his right to do so:
" 'Tis true, that where ever I have lik'd any story in a Romance,
Novel, or forreign Play, I have made no difficulty, nor ever shall,
to take the foundation of it, to build it up, and to make it proper
for the *English* Stage" (Preface, *Works*, 10:210). In the preface to
An Evening's Love Dryden mounts an elaborate defense against
charges that his plays are stolen. He proposes four interrelated
strands of argument to explain why taking the poetic work of
others is laudable, customary, authorized by the great names of
poetry, and to be considered "conquest" (as distinct from theft).
The first thread of his argument is exactly similar to Corneille's
final argument in his defense of *Le Cid:* that his thefts have pleased
"him" whom all drama must please. Dryden does not identify the
"him," but the reference to Caesar in the quotation from Juvenal
might permit us to think it the king: "There is one answer [to my
accusers] which I will not make; but it has been made for me by
him to whose Grace and Patronage I owe all things. . . . *Et spes
& ratio studiorum,* in Cæsare *tantum,* and without whose command
they shou'd no longer be troubl'd with any thing of mine; that
he only desir'd that they who accus'd me of theft would always
steal him Playes like mine" (*Works*, 10:210). In a monarchy—and
in a theatrical climate—where the king's likes and dislikes constituted a kind of law,[21] to say that one's "incorrect" productions had
pleased the king was to plead an overridingly higher standard of
correctness against which there could be no serious argument.

Dryden's second line of defense is that the plot is the least part
of a successful literary work; the author's wit and fancy are what
set the work off, and these, Dryden untruthfully insists, he has
never borrowed.[22] More accurately, he goes on to claim that the demands of English taste are such that any borrowed foundation of a
play must be so reworked as to make it completely new "since no
Story can afford Characters enough for the variety of the *English*
Stage, it follows that it is to be alter'd, and inlarg'd, with new
persons, accidents, and designes, which wil almost make it new"
(*Works*, 10:212). Thus the improving of a seized-upon work is

improvement of a play effectively makes it new.   The 'materials' of a poem not the author's property.

Onely Victory in Him

enough, in the language of Dryden's critical vocabulary, "almost" to "make it new." He shifts the argument here from the ethics of imperialism to the more radical notion (which we see embodied in the character of *An Evening's Love*'s Aurelia) that theft, per se, is artistically indefensible; only remaking appropriated material until it is "almost new" satisfies the demands of England's particular taste in drama and removes the stigma of simple plagiarism.

Taking the preceding approach a step further, Dryden mounts a potentially radical defense of poetic appropriation. He reasons that since the value of any poem lies in the "ornamentation," the story itself is, if not valueless, the least part of the poetic enterprise, a property as common to the nation of poets as language itself. Here, in the most far-reaching of the four arguments, Dryden attacks the entire notion of poetic property, arguing instead that the poet is a craftsman who fashions beautiful artifacts with materials that pass through his hands but do not belong to him, materials that, valuable or not as they may be, are the least valuable part of the finished artifact: "The employment of a Poet, is like that of a curious Gunsmith, or Watchmaker: the Iron or Silver is not his own; but they are the least part of that which gives the value: The price lyes wholly in the workmanship" (*Works,* 10:212). And in the following lines from the epilogue to *An Evening's Love* Dryden uses a similar metaphor of poetic currency passing altered through the hands of the artisan:

> He [the poet] still must write; and Banquier-like, each day
> Accept new Bills, and he must break, or pay.
> When through his hands such sums must yearly run,
> You cannot think the Stock is all his own.
>
> (*Works,* 10:314)

Dryden vigorously attacks the concept of poetic property, holding that the finished work of one's predecessors becomes the essentially valueless raw material from which one fashions one's own work, which then, it is to be assumed, becomes near-valueless material in the hands of one's successor artisans; if pursued far enough, such an approach would have made unnecessary Dryden's reliance on a poetic lineage, with its attendant literary history.[23] Had he articulated some of the implications of this ap-

③ all great poets adapt their predecessors : his great predecessors
'imperialists' too. ④ pillage justified if it enriches one's nation.

THE IMPERIAL DRYDEN

proach, he might have argued that we could think no poet's stock "all his own," that all poetry was the reworking of anterior poetry, that pure ownership of a poetic artifact, and hence, pure poetry, was an impossibility. But like so much in Dryden's criticism, it is a tantalizing suggestion, seemingly tossed off upon the instant, mused upon an instant longer, and passed over in a rush upon the next point.

In his third line of defense, Dryden argues that he has done no more than what all great poets have done in translating the works of their own predecessors. To illustrate this he inventories a roll of ancients who borrowed from others yet more ancient: Virgil from Theocritus, Hesiod from Homer, Terence from Menander. Moving forward in time, Dryden cites Tasso's borrowings from Homer and Virgil, Shakespeare's from Cinthio's *Hecatommithi*,[24] Beaumont and Fletcher's from the Spanish novelists, and Ben Jonson's from all the ancients.

Here, in an extraordinary transformation, the imperial and mis-quotational modes conflate. The entire corps of Dryden's poetic genealogy, invoked whenever necessary as the originators of one or another type of poetic effect, authorities from whom Dryden derives his poetic legitimacy, are here transformed—misquoted—to a pack of borrowers from whom Dryden derives the authority to borrow. The entire notion of poetic legitimacy is thus effectively modified into a new mode of (literal) invention in which each takes from others whatever is needed. Dryden here metamorphoses his validating fathers from their habitual status as authorizing origi-nators into a group of authorizing *not*-originators, protoimperial-ists. Dryden derives a right not to be original, that is, a right to appropriate from others, from his fathers' own lack of originality.

The fourth and most briefly stated of Dryden's justifications is grounded in Ben Jonson's takings from the ancients. Revert-ing to a nationalistic mode in which the seizure of what enriches the patria is justified by the patria's enrichment, Dryden writes of Jonson's borrowings (and by extension, of his own): "No man has borrow'd so much from the Ancients as he has done: And he did well in it, for he has thereby beautifi'd our language" (*Works*, 10:212). Pillage is justified, Dryden argues, because when it is successfully done the home state is enriched with the ornaments of others: "he has thereby beautifi'd our language."

This, so briefly suggested, is the final argument of Drydenian imperialism, unnecessary for him to dwell upon since it underlies the other three arguments. Poetic imperialism, he claims, is justified by the mere fact of its increasing the overall poetic wealth of the native country. To justify poetic imperialism one need say no more than that a poet, by his takings, has "beautifi'd the language," as British privateers preying upon the Spanish plate fleet claimed only that they enriched the treasuries of the king, and as the Spaniards, in turn, claimed as they extracted the wealth of the native Americans.

In these four related arguments justifying the appropriation of poetic property from others (especially those of other nationalities), Dryden shows himself keenly aware of the proprieties of poetic depredation. He demonstrates his awareness of the correct modes of poetic borrowing representationally (within the drama) as well as discursively (in prefatory material). One type that Dryden uses to show his consummate awareness of the proprieties of transcultural importation is the character of the failed or second-rate borrower, a type with which the Restoration is greatly fascinated and a type of which Dryden gives us some of the greatest examples.

An example of the failed borrower type in *An Evening's Love* is Aurelia, the object of Don Lopez's affections. She is modeled after Cathos and Magdelon, the affected ladies of Molière's *Précieuses Ridicules* (1659), and like her models in the much-imitated Molière play, Aurelia's humour is that she imports language verbatim from one sphere to another. Finding her native language inadequate to express her desired social status, she seeks to adopt a new language, composed of elisions (ma'am for madam, parn for pardon), the too-frequent use of "furiously," elaborate circumlocutions for simple objects, and a number of importations from the French. Not only are many of her affectations of speech borrowed from the French language, but her very character—indeed, whole speeches —are borrowed without acknowledgment from the Molière play.

In the following conversation between Aurelia and her maid, each of Aurelia's lines contains some affectation of speech; two (and possibly all) of the three are borrowed from the French either at the level of French vocabulary ("spiritual" for "clever"), or are borrowed closely from Molière's *Précieuses:*

Aurelia's borrowings / inept and obtrusive ; Dryden's equal
extensive , but skilful and covert.

A. Welsch

Aurelia. How am I drest to night, *Camilla?* is nothing dis-
order'd in my head?

Camilla. Not the least hair, Madam.

Aurelia. No? let me see: give me the Counsellor of the Graces.

Camilla. The Counsellor of the Graces, Madam?

Aurelia. My Glass I mean: what, will you never be so spiritual as to understand refin'd language?

(*Works,* 10:250–51) [25]

Here is Dryden's unacknowledged model in Molière:

Magdelon. Vite, venez nous tendre ici dedans le conseiller des
grâces.

Marotte. Par ma fois, je ne sais point quelle bête c'est là: il
faut parler chrétien, si vous voulez que je vous entende.

Cathos. Apportez-nous le miroir, ignorante que vous êtes, et
gardez-vous bien d'en salir la glace par la communication
de votre image.

(*Les Précieuses Ridicules,* Molière, 1:271) [26]

The passage shows two kinds of borrowings from the French;
the first type, in Aurelia's language, is borrowed intact from the
vocabulary of France, and is accordingly ridiculous as it is mal-
absorbed. The larger borrowing of the entire speech from Molière,
a secret, or at least unannounced, draws no attention to itself in
the context of the play. It is reworked into English so that the language that is foregrounded in the French remains foregrounded
in the English, but with differences that suit the context both of
the play and of English culture. It would not have done to have an
English maid speak so to her mistress, nor would it have been in
character for Aurelia to waste such a delicious insult ("gardez-vous
bien d'en salir") on her maid, unobserved. The reader is ever aware
of Aurelia's affectations of borrowed language, never Dryden's.

Aurelia, as an intermediary between the old "low" culture of her
maid and the new "high" culture she wishes to assume by introducing more polite kinds of language into her circle, shares certain
similarities with her raptor, Dryden, similarities of which Aurelia
herself is a kind of inverted instance. Aurelia, though borrowed,
is herself a borrower, and to that extent is an image in miniature

Aurelia as 'parody - imperialist'

of Dryden; what she does badly to language is what Dryden does well to Molière in the act of borrowing her. Aurelia is a kind of importer-exporter in language, introducing forms of speech, nominally French, intended by her to demonstrate her membership in an elect group presumed to exist outside the play's action (for we assume that she does not invent this affected speech, but exports it from a circle where it is currently in use).[27] By his borrowings (and in particular, in his borrowing of Aurelia), Dryden shows a similar determination to innovate, not by the fruits of his own endeavors, but by introducing what is taken from others. Through Aurelia a myth of imperialism is transmuted yet again, this time into another kind of parody of itself, the greedy barbarian taking what she does not understand and what she has not made her own by understanding, and introducing this borrowed material in an undigested form.

In the undigestedness of Aurelia's innovations we see Dryden's principal differences from her: she imports uncritically and whole, thinking to present an elevated image of herself merely by importing what had value elsewhere; the language is borrowed but not conquered, quoted but not remade. Dryden, on the other hand, claims to have gone (and apparently has gone) to some trouble to make his poetic booty "his." He describes the inadequacy of simple conquest and the subsequent degree of reworking in the epilogue to *An Evening's Love,* reporting his own speech in the third person:

> But should he all the pains and charges count
> Of taking 'em [French plays], the bill so high wou'd mount,
> That, like Prize goods, which through the Office come,
> He could have had 'em much more cheap at home.
>
> *(Works,* 10:314)

Dryden again emphasizes that "pains and charges" are needed for successful taking; uncritical importation of language or dramatic forms will result in failure as pretentious and comic as Aurelia's.

Though the distance between Aurelia and Dryden is large, it is by no means infinite; with her he parodies himself and his process of conquering by showing us not a conqueror, but an industrious importer whose principal characteristic is exactly what Dryden's

Absurd results when 'importation' are not fully 'naturalised' and reworked in the native language. —

enemies accused him of: plagiarism. He mocks her failure to assimilate what he has assimilated so well, and with such "pains and
charges." The proud imperialist reminds us yet again: not till an
importation is reworked, improved, made one's own, truly translated into one's own language, does it cease to be ridiculous.

As we leave the play through the back door of the epilogue, we
meet another Aurelia-figure seated, not onstage, but among ourselves:

> Up starts a *Monsieur* new come o're; and warm
> In the *French* stoop; and the pull-back o'th' arm;
> Morbleu *dit il,* and cocks, *I am a rogue*
> *But he has quite spoil'd the* feint Astrologue
>
> (*Works,* 10:313)

Dryden's miniature of the misborrowing English Monsieur is a
little gem; we see the fop's attitude exactly staged, stooped over so,
arm held back thus; his language is a marvelous blend of English
and French (rhyme of "rogue" and "astrologue"); his accusation
of spoiling-by-translation is false, but exactly the cultural crime
of which he is himself guilty, for he has imported a set of forms
(social and linguistic, instead of dramatic) and, in so doing, has
parodied whatever value they might have had in France. Concluding the play with the English Monsieur completes the circle of
representations of borrowing; the failed importer/audience member scorns the work of the backstage creator-borrower of the onstage verbatim importer; fiction is heaped on fiction in a tableau
of figures who seem almost frantic to import, to blazon forth their
importations, figures who finally remain ridiculous by failing to
make these importations their own. Standing back like a puppet-
eer behind a stage, the age's great cultural imperialist can afford
to let his parodies mock him.

Aurelia is a naive plagiarist; she takes a language not hers and
offers it as her own, as if such unlicensed importation of language
would elevate her social status. Dryden knows better, as do we;
he knows that the only kind of appropriation that is artistically
justifiable is what the character of Aurelia represents herself—a
theft that is a victory, not surreptitiously offered as one's own, but
a seizing, reworking, and improving upon the work of others. In

Melantha (Marriage A-la-Mode) as parody innovator

the prologue to *Albumazar* (1668), Dryden shows us a world in
which authors, like Aurelias, take from others only to claim what
they take, unaltered and untransformed, as their own:

> But this our age such Authors does afford,
> As make whole Playes, and yet scarce write one word:
> Who in this Anarchy of witt, rob all,
> And what's their Plunder, their Possession call;
> Who like bold Padders scorn by night to prey,
> But Rob by Sun-shine, in the face of day;
> Nay scarce the common Ceremony use,
> Of stand, Sir, and deliver up your Muse;
> But knock the Poet down; and, with a Grace,
> Mount *Pegasus* before the owners Face.
>
> (*Works,* 1:141)

In the "Anarchy of witt," which is Dryden's literary milieu, only
conquerors such as Ben Jonson and Dryden, not mere petty thieves
of verse, have the required poetic strength to refashion their appropriated poetic material. Dryden's quarrel with these "bold
Padders" is not that they are bold (after all, "bold" is his favorite adjective to describe himself), or that they steal (for Dryden
admits to taking plots from others), but that in stealing, they
"scarce Write one word"; they do not make what they have stolen
their own by a secondary appropriation that is, in effect, a new
act of creation. Language, like plots, must not simply be transported from one place, from one poet's work, from one country,
to another; the raptor must make his prey his own. By the char-
acterization of Aurelia, Dryden shows himself splendidly capable
of just such a thorough seizing of another's work.

The failed Dryden-figure of the parodied innovator appears
again, a better developed and more sympathetic character, as
Melantha, in *Marriage A-la-Mode.*

Much has been said, and much of that well, of the heights of
wit-writing attained in *Marriage A-la-Mode,* heights Dryden never
again reached in his drama. Langbaine characteristically insists
that the entirety of the play is borrowed, two separate stolen
plots "tackt together" to form, not a "Comedy," as it is titled,
but, Langbaine insists, a "Tragi-Comedy" (166). Subsequent exe-

getists have corroborated half of Langbaine's charge (the romance plot is taken whole from Mlle. de Scudéry) but virtually all commentators exonerate Dryden of plagiarizing the wit-writing, that for which most of us continue to treasure the play. Small but precise echoes of earlier works occasionally intrude, but the most dogged of source-hunters has not been able to wrest the comedy from Dryden (see *Sources,* 113).

Of all the gems of unexpected wit and unlikely character studded unevenly throughout *Marriage A-la-Mode,* one of the most precious—and unlikely—is the character of Melantha. Melantha is engaged to Palamede and pursued by Rhodophil; her humour consists principally in her love of things French. She is gripped by the delusion that French words possess a kind of magic that will lend her character a dignity she feels she needs (coming, as she does, from the town) and will ingratiate her with the court notables she so assiduously woos. In the words of Rhodophil: "No Lady can be so curious of a new Fashion, as she is of a new *French* Word; she's the very Mint of the Nation; and as fast as any Bullion comes out of *France,* coins it immediately into our Language" (*Works,* 11:234).

Melantha's knowledge of French is mediated by her maid, Philotis, who is steeped in the French language and literature. In the following passage Melantha restocks herself with new language from Philotis, a scene that, it is suggested, is repeated daily:

> *Philotis.* Indeed, Madam, I have been very diligent in my vocation; but you have so drain'd all the *French* Plays and Romances, that they are not able to supply you with words for your daily expences.
>
> *Melantha. Drain'd?* what a word's there! *Épuisée,* you sot you. Come, produce your morning's work. . . .
>
> *Philotis. Sottises.*
>
> *Melantha. Sottises: bon.* That's an excellent word to begin withall: as for example; He, or she said a thousand *Sottises* to me. Proceed.
>
> *Philotis. Figure:* as, what a *figure* of a man is there! *Naive,* and *Naiveté.*
>
> *Melantha. Naive!* as how?
>
> *Philotis.* Speaking of a thing that was naturally said; It was so

naive: or such an innocent piece of simplicity; twas such a *naiveté.*

(*Works,* 11:263–64)

Armed with her new vocabulary for the day, Melantha introduces French words into every conversation she can; when she is forced to use a new word on a person of lower social status than the one for whom the word was destined, the word is "wasted."

Melantha's immediate source is to be found in Dryden's own *An Evening's Love.* [28] Aurelia's affected language and inappropriately imported French is clearly the basis for Melantha's humour, though Melantha's character—and humour—are conceived on a larger scale. Aurelia, though of a wealthy family, is not independent; Melantha, by contrast, rules herself, decides how she will spend her money, and whether she will marry. Melantha, though of the town, has larger ambitions than Aurelia; she wishes to be recognized by the greatest personages in Sicily—Aurelia wishes only to have Don Melchor. Though both characters specialize in borrowing language to which they are not entitled by birth or breeding, Melantha is admirably organized about it, spending time, energy, and substantial amounts of money on daily obtaining the newest-coined words from France.[29] Although Aurelia herself is a daughter of Molière's *précieuses,* the much greater Melantha, in effect a granddaughter of Molière, is emancipated from her literary genealogy; she lives with a kind of zany authority denoting her as Dryden's own.[30]

Marriage A-la-Mode, like *An Evening's Love,* exhibits Dryden's own fascination with things Gallic both on and beneath the surface. Of the two "tackt together" plots, the heroic (duller) plot, concerned with the precociously and tediously heroic Leonidas's attempts to regain his throne from the usurper Polydamas, is borrowed directly from Mlle. de Scudéry, though this borrowing is unacknowledged.[31] Because fully one-half of *Marriage A-la-Mode* is silently borrowed from the French, the comic half, concerned with keeping the French incursion at a distance, is very much complicated; Dryden, in fashioning the play from a popular romance (or, as Philotis says of Melantha, having "so drain'd all the *French* Plays and Romances"), has committed what his own characters disdain.

Accordingly, a much deeper look is required into the play's relations with the French tradition than merely to claim (as some have) that *Marriage A-la-Mode* is concerned only with ridiculing the French influence on English dramatic and cultural life. Ultimately the play is concerned not with keeping the foreign at a distance, but with examining means of adopting and adapting it. The French element, so bitterly fought against elsewhere in Dryden, is treated with fondness here, not only by means of a character, lovingly drawn, who believes in and loves her very words with a kind of passion foreign to anyone but a poet, but with a mild bemusement that suggests nothing so much as affection. In *Marriage A-la-Mode* French language and culture are mocked into the margin, then wrested back to the center; the play seems less concerned with the quality of the French contribution to English culture than it is concerned with the manner of its appropriation by the English.

Marriage A-la-Mode, for the first time in Dryden's oeuvre, contrasts the good borrower with the bad; this dramatic juxtaposition, itself a kind of object lesson, grows fairly common in Restoration representations of misborrowing, representations that themselves were fairly common (the modish fop just back from France, for example), indicating a continuing interest in cultural misappropriation throughout the period.[32] Doralice describes the type during her first encounter with Palamede: "You travelling Monsieurs live upon the stock you have got abroad, for the first day or two: to repeat with a good memory, and apply with a good grace, is all your wit. And, commonly, your Gullets are sew'd up, like Cormorants: When you have regorg'd what you have taken in, you are the leanest things in Nature" (*Works,* 11:229). And Melantha, though neither a traveler nor a Monsieur, admits to Philotis that she too, in her own poverty of native language, is related to the Cormorant: "Are not you a most precious damsel, to retard all my visits for want of language, when you know you are paid so well for furnishing me with new words for my daily conversation? Let me die, if I have not run the *risque* already, to speak like one of the vulgar; and if I have one phrase left in all my store that is not thrid-bare *& usé,* and fit for nothing but to be thrown to Peasants" (*Works,* 11:263). Dryden juxtaposes cormorantic bad borrowers, those, like Aurelia, Melantha, and Doralice's "travel-

Onely Victory in Him

ling Monsieurs," who take French words and customs and use them unaltered, with those who have also integrated the French language and aesthetic but do not display this knowledge except as a kind of spice to normal discourse, or else to shame the verbatim misborrowers by showing that they too have integrated the French language and aesthetic, and have done it better.

Explicit juxtapositions of bad with good borrowers occur twice in *Marriage A-la-Mode,* the first time between Doralice and Melantha. Melantha makes herself ridiculous in insisting even that her regards, or "service," be extended to the princess in the pretentious *"Baise mains"*:

> *Doralice.* Farewell, *Melantha.*
> *Melantha.* Adieu, my dear.
> *Artemis.* You are out of charity with her [the Princess], and therefore I shall not give your service.
> *Melantha.* Do not omit it, I beseech you; for I have such a *tendre* for the Court, that I love it ev'n from the Drawing-room to the Lobby, and can never be *rebutée* by any usage. But, hark you, my Dears, one thing I had forgot of great concernment.
> *Doralice.* Quickly then, we are in haste.
> *Melantha.* Do not call it my service, that's too vulgar; but do my *baise mains* to the Princess *Amalthea;* that is *Spirituelle!*
> *Doralice.* To do you service then, we will *prendre* the *Carosse* to Court, and do your *Baise mains* to the Princess *Amalthea,* in your phrase *Spirituellé.*
>
> (*Works,* 11:263)

Melantha, calling it a matter "of great <u>concernment</u>," insists upon her French substitution for a perfectly <u>good</u> English word; Doralice, hurried and unamused by Melantha's eccentricities, overwhelms Melantha's pretensions by showing not only that she speaks French fluently and idiomatically (without, we are sure, having to consult her maid each morning), but that she has so integrated the French language into her own that ostentatious display is unnecessary; Doralice proves that when the occasion demands she can speak the mot juste.

Such overwhelming of inferior by superior appropriation of the

cp. ↓.
on Ovid

foreign occurs once more in *Marriage A-la-Mode,* at a crucial juncture. When a wrinkle in the plot demands that Palamede either win Melantha immediately or be disinherited, Philotis counsels him to use Melantha's vocabulary against her. At first chagrined at his further appropriation of her appropriated language, Melantha is soon charmed by his superior grasp of French culture:

> *Melantha.* He mocks himself of me, he abuses me: ah me unfortunate! [*Cries.*
>
> *Philotis.* You mistake him, Madam, he does but accomodate his phrase to your refin'd language. *Ah, qu'il est un Cavalier accomply!* Pursue your point, Sir— [*To him.*
>
> *Palamede. Ah, qu'il fait beau dans ces boccages;* [*Singing.* *Ah, que le ciel donne un beau jour!*
> There I was with you, with a *minouet.*
>
> *Melantha.* Let me die now, but this singing is fine, and extremely *French* in him: [*Laughs.*
> But then, that he should use my own words, as it were in contempt of me, I cannot bear it. [*Crying.*
>
> *Palamede. Ces beaux séjours, ces doux ramages—* [*Singing.*
>
> *Melantha. Ces beaux séjours, ces doux ramages,* [*Singing after him.* *Ces beaux sejours, nous invitent a l'amour!*
> Let me die but he sings *en Cavalier,* and so humours the Cadence. [*Laughing.*
>
> *Palamede. Voy, ma Clymene, voy soubs ce chesne,* [*Singing again.* *S'entrebaiser ces oiseaux amoureux!*
> Let me die now, but that was fine. Ah, now, for three or four brisk *Frenchmen,* to be put into Masquing habits, and to sing it on a Theatre, how witty it would be! and then to dance helter skelter to a *Chanson a boire: toute la terre, toute la terre est a moy!* what's matter though it were made, and sung, two or three years ago in *Cabarets,* how it would attract the admiration, especially of every one that's an *éveillé!*
>
> *Melantha.* Well; I begin to have a *tendre* for you.
>
> (*Works,* 11:302–3)

Here Palamede, like Doralice before him, demonstrates a mastery of French language and culture. That Palamede possesses this kind

Doralice both pro-English and fully assimilative of French culture (in the best sense).

of close acquaintance with France surprises us; we have seen no previous evidence of such a thorough (or indeed, any) knowledge of the French language, manners, poetry, and customs. The inhabitants of this courtly world must possess such knowledge, but the imperative carries with it a corollary: such knowledge must be possessed in secret.

Within the terms set forth in the play, Palamede's and Doralice's knowledge of French is clearly the model for the manner of assimilating French into English culture; each time a character besides Melantha shows knowledge of French, it is to demonstrate that French culture can be integrated into the larger English scheme without calling attention to itself—just as de Scudéry's plot is silently integrated into this English play. When Doralice and Melantha, disguised and hence incognita to one another, clash on the subject of the relative merits of French and English drama, Doralice, despite her infinitely greater understanding of and familiarity with the French tradition, is vehemently pro-English:

> *Melantha.* You are one of those that applaud our Countrey
> Plays, where drums, and trumpets, and bloud, and wounds,
> are wit. . . .
> *Doralice.* You are an admirer of the dull *French* Poetry, which
> is so thin, that it is the very Leaf-gold of Wit, the very
> Wafers and whip'd Cream of sense, for which a man opens
> his mouth and gapes, to swallow nothing: and to be an
> admirer of such profound dulness, one must be endow'd
> with a great perfection of impudence and ignorance. . . .
> *Melantha.* I'll sacrifice my life for *French* Poetry.   [*Advancing.*
> *Doralice.* I'll die upon the spot for our Countrey Wit.
>
> (*Works,* 11:291)

It is significant that the most explicitly pro-English voice in the play, that of Doralice, should also be the voice best informed by knowledge of the French language and cultural tradition.

The two exchanges between Doralice, Melantha, and Palamede illustrate the correct means of treating the French tradition and reflect Dryden's own notions—as exemplified in the body of *Marriage A-la-Mode* itself—of how French language and culture ought to be absorbed into English. French culture, Doralice and Pala-

Doralice's method close to D's own. Melantha a
cultural /linguistic / human 'outsider'.

THE IMPERIAL DRYDEN

mede show us, must be integrated invisibly; one *knows* French, one
speaks English. French language and culture should be a kind of
leaven to the English, a means to increase variety, one more strand
to be woven into the English tapestry. Moreover, the interchanges
between Melantha, Doralice, and Palamede could be taken as the
model for *Marriage A-la-Mode*'s construction. Borrowings from
the French, notably the entire romantic-heroic plot and the origin
of Melantha, are as invisible as Doralice's knowledge of French;
only when it is necessary to show some knowledge of capacity
in French does Dryden reveal his knowledge, as do Doralice
and Palamede. Dryden reveals his knowledge of French language
and literature in characteristically offhand style—by representing
interchanges between Melantha and those who know better.

The image of the faulty borrower, the failed imperialist, is given
a new twist with Melantha; she begins the play as the embodiment
of the outsider, champion of the ridiculous, the quintessential arri-
viste buzzing vainly from figure to figure, failure to failure, rebuff
to rebuff. But she does not remain outside; she is integrated by
marriage into the society she craves, and Palamede predicts—and
the reader is certain—that she will dictate language and poetic
forms to the newly, and now justly, reconstituted society. Not only
is she a gloriously powerful misreader of language's uses, but her
misreadings are so strong that they eventually become acceptable
readings. Reforming the manners of the court has long been on
her mind; at her first meeting with Palamede she expresses the
hope that his travels will serve to polish the manners of a group
that just barely suffers her acquaintance: "I suppose, Sir, you have
made the *Tour* of *France;* and having seen all that's fine there, will
make a considerable reformation in the rudeness of our Court: for,
let me die, but an unfashion'd, untravel'd, meer *Sicilian* is a *Bete;*
and has nothing in the world of an *honete homme*" (*Works,* 11:244).

During the course of the play, however, Melantha moves from
outside to inside, from failure to success, from ridiculous aper of
customs she hardly understands to a cultural legislator for a new
society. At the play's conclusion, her husband-to-be, Palamede,
says of her: "I find I must get her a place at Court; and when she
is once there, she can be no longer ridiculous; for she is young

enough, and pretty enough, and fool enough, and *French* enough, to bring up a fashion there to be affected" (*Works*, 11:313). Not only does Melantha knock on the doors of this closed world, which finally, magically, open to her, but her language is the lexical indicator of both her oddness and her eventual success. In a recapitulation of that success, her language has been accepted into our own. *Voyage, good graces, air, levé, figure, naive, foible, chagrin, double entendre, eclaircissement, penchant, ridicule, incendiary, billet doux, gallant, tendre, à propos, mal à propos* are all words we use, if not daily, at least often enough to admit that we speak them. The triumph of Melantha's vocabulary signifies her personal triumph in Sicily (where the action purports to occur, though the characters are English enough to quote Shakespeare); Dryden's personal triumph lies in his sensitivity to what language will become standard English and in incorporating such language, mocking yet stressing its eventual adoption, in his own writing.[33]

A full century after *Marriage A-la-Mode*, Dr. Johnson writes of Dryden in nearly the same terms that Dryden uses for Melantha: "He had a vanity unworthy of his abilities to show, as may be suspected, the rank of the company with whom he lived by the use of French words which had then crept into conversation—such as *fraîcheur* for 'coolness,' *fougue* for 'turbulence,' and a few more, none of which the language has incorporated or retained. They continue only where they stood first, perpetual warnings to future innovators (*Life*, 197). Johnson, however, was as wrong about Dryden as the characters in *Marriage A-la-Mode* are about Melantha; not only would a list of Dryden's introductions from the French be long indeed, but it would be found that many of his words, like Melantha's, have become standard usage.[34] Melantha's triumph in *Marriage A-la-Mode* is Dryden's in the larger world of language and poetry.

As much as Dryden, Melantha has drained, or as she would have it, *épuisé*, "all the *French* Plays and Romances" in order to provide herself with a vocabulary that will express what cannot be expressed in her native tongue, since, she claims, "I know not how to express it in our dull *Sicilian* Language" because "our damn'd language expresses nothing."[35] By using this imported language

λ?

she seeks to stress a connection between herself and France; this, of course, is a connection Dryden has no wish overtly to make for himself. That the serious part of the play is entirely derived from a French romance and that Melantha is the daughter of a character inspired by the French are not literary facts that would find their way into one of Dryden's self-serving genealogies or histories of literary influence.

Through Melantha, Dryden plays out a series of delicate in-jokes on himself, on the process of writing, and on the nature of his own literary imperialism. To make Melantha a grotesque like Sir Fopling Flutter, someone whose borrowings from the French were and would remain forever beyond the pale, would have been easy. But her attractiveness is essential, both to her success within the plot and, as a character, to us. The male characters in the play find her desirable (in the case of Rhodophil, enormously so), and that sexual desire should so join with desire for the importer of language says as much about Dryden's victories over the French as it does about a pair of young men being sexually attracted to a rich and beautiful young woman.

Weaving a borrowed French plot and borrowed French language into a play whose languages and tones vary so widely embodies Dryden's long-articulated critical desiderata. Elements of the French language and literary tradition, worthy but narrow, alluring but insufficient, are to be subsumed into a larger whole that includes them while transcending them. Alone, the French plots, the French characters, the isolated French words introduced into the language, impress neither Dryden nor the characters in *Marriage A-la-Mode*. But fully appropriated and improved, used as a means to achieve greater variety, the French element—always of enormous interest to Dryden and his time—becomes dramatically respectable and successful and, ultimately, worthy of qualified admiration. Only by an inclusion as total as Doralice's and Palamede's can Dryden take what he needs from the French while maintaining his own respectability as an English writer writing English plays for English audiences. Depredating imperially where he can, and misquoting where he must, Dryden shows an amazing versatility in adopting forebears from many nations and

Eventually assimilated.

times into a dramatic and critical scheme that includes them without claiming too much from or for them. The inclusion of Melantha into the highest court circles incarnates sexually Dryden's varied textual inclusions from the French, aptly justified with a term borrowed from the lexicon of international relations—victory.

CHAPTER THREE

Both Woo'd and Wooing: The Rhetoric of Translation

How can he show his Manhood, if you bind him
To box, like Boys, with one Hand ty'd behind him?

Prologue to *Amphitryon*

Following the revolution of 1688, Dryden, suddenly of the wrong faith and political persuasion, was unceremoniously thrust outside the structures of official religious, political, and economic power that had hitherto supported him. Communicant of a proscribed faith, stripped of his titles of Poet Laureate and Royal Historiographer (and the substantial, though fitfully paid, stipends that accompanied them), reduced by need to return to writing for "th'Ungrateful Stage," Dryden after 1688 found himself in a situation not unlike Milton's after the Restoration, apologizing for an ousted and unpopular regime. Being of the defeated party required radical shifts of perspective for the suddenly laurel-less poet, and Dryden accordingly devised new ways to speak of himself in relation to the structures that confer power on poet, male, and citizen. Whereas in better days he had represented himself as the creation of and agent for the great power-conferring hierarchical systems—that is, the genealogy of poets, masculinity, military force, and political power—after the revolution, Dryden represents himself as identifying with individuals who are denied power and authority by those same great systems of poetic paternity, gender, force, and politics. The multiple shifts of self-presentation, from confident male to vulnerable neuter, privileged heir to belated mediocrity, laureled conqueror to bitter subject and, ultimately, from rapacious conqueror of the poetic past to

116

Recent accounts of the 'indirection' of the late Dryden. D's 'gendered' discussions of power.

(?) self-abnegating translator, all combine to produce a Dryden we might safely call a new figure.

Critical interest in Dryden's late period has come into its own only lately. Alan Roper, Steven Zwicker, Michael McKeon, and others have shown us the subtle ways that such poems as *Annus Mirabilis* and *Absalom and Achitophel* both reflect and are constituted of the texture of political day-to-day existence;[1] applying such methods to the more problematic works of the later Dryden has recently yielded several book-length studies. Judith Sloman, Cedric D. Reverand II, David Bywaters, and the final chapters of James Winn's *John Dryden and His World* all treat the social and political climate of Dryden's late period;[2] all stress Dryden's development of a "literary form through which he could reveal and conceal himself at the same time" (Sloman, 7), for it was a period in which the poet, owing to the unpopularity of his religion and persistent loyalty to the Stuarts, had to code his utterances of discontent. Reverand, who fixes his attention principally on Dryden's last work, *Fables* (1700), describes the poet's concealment even of his own rhetorical indeterminacy: "indirection was always part of the game, but now the game went underground" (204). Few critics, with the conspicuous exception of Jean Hagstrum and James Winn,[3] have treated the subject of Dryden and sex—an odd omission considering Dryden's evident concern with the subject. This chapter, focusing precisely on those elements in Dryden's works that generations of readers have dismissed as reflections of the low taste of a debauched age, aims to show how the poet keeps translating his relationship to formally constituted structures of power (politics, religion, and force) into a gendered language too easily confused with, and traditionally dismissed as, mere bawdry. Dryden's practice seems to answer Gilbert and Gubar's opening query—"is a pen a metaphorical penis?"[4]—with a resounding affirmative, for to Dryden the pen is always a sexual instrument, even when historical accident constricts the manner in which he may wield it, or even deprives him of its use.

The differences between Dryden's modes of self-presentation before and after the revolution of 1688 show how much his altered circumstances themselves altered his views on his own relation to

Before 1688 : D's writing depicted as a 'masculine' activity.
(as frequently in the period)

THE IMPERIAL DRYDEN

the world of poetry. Before the revolution Dryden's self-presenta-
tions were unremittingly masculine, and he represented the act of
writing—and the act of helping himself to other writers' writing
—as an essentially virile activity. His gendering of poetic activity
was grounded in the figural language of his time, for the eroti-
cized poetics of literary conception was not an uncommon genre
of fable, especially among the courtier poets and their admirers.
For example, Samuel Butler plays with notions of sex and poetic
conception, impotence, adultery, and sexual/poetic "offspring" in
his characteristically bilious "Satyr Upon Plagiaries":

> The World's as full of curious Wit
> Which those, that father, never writ,
> As 'tis of Bastards, which the Sot
> And Cuckold owns, that ne'er begot;
> Yet pass as well, as if the one
> And th' other By-blow were their own.[5]

For Butler, texts go astray as bodies do, with no better or worse
results—adultery may produce a "legitimate" child, as plagiarism
may produce a "legitimate" poem. Butler invalidates categories
of poetic ownership as he expands notions of poetic engendering;
poetic origin, in his view, is as slippery and impossible to trace as
a person's own—genealogy and authorship must both be taken
on faith, and both, he caustically suggests, should probably not be.

For the Earl of Rochester (who also equates writing with the
quill and with the pen of the body) the pleasure of reception
enters into the sexual/textual equation. Poems may be directed *to*
readers (in the following case, Phyllis), but are *for* the pleasure of
the author's genitals, a circuitous autoeroticism of text and sex that
keeps authorship and ownership strictly in the hands of the poet:

> A song to Phyllis I perhaps might make,
> But never rhymed but for my pintle's sake.[6]

And if Rochester, as he here claims, writes only to please a part
incapable of being so pleased, so Aphra Behn, using similar terms,
but transcending Rochester's autoerotic model for a more generous view of the uses of writing, devises alternative—and specifically female—mythologies of poetic conception. Some of these

fables of conception authorize women to write based upon their ability to provide men with pleasure:

> Quickest in finding all the subtlest ways
> To make your Joys, why not to make you Plays?[7]

In Behn's scheme, pleasure—joy—floats free of specific meaning as it suggests a gender-based ability to please the other. Indeed, Behn, Rochester, and even Butler come down firmly on the sweet side of the Horatian dichotomy between utile and dulce; poetic engendering has for them all the tantalizing erotic quality of crossing, as Anne Carson puts it, "the boundary of flesh and self between you and me."[8]

Dryden found congenial his contemporaries' language of mutually signifying sexual and textual desire, and he refers to his own sexuality (and specifically to a phallus that, textually incarnate as it is, I shall oxymoronically refer to as the "poetic phallus") throughout his prologues and epilogues. Dryden accords the poetic phallus a range of complementary significations and rhetorical uses, the study of which reveals many of his concerns and anxieties in the related realms of poetic conception and poetic strength. He recurs almost reflexively to the sexual body as a system of textual signifiers and works out such connections and their implications more extensively and rigorously than any other poet of his (or perhaps any) period. Examining Dryden's shifting uses of the sexual body, we shall come to see his shifting relation to the world of textuality.

Before 1688 Dryden sometimes uses the poetic phallus to celebrate his masculinity and to depict erotic pleasure (a phallus sometimes being just a phallus), but more often he uses the poetic phallus to express his satisfaction in the creation of his own poetry, and his joy in the appropriation of others'. This early Dryden uses the poetic phallus to express aggressive or penetrative gestures toward readers (taken in the aggregate to include theatrical audiences) and toward the work of other poets. The forms taken by these celebrations of poetic engendering are various, carefully worked out, and often startlingly witty in their "postmodern" play with pens and penises, sex and text. Dryden imagines himself— or at least a persona of the poet—persuading his Muse to sing to him through the agency of vigorous copulation, as in the opening lines to the prologue of *An Evening's Love* (1668), in which his early career is rendered in terms of a honeymoon with the Muse:

> When first our Poet set himself to write,
> Like a young Bridegroom on his Wedding-night
> He layd about him, and did so bestir him,
> His Muse could never lye in quiet for him.
>
> *(Works,* 10:214)

In this brief fable of poetic conception, Dryden evokes both masculine and feminine elements as constitutive of poetic production, but it is the actively male element that lays about and bestirs, that induces song in a generally passive Muse, a female entity described not as an aspect of the poet himself, but as a discrete object. The poet begins by boasting of his poetic energy, but next informs us that he has tired of his conjugal duties, and now feigns pleasure in the act, straining himself to please his audience in the manner of a bored husband:

> But now his Honey-moon is gone and past,
> Yet the ungrateful drudgery must last:
> And he is bound, as civil Husbands do,
> To strain himself, in complaisance to you:
> To write in pain, and counterfeit a bliss,
> Like the faint smackings of an after-kiss.
>
> *(Works,* 10:214)

It is indeed a sorry picture of a marriage gone stale (a marriage such as he is soon to describe so vividly in *Marriage A-la-Mode*). We, as readers, demand of him what he is bored with providing; pleasing us forces him into the somewhat ridiculous posture of feigning joy, counterfeiting bliss—a counterfeiting that Dryden, ever the worst keeper of his own secrets, must reveal to us.[9]

In the androgenetic fiction of Dryden's early career, in which texts are the result of sexual activity, poetic production does not absolutely require the agency of a female persona in the guise either of Muse or audience. Recounting the story of his poetic maturation, Dryden begins by describing his early efforts at poetry as a kind of closeted masturbation, from which he progresses only

writer as masturbator / penetrator of audience (!)

over years into his present condition of stylishly public dissolution:

> As some raw Squire, by tender Mother bred,
> Till one and Twenty keeps his Maidenhead,
> (Pleas'd with some Sport which he alone does find,
> And thinks a secret to all Humane kind;)
> Till mightily in love, yet halfe afraid,
> He first attempts the gentle Dairymaid. . . .
> By such degrees, while knowledge he did want,
> Our unfletch'd Author, writ a *Wild Gallant.*
> (Prologue to *The Wild Gallant, Works,* 8:6)

In Dryden's sexualized poetics, private masturbatory writing obviates the need for a participating other; public writing, on the other hand, Dryden imagines as a kind of intercourse in which he again plays the male part, as we, the readers, play the female. Limning out the metaphor of public writing as a kind of consensual sex act between poet and reader, he imagines the pen (and hence the process of writing) as a poetic phallus that evokes our pleasure by penetrating us in ways and places hitherto untried and untouched:

> Your several Poets work with several tools,
> One gets you wits, another gets you fools:
> This pleases you with some by-stroke of wit,
> This finds some cranny, that was never hit.
> (Prologue to *An Evening's Love, Works,* 10:214)

In this elaboration on the scheme of poetic begetting, each poet's dramatic forte is a tool that both engenders dramatic characters and penetrates readers, functions that operate separately. That with which the poet reaches the audience no longer fathers children, but induces pleasure—we are pleased with its by-strokes, and hit in hitherto untouched crannies. Dryden casts our enjoyment of dramatic novelty in terms of sexual experimentation, likening the most public of onstage surprises to the most private of explorations. With characteristic verve, he links the public and private spheres, and the form of his dual discussions of private and public acts of creation and reception persists essentially unmodified throughout this early period: we readers are feminized as the poet breeds pleasure in and through us; Dryden wields his tool with full male authority.

The younger Dryden strikes a similarly aggressive attitude toward those he reads, describing his appropriations from poets and critics in language similar to that with which he describes his unions with us; the imperial mode of open plunder from other poets is very much a gendered one. According to Dryden, other poets are conquered, vanquished with the pen, their work is seized, made prize, invaded, wrested away from them. Dryden refers to what he reads, his own readers, and women in essentially inter-changeable terms, approaching femininity, textuality, and us, his readers, with a conventionally male appetite.

Dryden seems to take real pleasure in this poetically imagined masculinity, judging from the frequency with which he brandishes the poetic phallus while likening reception to the female sexual rôle. In this early model of gendered production and reception, the male rôle is always privileged over the female, for in all Dryden's fables of androgenesis, the male chooses the time and manner of union, and initiates all contacts. The female rôle—our rôle—is to spread wide the mind and conceive the products of his pen, ac-companied, Dryden hopes, with the pleasure appropriate to poetic union. The scheme is wittily worked out, and Dryden rings the changes on it throughout a twenty-year span. But almost precisely contemporaneous with the revolution of 1688, Dryden assumes a different view of his relations to those poets and readers with whom he carries on his poetic transactions, and to express this new attitude Dryden employs a wholly novel set of images to rep-resent self, other, writer, and reader.

His party ousted from power, those to whom he held allegiance exiled, his own faith proscribed, himself deprived of his prestigious and sometimes remunerative positions—what impression such a collective catastrophe must have made on the time's greatest poet, we can only guess. Yet the new language Dryden uses to describe himself hints at a personal transformation, or a series of them, as profound and disturbing as the political upheavals were for him catastrophic. No longer, after 1688, does the poet characterize his poetic persona as active, phallic, aggressive, and "bold"; from his new vantage point outside the official systems of power, he employs a new language of weakness, constraint, even castration. He questions the virtues of what had been an unquestioning masculinity, and in so doing he begins to clothe his poetic persona in a new garb of androgyny, even outright femininity, with all the deficits of power and all the benefits of insight and capacity that such a transformation might imply. In this dark time the poet no longer copulates with his once-darling Muse; now he himself is filled with the spirits of others as he translates and adapts; no longer does he claim in the audience "an Husband's right," for now the audience, which has changed gender along with Dryden, treats him like a whore, uses him for its own pleasure, then casts him off without pay; the poetic phallus that Dryden had so proudly displayed as a symbol of his poetic strength is now ripped from his body by the censors, by the bad times, by ill health, by advancing age.

Soon after 1688 Dryden begins referring to his poetic persona as an emasculated figure. The prologue to *Amphitryon* (1690) commences with that familiar emblem of poetic integration, the bee—now, however, stripped of its ability to hurt.

> The lab'ring Bee, when his sharp Sting is gone,
> Forgets his Golden Work, and turns a Drone:
> Such is a Satyr, when you take away
> That Rage, in which his Noble Vigour lay.
>
> (*Works,* 15:227)

From the gathering of pollen and production of honey—itself, for Dryden, a new view of poetic appropriation and synthesis, in which the poet ranges wide to cull the nectar from others' poetic flowers, then synthesizes them in his own body into a new, more highly refined poetic honey—the lines soon modulate to a characteristically Drydenian correspondence between the organs of generation and those of poetic production, the capacity for both of which is now stripped from him by fearful censors and a politically unsympathetic audience.

> What gain you, by not suffering him to teize ye?
> He neither can offend you, now, nor please ye.

> The Honey-bag, and Venome, lay so near,
> That both, together, you resolv'd to tear;
> And lost your Pleasure, to secure your Fear.
>
> *(Works,* 15:227)

The poet's "Honey-bag" (an obvious reference to the testicles) has been torn to deprive him of his "Venome." Male corporeal integrity signifies the power to write freely, and when that integrity is impaired by the restrictive violence of a censor, sweetness and generation, poetic pleasure and poetic utility, must disappear. The poet becomes a "Drone"; his "Golden Work" is done. Dryden, for whom the phallus had always connoted poetic paternity and poetic aggression, poetic theft and poetic pleasure, must now find a way to do without its metaphoric aid; Dryden's poetic phallus appears after 1688 only in laments over its absence.

James Winn observes that Dryden refers to the censorship of his writing in terms of castration (453), and images of compromised corporeal integrity proliferate in Dryden's writing of this period. Not long after the elaborately figured bee of *Amphitryon*'s prologue, his references to censorship as genital mutilation grow matter-of-fact. In 1692 he complains that the "superiors of the play-house" were driven "to geld it [*Cleomenes*] so clearly in some places, that they took away the very manhood of it" (Preface, Scott, 8:199), and in a play whose eponymous character's life contains so many parallels with its creator's,[10] Dryden's reference to gelding Cleomenes takes on additional significance.

Even when Dryden does not employ terms specifically connoting castration, he continues to evoke a sense of compromised masculinity in the related language of impotence and restraint; he is "disenabl'd" and "bound" by censors and by the times, complaining of his inability to undertake an epic that "Want . . . through the Change of the Times, has wholly disenabl'd me" (*Discourse Concerning Satire, Works,* 4:23), and the poet, who had already given up the stage, in 1695 says he would write a tragedy on the condition "That my Hands were not bound behind me, as now they are" (*A Parallel betwixt Painting and Poetry, Works,* 20:68). Explicitly yoking the categories of masculinity and physical unconstraint as he implicitly yokes their contraries, Dryden asks:

Or as androgyne.

How can he [the poet] show his Manhood, if you bind him
To box, like Boys, with one Hand ty'd behind him?
(Prologue to *Amphitryon, Works,* 15:227)

Dryden's references to the fettering of the poet's persona recall the
scene of Montezuma's racking written twenty-five years earlier,[11]
in which a great figure, defeated by a moral inferior of superior
strength, is first bound, then obliged to defend himself; as in the
earlier scene, representatives of officially constituted systems of
authority attempt—by means of binding and attendant coercion—
to prohibit the production of speech antithetical to their interests,
while the defeated object insists upon his persistent capacity to
speak and his capacity to persist through speech.

As part of his new tendency to explore the less privileged side
of those dichotomies that had once conferred power on him (con-
queror/defeated; aggressive reader/defensive text; agent for constituted powers/disenfranchised individual), Dryden at about the
time of the revolution begins to explore the other side of the dichotomy between male and female. With the benefit of hindsight,
it seems a necessary conclusion to his sexual poetics; if to conquer,
seize, penetrate, and overwrite is the province of the male, then
to be defeated, compromised, to have one's defenses penetrated
and one's own writing overwritten is logically—using Dryden's
scheme—that of the female. Accordingly, if we visualize a continuum of gender representations stretching from male to female
(each endowed with those characteristics bestowed upon them by
late seventeenth-century custom) and then plot Dryden's references to himself and other poets along this axis of gender, we
discover that Dryden's representations of the poet, beginning in
the late 1680s, travel in a swift straight line across the continuum
from male to female. As we have seen, Dryden came to represent
his poetic persona in such terms of compromised masculinity as
incapacity, castration, and bondage, and he travels further across
the continuum from compromised masculinity into an exploration
of androgyny and its poetic implications.

Whereas he had once imagined the young poet's progress as
one from closeted masturbation to fashionable heterosexual pro-
miscuity, in a later prologue to a first play of a fledgling poet (both

Poet as hermaphrodite, capable of offering different kinds of poetic pleasure.

unidentified), Dryden now imagines the state of the young poet as one of hermaphrodism:

> He makes this difference in the Sexes too,
> He sells to Men, he gives himself to you.
> To both, he wou'd contribute some delight;
> A mere Poetical Hermaphrodite.
> Thus he's equipp'd, both to be woo'd, and woo;
> With Arms offensive, and defensive too;
> 'Tis hard, he thinks, if neither part will do.
>
> (Prologue, *Works*, 3:252)

Situating the young poet where Dryden once situated himself (at the beginning of a career in poetry), he now imagines the poetical state to be both androgynous and bisexual, contributing delight to either sex. In this poetic/erotic fantasy of textual engendering, Dryden, for the first time, moves away from a strict poetic androgenesis and experiments imaginatively with being "equipp'd, both to be woo'd, and woo." Both wooed and wooing, the poet penetrates the reader and is penetrated by us; he gives and takes, fills and is filled, finds crannies that were never hit and provides crannies for us to hit ourselves. As imagined by Dryden, the new-found androgyny of the poetic state permits the poet a greater imaginative range of imparting pleasure to the reader, for the androgyne may provide varied types of pleasure to various types of readers; as the poet assumes the capacity to perform the function of either sex, so the audience now possesses either male or female characteristics. Dryden's simple androgenetic fable evolves toward a more complex series of interlocking myths of poetic creation; the midpoint, and perhaps the most privileged position—as the figure of Tiresias enjoyed a privileged position in the realm of sexual epistemology—is that of the hermaphrodite poet, capable not only of every sexual/textual permutation, but capable as well of knowing the other because the androgyne is the other.[12]

Imagining one's self to be both sexes simultaneously is, of course, only an intermediate point as one passes along the continuum of gender, and in a 1690 prologue that was itself banned for its political content, Dryden finally crosses gender-identification into a fable of degraded authorship (and actorship) in which female-identified males are used and abandoned by fickle—if not actually prematurely ejaculating—English men.

> False Men, even so, you serve your Mistresses;
> . . . you love not long enough,
> To pay the Rigging, e're you leave 'em off:
> Never content, with what you had before;
> But true to Change, and *English* Men all ore.
> (Prologue to *The Prophetess, Works,* 3:255)

Whereas Dryden had once represented himself as the audience's male lover, enjoying the spectators with all the vigor of a sailor home on shore leave,[13] now it is the audience who has their way with him (and the actors), failing even to pay them for their services before leaving them for others. The quondam conqueror, now whore, is victimized by the very category of person with which he had once proudly identified himself; the state in which Dryden had once gloried, that of being an English man, is now become a term of disparagement.

As a playwright he may have come to think of himself in terms of prostitution, but as a translator he referred to himself in the more benign terms of motherhood; being filled with the spirit of his (always male) author, he imagined himself impregnated, and finally giving birth to the work of translation; it is an apt metaphor for the work of a translator and for the status of the product spawned of a poetic father and a translating mother. Dryden plays with bits of the metaphor throughout his late career: attempting to flatter the Earl of Chesterfield into serving as dedicatee for the *Georgics* (with the financial obligation such a rôle would entail), Dryden likens himself to a pregnant ("becoming") woman who must speak her desire (the sharp "longing" of pregnancy), or run the risk of not receiving it: "Twas upon a just diffidence of my success in this presumption that I have humourd my natural bashfulness, in not addressing to you sooner, But as becoming Women must speak at last or loose their longing so I am constrain'd to beg that I may not miscarry of my translation" (*Letters,* 86–87). That men should give birth to the immaterial is, after all, an old idea; Zeus's headache resulted in Athena, and Socrates styled himself a midwife of ideas. But Dryden's assumption of the feminine is of a different kind than Zeus's and Socrates's confident participation in the births of abstractions; he represents himself as a diffident and bashful mother; she is "constrain'd," begging help for an infant of dubious paternity; she supplicates in a kind of genteel desperation —in danger of losing the very thing for which she longs, in danger of miscarrying her womb's treasure. The poet, not much given to punning, cannot resist the play with "miscarry"—the translation might go astray, it might not yield him what he had planned for it and, as the fruit of his poetic womb, it might not be born alive.

Dryden comes to represent his poetic persona as defeated, bound, castrated, androgynous, woman, whore, pleading mother of a threatened child; no longer an aggressive reader, he is aggressively read. These are the terms we require in order to understand his new attitudes toward previous poets, for Dryden now shows a new subordination to the work of his predecessors and manifests a novel desire to possess himself of their works in a legitimate and peaceful fashion, a fashion he would once have disdained as ignoble. No longer is he, in Langbaine's scornful phrase, "this Poetick *Almanzor*" (Langbaine, 133)—the "noble savage" of Dryden's *Conquest of Granada* (1670)—taking what he needs as he needs it "because he dares." Now, as he always has, employing gendered language to describe his relations with others, instead of seizing the works of other poets, he is seized by them. Instead of rushing in, he is rushed in upon. Instead of entering into the spirits of great predecessors, their spirits enter into him. Instead of penetrating, like the poetic conqueror or the poetic lover, now he is penetrated. Dryden's new relation to textuality, using the terms he set out for himself over decades, is decidedly feminine.

"In nothing else must a poet submit as much to a predecessor as in translation," Earl Miner writes,[14] and an introductory example of Dryden's new submissive attitude toward his predecessors, not feminine itself but of a markedly different cast from his earlier Almanzorian forays into his antecedents' works, is the following passage, in which he now claims to find the ideal model for enriching the language to be, not what he earlier described as Ben Jonson's imperial plundering, but the more prosaic one of commercial exchange. "I carry not out the Treasure of the Nation, which is never to return: but what I bring from *Italy,* I spend in *England:*

Here it remains, and here it circulates; for if the Coyn be good, it will pass from one hand to another. I Trade both with the Living and the Dead, for the enrichment of our Native Language. . . . If we will have things of Magnificence and Splendour, we must get them by Commerce" (Dedication of the *Æneis, Works,* 5:336). Linguistic transmission, according to Dryden, is now a matter of agreement between transmitter and receiver, writer and reader, and linguistic enrichment arises through a concordance of wills. Shifting from metaphors of international conquest to international trade, Dryden sketches out a newly pacific model of textual transmission. Only through such "Commerce" are magnificent and splendid things obtained; only by trading "with the Living and the Dead" can the total poetic capital be increased. Although the poetic riches Dryden describes may not differ as much as the terms suggest (after all, identifying and transmitting good "Coyn" demands a poetic force similar to that required to plunder imperially), the point is that he now regards the poetic enterprise in wholly different terms; he is a reformed plunderer, a law-abiding merchant who moves goods—literally, *translates*—from one place to another.

Dryden's newly pacific model of textual transmission is accompanied by representations of a radical drop in his own poetic status. The poetic Almanzor is gone, replaced by a translator whose uttermost aspiration is to attain the same heights as were reached by the respected, but hardly never-to-be-equaled "Sir *John Denham,* Mr. *Waller,* and Mr. *Cowley;* 'tis the utmost of my Ambition to be thought their Equal, or not to be much inferiour to them, and some others of the Living" (Dedication of the *Æneis, Works,* 5:325). For the first time in his criticism, Dryden admits the desire to equal his (near) contemporaries, suggesting that he now finds himself below even the standard of his own era. And the hope for mere equality with coevals seems the greatest optimism, if not presumption, when compared to his expressions of veneration for, and abjection in the face of, those he translates. Referring to his translation of the *Georgics,* he confesses "I have too much injur'd my great Author, to expect he should intercede for me. I wou'd have Translated him, but according to the litteral *French* and *Italian* Phrases, I fear I have traduc'd him. 'Tis the fault of many a well-meaning Man, to be officious in a wrong place, and do a prejudice, where he had endeavour'd to do a service" (Dedication to the *Georgics, Works,* 5:137–38). Even when Dryden imagines making a translation of a phrase from Horace, he instantly imagines Horace's spirit looking on in disapproval: "When I have leisure, I mean to try how near I can raise my English to his Latin; though, in the mean time, I cannot but imagine to myself, with what scorn his sacred *manes* would look on so lame a translation as I could make" (Dedication to *Cleomenes,* Scott, 8:193). When he thinks of his own *Amphitryon* in the context of Molière's and Plautus's, he can only condemn himself: "But I am affraid, for my own Interest, the World will too easily discover, that more than half of it is mine; and that the rest is rather a lame Imitation of their Excellencies, than a just Translation" (*Works,* 15:225).

but he'd / praised / french / critics.

And for the first time in his criticism, he writes an encomium for a French poet (living, no less) in terms previously reserved only for long-dead English or antique writers. In the *Discourse concerning the Original and Progress of Satire* (1692), he writes of his French contemporary: "But if I wou'd only cròss the Seas, I might find in *France* a living *Horace* and a *Juvenal,* in the Person of the admirable *Boileau:* Whose Numbers are Excellent, whose Expressions are Noble, whose Thoughts are Just, whose Language is Pure, whose Satire is pointed, and whose Sense is close; What he borrows from the Ancients, he repays with Usury of his own: in Coin as good, and almost as Universally valuable" (*Works,* 4:12). Dryden's mustering of such a string of periods for a living Frenchman is simply

?

unprecedented and betokens a novel willingness to allow other contemporaries besides himself and Congreve to be great; moreover, he now finds that many with whom he once compared himself favorably are now his poetic superiors. Stripped of his crown of laurels, he abdicates his position as the king of living poets.

Dryden also is now content with second-class citizenship in the republic of letters in the related area of innovating poetic form, for instead of generating new rules for English poetry—new rules that were once Neander's pride—he is satisfied to follow in the footsteps of the masters, explicitly rejecting formal innovation: "Not to make new Rules of the Drama, as *Lopez de Vega* has attempted unsuccessfully to do; but to be content to follow our Masters, who understood Nature better than we" (*A Parallel be-*

twixt Painting and Poetry, Works, 20:62). Modern-day poets should be content to follow where Dryden (by example—he rarely legislates) had once hoped to lead; in accordance with his pessimistic view of the moderns' accomplishment, Dryden now holds that nature is best understood refracted through the understandings of predecessor poets "who understood Nature better than we"; nature now veils her face at the approach of Dryden and his contemporaries.

One telling exception to Dryden's abjection in the face of patterns set by his great predecessors is his newfound disdain for the heroic code as it was first articulated by Homer and perpetuated into Dryden's present, even by the young Dryden himself. His new rejection of violence, war, and "the most degenerate Vice, which is that of Ruggedness and Harshness to our Fellow Creatures" (Dedication to *Amphitryon, Works,* 15:223) comes accompanied by a contempt for the glory-purchasing but gratuitous violence so characteristic of the heroic plays; Dryden, befitting his new seriousness as a Catholic and his new status as a member of a defeated party exiled from the centers of power, voices a novel opposition to the lessons of epic poetry: "For *Homer,* as I observ'd before, can move rage better than he can pity: He stirs up the irascible appetite, as our Philosophers call it, he provokes to Murther, and the destruction of God's Images; he forms and equips those ungodly Man-killers whom we Poets, when we flatter them, call Heroes; a race of Men who can never enjoy quiet in themselves, 'till they have taken it from all the World" (*Examen Poeticum, Works,* 4:374). The combination of Dryden's new elasticity of gender, his new renunciation of the violence of poetic conquest, and his new, lower appraisal of his own stature with regard to other poets, concord to yield a new tone in which he discusses his manner of assimilating the works of other poets. He approaches others deferentially: instead of assaulting the slopes of Mount Helicon, "rushing in," "invading," "pillaging," "seizing," he opens himself for such assault and invasion; he is himself filled by the spirits of dead poets—as well as the spirit of poetry. "We, who are Priests of *Apollo,* have not the Inspiration when we please; but must wait till the God comes rushing on us, and invades us with a fury, which we are not able to resist: which gives us double strength while the

Fit continues, and leaves us languishing and spent at its departure" (Preface to "Eleonora," *Works,* 3:231). Dryden's language for poetic inspiration is similar to that with which he formerly described the ravishment of women; they too used to be "invaded with a fury" that they were "not able to resist," and upon completion of the act, they were left "languishing and spent." Indeed, although Dryden does not specify the gender of Apollo's priest, he clearly—though tacitly—casts himself in another female role, that of the sibyl of *Æneid,* book 6.[15] Dryden was soon to translate the passage to which he refers:

> Aloud she cries,
> This is the time, enquire your Destinies.
> He comes, behold the God! Thus while she said,
> (And shiv'ring at the sacred Entry staid)
> Her Colour chang'd, her Face was not the same,
> And hollow Groans from her deep Spirit came.
> Her Hair stood up; convulsive Rage possess'd
> Her trembling Limbs, and heav'd her lab'ring Breast.
> Greater than Human Kind she seem'd to look:
> And with an Accent, more than Mortal, spoke.
> Her staring Eyes with sparkling Fury rowl;
> When all the God came rushing on her Soul.
> (*Works,* 5:529)

Dryden's Sibyl is nearly crushed by the weight of a god inside her; she tries to shake off her burden. In his translation he suggests a powerful woman struggling vainly against the superior strength of a man determined upon rape:

> Strugling in vain, impatient of her Load,
> And lab'ring underneath the pond'rous God,
> The more she strove to shake him from her Breast,
> With more, and far superior Force he press'd:
> Commands his Entrance, and without Controul,
> Usurps her Organs, and inspires her Soul.
> (*Works,* 5:530)

In Dryden's new fable of poetic conception, the Poet who once "layd about" with the Muse is transformed to the Priestess who

Poet as conduit for annihilating powerful past masters.
Defeat of the virtuously powerful as a theme in D's late plays.

opens herself up to penetration by "the God," who, "with an Accent, more than Mortal," speaks the words of greater spirits who possess her frame; even if she wishes to resist, the God will have his way. The sibylline Dryden, during "the Fit" doubly endowed with her own and another's strength, refers to herself as "languishing and spent" (terms of erotic exhaustion) when she returns to herself, by herself.

Through the sibyl, Dryden imagines one more way to describe the fashioning of himself into the poetic conduit for the linguistic semen of the greater dead; the priestess whose organs are usurped is yet another version of the supplicating mother, swollen to bursting by another's impregnation, begging another to relieve her of her load. Dryden's new poetics of reception, in which spirits of the dead enter into and impregnate his aged and decrepit frame to be reborn in a belated and unworthy manner (throughout the late criticism and letters, Dryden uses the word "barbarous" again and again to describe the English language), reflects a desperate desire, not to fight the past but to unite with it. The sibylline Dryden is very far from Bloomian notions of Oedipal anxiety regarding other poets; she is unbowed by what W. Jackson Bate called "the burden of the past." In Dryden's terrifyingly generous vision of his relation to the great spirits of poetry, he opens himself so wholly that he dies as they live, fights his own will to speak so that "the God" can usurp his organs, forces his own resisting poetic sensorium in order that what emerges might truly be the words of a God, the words of a Virgil, spoken in the voice, "with an Accent, more than Mortal," of a Dryden.[16]

Melding identities with and speaking in the words of more than mortals reflects a particular relation to the various systems of power that first celebrated him, then abruptly sent him packing. Dryden's late plays, their prefaces, dedications, and prologues, also reflect his new status, no longer as the acolyte of power, but as its victim; each casts a new light on Dryden's own position on the margin of a newly reconstituted political structure. *Don Sebastian* (1689), *Amphitryon* (1690), and *Cleomenes* (1692) all concern the plight of a virtuous leader (a general in each case) who finds himself defeated either in a foreign land or by invaders in his own. At the end of each play his dilemma is to discover a way to endure his reverse with honor; in *Don Sebastian* this means abjuring king-ship and living alone in a monastery in exile. In *Amphitryon*'s trans-position of the tragic dilemma, the hero must learn to live with a cuckoldom of which his wife was ignorant and volitionally inno-cent. In *Cleomenes* the hero must die in exile while trying in vain to incite to rebellion a stubbornly pusillanimous and self-satisfied populace. In all three dramas the victorious powers are portrayed as unsympathetic at best and, more typically, self-centered, ca-pricious, and gratuitously cruel. All the late heroes and heroines meet their fate not with the splendid resignation of Montezuma and St. Catherine, but with the tough, bitter, human-scaled deter-mination to salvage what is good and right out of a situation not of their making, a situation that has been personally disastrous. In the words of J. Douglas Canfield "Dryden portrays a world where the ultimate betrayal is 'the Fault' of Heaven Itself. Frustrated at Heaven's tardy vengeance, one can only adopt the stance of the One Just Man and rail at a faithless world."[17]

Of the prefatory material associated with the final plays, the dedication to *Amphitryon* is of unusual interest for its complete ar-ticulation of Dryden's new fable of poetic influence; in it he spells out fully what he had previously scattered in such hints as are col-lected above. The dedication recapitulates many of his new themes regarding the related categories of his own ontological status, his standing relative to others, his manner of appropriating poetic ma-terial, and the quality of his work.

Voicing the mood of poetic self-abnegation so characteristic of later critical self-representations, Dryden comes to speak of his, and *Amphitryon*'s, relation to Plautus and Molière: " 'Tis true, were this Comedy wholly mine, I should call it a Trifle, and perhaps not think it worth your Patronage; but when the Names of *Plautus* and *Moliere* are joyn'd in it; that is, the two greatest Names of Ancient and Modern Comedy, I must not presume so far on their Repu-tation, to think their best and most unquestion'd Productions can be term'd Little" (*Works,* 15:224–25). In an extraordinary shift re-specting the work of those from whom he translates, borrows, and adapts, Dryden dons the persona of the craven poet, meekly seek-ing approval by associating his own confessedly mediocre work with that of his poetic betters. What is his own, Dryden states,

is trifling; what is borrowed, he implies, cannot be thought unworthy, since it is not by him.

In that passage Dryden again reveals his putative demotion in
the hierarchy of poets, for he had not always admired Molière and
Plautus as much as he here claims. He had formerly held Molière
to be only a clever practitioner of an inferior genre (a dramatist
who, Dryden once claimed, had begun to copy tricks from the
English). Plautus, according to Dryden, was a rough poet ("infinitely too bold in his Metaphors and coyning words; out of which
many times his wit is nothing" [*Essay, Works,* 17:29]), a dramatist
whose punishments and rewards are not well distributed.[18] Now,
however, "the two greatest Names of Ancient and Modern Comedy" attest to the quality of a play for which Dryden wishes to
take little credit. He refers to his own contribution as a necessary
degradation. "I will not give you the trouble, of acquainting you
what I have added, or alter'd in either of them, so much it may be
for the worse; but only that the difference of our Stage from the
Roman and the *French* did so require it. But I am affraid, for my
own Interest, the World will too easily discover, that more than
half of it is mine; and that the rest is rather a lame imitation of
their Excellencies, than a just Translation" (*Works,* 15:225). His
additions and alterations are "for the worse," necessitated by the
demands of the English stage (which, since it demands alterations
which are "for the worse," may be thought of as "worse" itself).
Dryden disclaims all responsibility for whatever poetic quality the
drama might possess, carrying his disclaimer so far as to decline
all credit for the play's success; such praise he grants to Plautus
and Molière, Henry Purcell, composer of the incidental music, and
the play's actors—all, in short, but himself: "I neither deserve nor
desire any Applause from it: If I have perform'd any thing, 'tis
the Genius of my Authors that inspir'd me; and if it has pleas'd
in Representation, let the Actors share the Praise amongst themselves. As for *Plautus* and *Moliere,* they are dangerous People; and
I am too weak a Gamester to put my self into their Form of Play"
(*Works,* 15:225).

By claiming that anything good to be found in *Amphitryon* is the
result of having been inspired by "the Genius of [his] Authors,"
Dryden insists upon his new status as a poetically inert transmit-

The English genius now turn as one for improvement rather than invention of material.

ter of others' genius, a small poet of modest ambition, steering his diminutive craft by the blazing light of astronomical bodies hung unreachably high in the poetic firmament. No longer does the modern English adaptor, Dryden implies, at substantial trouble to himself, break down a received French (or antique) drama and remake it as if from scratch.[19] In 1690, according to Dryden, adapting foreign plays to the English taste involves taking in and being inspired by the genius of the plays' authors, and, Dryden suggests, his work is good to the exact extent to which he has let the spirits of his authors into his own. The previous course of Dryden's poetic influence—that of reaching out, of seizing what was needed, of recreating and inventing his "ancestors" and "history"—is reversed. Dryden, according to his own testimony, becomes the empty vessel, vacant receptor of millennia and nations' worth of poetic tradition that, once received, he then lightly and reverentially works over to suit the low tastes of the English playgoing audience. French and antique poets, in Dryden's new fable of reception, suddenly acquire an aura of power and menace; they threaten him with poetic annihilation—Plautus and Molière "are dangerous People"; Dryden is "too weak a Gamester to put [himself] into their Form of Play." Their "Form of Play," a pun, apparently, upon *originating* plays, is an approach to textuality from which Dryden seems to wish to distance himself in this last period.

Dryden, suspicious of this form of play—and adept as ever at deriving theory from predilection—comes to contend that English writers' true poetic genius is for improving what they find in the hands of others, not inventing ex nihilo. He vigorously argues the existence of this improving trait in the English poetic character, not only justifying the fact that he now translates rather than invents, but justifying, as he always had justified, his own work among the work of others: ". . . the Genius of our Countrymen in general being rather to improve an Invention, than to invent themselves; as is evident not only in our Poetry, but in many of our Manufactures" (Preface to *Fables, Poems,* 4:1450). Dryden, in *not* originating, claims to exemplify the best spirit of his country's genius, as exhibited in its poetic and material goods. He has learned to pride himself upon this lack of originality (formerly, "with want of Genius, curst"), and at the end of his life he finds

The Fables in a long (and worthy) line of non-original poetry.

that as a *not*-originator he follows in the footsteps of the great poets he translates, discovering that they, too, with the exception of Homer, were not original. Dryden's former darling, Virgil, only continued what Homer had begun. *"Homer's* Invention was more copious, *Virgil's* more confin'd: So that if *Homer* had not led the Way, it was not in *Virgil* to have begun Heroick Poetry: For, nothing can be more evident, than that the *Roman* Poem is but the Second Part of the *Ilias"* (Preface to *Fables, Poems,* 4:1448). Chaucer and Ovid were equally owing to others. "Both [Ovid and Chaucer] writ with wonderful Facility and Clearness; neither were great Inventors: For *Ovid* only copied the *Grecian* Fables; and most of *Chaucer's* Stories were taken from his *Italian* Contemporaries, or their Predecessors" (Preface to *Fables, Poems,* 4:1450). And Boccaccio, too, is demoted to the category where Dryden places himself, a transcriber and improver of others' stories. "Those of *Boccace* were not generally of his own making, but taken from Authors of former Ages, and by him only modell'd" (Preface to *Fables, Poems,* 4:1459). Dryden suggests that in creating the *Fables* he is the latest in a long and distinguished line of European *not*-originators, great transcribers and improvers upon the works of others. Moreover, he discovers, the English have a kind of genius for just the kind of work he has chosen to do. Furthermore, in his last period he also discovers that, of all translators and transcribers, he, best and alone, is suited to receive Virgil's spirit into him, and to clothe it in his own poetic flesh. As he describes his accomplishment, he recurs to his favorite critical adverb—"boldly" —not much in evidence during his last period: "And therefore I will boldly own, that this *English* Translation has more of *Virgil's* Spirit in it, than either the *French,* or the *Italian"* (Dedication of the *Æneis, Works,* 5:325). In his final phase Dryden not only comes to see himself the last in a long line of writers of others' stories (Virgil, Ovid, Boccaccio, Chaucer), but he prides himself on precisely that which the earlier Dryden would have despised—the transmission of another's *spirit* through his own.

Dryden's figure for himself as translator is more telling than anything a literary historian would dare devise: the pregnant woman with a longing, her poetic womb quick with the spirit of another poet, proud of the conception, and fearful of miscarrying.

(but he also says he now prefers Homer)

D. as happy receives/transmitter of his predecessors.

Dryden now gladly takes the works of other poets inside him, is penetrated by them, lets them gestate into new births of which, if he is not the father (which of course he is not of the *opera* of Virgil), he may style himself the mother, as the *opera* are reborn through him into a new tongue bearing more of Virgil's spirit in it, the proud mother avers, "than either the *French,* or the *Italian.*"

Dryden's translation of presented identity from the male to the female, from phallic plunderer to nurturing mother, betokens not only a synthesis of gender but a poetic synthesis as well. In his final phase Dryden looks back to his precursors to fill him with their spirits; he refines and revises them into such new births as the translations of Juvenal and Persius, Virgil and *Fables;* the spirits of father poets live and breathe anew, transmitted through his poetic flesh. Fashioning a gynogenetic myth permits Dryden a whole new discourse of textuality; in his final phase all his predecessors and competitors, his anxieties of influence and his fathers, come to be internalized in a peaceable conjunction in which his poetic fathers come to speak with the voice of Dryden. It is in this last series of works that Dryden finally comes to a kind of late and luminous peace with his predecessors, in which he finally assimilates them even as he is possessed by them. He incorporates the sensibilities of man and woman, victor and vanquished, Homer, Virgil, Ovid, Boccaccio, and Chaucer—and his own mature poetic voice and sensibilities—in a magnificent conjunction of sex and text. In Dryden's final synthesis of the poetic, historic, and personal, the heights and depths of human experience seem finally to be known, and uttered in a language so full that it seems, not just the final sum of his own lifetime of poetic accomplishment, but the final sum of a civilization's.

The early J. : images of literary commerce as imperial competition / aggression

The Stilling
of the Cannon

It was that memorable day, in the first Summer of
the late War, when our Navy ingag'd the *Dutch:* a day
wherein the two most mighty and best appointed Fleets
which any age had ever seen, disputed the command of
the greater half of the Globe, the commerce of Nations,
and the riches of the Universe. . . . The noise of the
Cannon from both Navies reach'd our ears about the City.

Essay of Dramatick Poesy, Works, 17:8

As befitted the official poet of a newly restored monarchy, poor,
as monarchies go, and aggressive, Dryden looked outward from
his fortress island with a gaze of appropriative ferocity. When
he imagined early imperial England in contact with Europe (the
Dutch, the French, the Spanish), and when he imagined a greater
Europe in contact with other cultures, those contacts were uni-
formly imagined in terms of comparison, competition, struggle,
and victory; many of these contacts begin and end with the roar-
ing cannon of imperial warships. The poet made of that sound
a distinctive song that caught his country's ear with an anthem
of its liking; an England bent on following the restoration of its
monarchy with an expansion of its political and economic domin-
ion seemed pleased to hear its presence announced, and its poetry
punctuated, by the booming of artillery.

> The Duke, less numerous, but in courage more,
> On wings of all the winds to combat flies:
> His murdering Guns a loud defiance roar,
> And bloudy Crosses on his Flag-staffs rise.
> (*Annus Mirabilis, Works,* 1:68)

The cannon's roar is the imperialist's vocative. Seen either from inside or outside the ambitious empire whose praise he sang for nearly thirty years, the desires of the empire, be they territorial or poetic, are articulated in the language of war and forcible seizure, muzzle blast and hurtling ball:

> Some preciously by shatter'd Porc'lain fall,
> And some by Aromatick splinters die.
> (*Annus Mirabilis, Works,* 1:64)

Dryden's poetic cannons work imperial metamorphoses, transfiguring items of foreign wealth (objects of envy) into instruments of revenge upon those who dare possess what the poor but ambitious empire lacks. Nor is this transfiguring magic limited to material goods, for Dryden trains his poetic artillery upon the works of foreign writers with equal vigor.

To the ambitious young poet, cannons speak the imperial tongue of appropriation and sway. Gold-hungry Spaniards announce their arrival to the native Americans with massed firing of the ships' cannon, a call at first indecipherable to the natives.

> *Montezuma.* What Divine Monsters, O ye gods, are these
> That float in air and flye upon the Seas!
> Came they alive or dead upon the shore?
> *Guyomar.* Alas, they liv'd too sure, I heard them roar:
> All turn'd their sides, and to each other spoke,
> I saw their words break out in fire and smoke.
> Sure 'tis their voice that Thunders from on high,
> Or these the younger brothers of the Skie.
> (*The Indian Emperour, Works,* 9:36)

The poet imagines the imperial challenge falling upon an innocent ear, accustomed only to the subtler tonal palette of nature's murmurs; this European thunder inspires awe in its ingenuous hearers—and chastened envy in its overhearers, the poet and his audience. The Indians' lack of cultural context for interpreting this imperial speech foredooms them; too late do they come to linguistic competence, understanding the import of those words that "break out in fire and smoke" only when their civilization is destroyed. Dryden presents the attractiveness of western armament and the almost comic interpretational impotence of the imagined other with a mingled reverence for might and disdain for linguistic incapacity. His explicit sympathy is with Montezuma—but if *The Indian Emperour* shows anything of its author, it shows that his heart is with Cortes, the man who directs the cannons.

The young poet imagines his relations with foreign poets in exactly this mode of imperial comparison, competition, struggle, and victory. He wishes English poetic sea-lanes protected, foreign goods either seized for England or destroyed. Even though the products of English poets have no value whatever on the world market (Dryden declares native plots to be "weav'd in *English* Loomes" but no foreign buyer wishes such homespun wares), Dryden claims to wish to follow a protectionist policy regarding trading with the living. He claims to despise the cultural and poetic wealth of the French, claims to wish it no place in his native England. He repeatedly voices his contempt for the foreign wealth the English so desperately feel themselves to lack; he resentfully wishes away individual French words, customs, manners, music, mores, ideals, poetry, plays, and playwrights. The young poet trains his rhetorically metamorphosing cannon upon and fires away at these chimerical targets—chimerical because, after all, the actual elements of French literary culture (deriving from Versailles, the theaters of Paris, the savants of the Académie Française) are well beyond the reach of Dryden's gunnery. He can blow up Corneille's unities in England without the destruction being noticed in France.

Although his disdain for the products of the foreign pen was often and vigorously stated, the young Dryden asserted his imperial right to seize upon whatever elements of foreign poetry came his way: "Where ever I have lik'd any story in a Romance, Novel, or forreign Play, I have made no difficulty, nor ever shall, to take the foundation of it, to build it up, and to make it proper for the *English* Stage" (Preface, *Works,* 10:210). The imperialist's poetic license is in some ways like that of the privateers licensed by British monarchs who stole from foreign powers with the understanding that both the monarch and the pirate would be enriched; linguistic theft is licit if it benefits king and country. As Dryden says of Jonson, his authorizing figure in plunder, "No man has bor-

An appropriative approach to 'borrowed' poetry justified.

row'd so much from the Ancients as he has done: And he did well in it, for he has thereby beautifi'd our language" (*Works,* 10:212). "Borrow'd" poetry (the term oddly suggests that the item will be returned) embellishes the language of the borrower, thereby enriching it, increasing the national linguistic capital. Moreover, borrowing from foreign poets may increase the capacity for royal and aristocratic pleasure. In a newly restored political and poetic climate where the king determines what is beautiful or pleasing, the royal pleasure is of paramount importance, and may be served by even a poet's piracy. "He [Charles II] only desir'd that they who accus'd me of theft would always steal him Playes like mine" (*Works,* 10:210). Foreign pillage is licensed so long as the native sovereign is pleased and the native land enriched. With the understanding that he wishes such poetic treasure not for himself, but only to please his sovereign and time, Dryden forages through the works of French critics, romance writers, and playwrights—Georges and Madeleine de Scudéry, Molière, Pierre and Thomas Corneille, Quinault, and a host of others—seeking spoils to "make 'em prize." Training the cannons of imperial poetic desire upon the works of these writers was no more theft than any other duly declared act of war: it was, in his own words, "onely victory in him," and he reveled in such imperial depredations.

The young poet with a name to make, and then to protect, adopts his country's imperial mode (relatively poor, ambitious, aggressive) in his own linguistic trade. When Dryden imagines a discussion concerning the correct way to fashion a play, when he wishes to consider the role of the unities, the rules, the ancients, the need for decorum and verisimilitude, the necessity for rhyme, he frames that discussion as well in the context of imperial cannon fire, as in the beginning of the *Essay of Dramatick Poesy.* The elegantly balanced debate between the nativist poet and apologists for the stifling greatness of Greek, Roman, and French playwrights and critics is conducted against a heroic backdrop wherein is fought a noisy sea battle for no less than "the command of the greater half of the Globe, the commerce of Nations, and the riches of the Universe" (*Works,* 17:8). Who would possibly win "the command of the greater half of the Globe," either at sea or in the realm of poetry, but Dryden and his imperial metonym, the Royal Navy?

Extensive borrowing from alleged despised authors
Refashioning of 'authorities' to argue very different positions to those which they actually argued.

Yet the story, as we have seen, is more complicated. At a remove of three centuries we can only imagine how galling it must have been to young poets like Dryden, eager to make a name and a living in the newly unfettered poetic climate of the Restoration, to be told that the king, "whose example gives a law to it," wished to have plays written in the French style. Courtiers and would-be courtiers would have had to write in this exotic manner as well as they could; such a rarefied poetic artifact as the rules-obeying rhymed Cornelian drama of love's predictable contentions with honor could be grafted only awkwardly onto the sturdy native stock of Shakespeare, Marlowe, Jonson, and Webster.

Because no professional poet could afford to ignore the taste of the court, the young Dryden was obliged to borrow from the very foreign pens he so frequently disdained. The pressure to honor the past of English dramatic poetry was great, but not so great as the need to assimilate many elements of French literary and dramatic culture. Hence the necessity of dissimulating sources, disguising models, claiming to imitate one thing as he imitated another. To honor the present, one had to emulate the French style (but never admit it); to honor the past, one had to extol the tradition of the great English poets (but never imitate them). Especially in his drama—the genre that most depends on pleasing an audience in the very moment of its hearing—Dryden constantly borrowed and adapted even as he claimed to despise those authors from whom he claimed never to wish to borrow a syllable; he faithfully copied the lineaments of their poetic and critical forms even as he claimed that his patterns were all native. The frequent misquotations of his early period reveal the strain between the cultural exigencies of the past and the practical ones of the present, the need to justify himself to a lineage of poetic forebears and to a court (and a courtly theatrical audience) whose eyes were set on Versailles and Paris.

The charms of imperial war are less in evidence in Dryden's work through the decade preceding the revolution of 1688, and are utterly gone by the time of the revolution itself. His conversion to Catholicism (evidently sincere, in spite of the religion's fashionability at court) brought a new moral seriousness to his work (as well as a new use for cannons: the last to appear in his poems is a rhetorical one aimed by the Panther at the Hind [*Works*, 3:141]).

Moreover, the revolution of 1688, in which the spectacularly un-popular James II (about whom Dryden too had grave reserva-tions) was replaced by the Protestant monarch of a former enemy to England, substantially worsened the cultural climate in which the unrepentant Jacobite and Catholic would spend the rest of his life. No longer was he the darling of the court set; his party chased from power, his religion proscribed, his loyalty called into ques-tion, stripped of his official posts, his health deteriorating, Dryden found the conditions for writing forever altered, and from these new conditions arose his need to develop a new voice, and with that, a new relation to the works of other poets.

Because of the climate of suspicion and constraint surround-ing the now-aging poet (Dryden was twenty-eight at the time of the Restoration, fifty-seven in 1688), he could no longer speak openly. The new political culture required that he devise a way to veil his views even as he uttered them, to speak his discon-tent in such a way that he would not be vulnerable to legal or political charges. For this reason his late writings contain figures of castration and restraint; they brim with sullen resentment and philosophical scorn for the social and political currents that had swept him from his official poetic eminence as quickly and firmly as those currents had swept away the former king.

Dryden's voice changes tone gradually throughout the decade of the 1680s; by the end the alteration is complete. Neander, the *Essay of Dramatick Poesy*'s confident new man, is replaced by a still-newer persona of the poet, but this figure (perhaps no less confident) is compromised and constrained by the time's great political and cultural shift. Instead of arguing for his time's superi-ority over the ancients in whose tongue he once named himself, the later Dryden deprecates his poetic talents even as he had for-merly deprecated the talents of others. He finds that everything important has already been said by the ancients better than it can ever be said again; his native tongue is barbarous, his audiences vulgar, his countrymen fit for adapting, not originating. Circum-stances demand that he come to a deeper understanding of those outside the official structures that confer authority on male, citi-zen, and poet; as an element of this understanding he experiments with different configurations of gender for himself, finding that a female poetic persona often befits his new poetics of reception.

Chased from the present, Dryden returns to the ancients to fashion a suitable poetic voice. He reverts to associating his persona with those of predecessor poets, yet this appropriation of the past is now conducted with a different end. Where he had once adopted poetic fathers that authorized his literary practices in an imperial gesture that refashioned Shakespeare into the inventor of blank verse and Aristotle into preferring epic to tragedy, in his later period he adopts ancient voices that blend with and to some extent disguise his own. He shifts from a model of imperial appropriation to one of female reception; he prides himself on the degree to which he can take the spirit of the ancients into himself; his biological model for his late poetics is childbirth.

So smoothly that one is hardly aware, the voice of Dryden modulates into, then out of, a translation from the past; whenever the past seems to speak directly of the present—where priests are ridiculed, where kings are held in suspicion, where patriots' motives are questioned—there one will probably find that Virgil or Juvenal or Ovid has left off or has been subtly adapted. The shifts in tone are so subtle, and the translations themselves so supple and vigorous, that the voices of the ancients seem living and young— in contrast to that of Dryden, which, when he speaks in propria persona, seems aged and weary.

Yet the late translations are far more than a vehicle for covert carping against a regime the poet did not favor, for in them the aged poet, mature in years and poetic judgment, adopts an entirely different point of view with regard to his great predecessors, the scattered voices of a disunited Europe. In his late works, and particularly in his last great poetic effort, *Fables Ancient and Modern* (1700), disparate voices from various times and places throughout Europe are reconciled in an act of poetic integration so massive as to constitute in itself an act of new creation.

By the end of his life Dryden has long lost the boyish confidence that led him to declare that the present-day English, the greatest dramatists ever to have lived, also possessed the right to appropriate whatever poetic wealth they wished. Although we

The poet an worker in a received material.

might call the *Fables* a last great effort of Drydenian imperialism, the character of *Fables,* it seems to me, is altogether unlike the improving depredations upon the work of others that *An Evening's Love* or *All for Love* once represented. *Fables* does not attempt to steal the glory of composition, or adaptation, for the poetic raptor. On the contrary, even though Dryden's voice is close-woven with the voices of Virgil and Homer, Chaucer and Boccaccio, in *Fables* Dryden affirms not so much the greatness of the translator, but the greatness of European poetry, and of the poetic process itself. In *Fables* Dryden finally enacts, in a movement whose causes and implications seem as much spiritual as poetic, his earlier, generously intertextual view of the origins of poetry, and of the impossibility of owning the materials with which the artisan of language fashions his work. Dryden will have the last word regarding the relation of poets to all the poetry that has come before them:

> The employment of a Poet, is like that of a curious Gunsmith, or Watchmaker: the Iron or Silver is not his own; but they are the least part of that which gives the value: The price lyes wholly in the workmanship.
>
> (*Works,* 10:212)

Dryden and the French:
A Chronology

Dates are for first performances of plays and publications of non-dramatic works. Asterisks denote approximate dates.[1]

YEAR	ENGLISH	FRENCH
1622	Middleton and Rowley, *The Changeling**	Molière born
1623	Shakespeare, First Folio	Sorel, *Histoire comique de Francion*
1624	Donne, *Devotions upon Emergent Occasions*	Richelieu ascends to power
1625	Purchas, *Purchas his Pilgrims* James I dies	Racan, *Les Bergeries*
1626	Sandys, trans. of Ovid's *Metamorphoses*	Madame de Sévigné born Mairet, *Sylvie*
1627	Bacon, *Sylva Sylvarum*	
1628	Bunyan born	Ogier, preface to *Tyr et Sidon*
1629	Hobbes, trans. Thucydides Brome, *The City Wit**	Corneille, *Mélite**
1630		Corneille, *Clitandre** Mairet, *La Sylvanire**
1631	Dryden born Katharine Philips born Donne dies	Corneille, *La Veuve**
1632	Massinger, *The City Madam**	Corneille, *La Galerie du Palais**
1633	Donne, *Poems* Herbert dies	Corneille, *La Place Royale** ———, *La Suivante**

YEAR	ENGLISH	FRENCH
1634	Webster dies	Corneille, *Médée**
	Chapman dies	Mairet, *La Sophonisbe*
	Marston dies	
1635	Quarles, *Emblems*	Corneille, *l'Illusion Comique**
		Académie Française founded
1636	Brome, *The Queen and Concubine**	Boileau born
1637	Ben Jonson dies	Corneille, *Le Cid*
	Rutter, trans. of *Le Cid*	querelle du Cid
	Hobbes, *Art of Rhetorique* [trans. of Aristotle]	Descartes, *Discours sur la méthode*
1638	Milton, *Lycidas*	Tristan, *Les Amours*
1639		La Ménardière, *Poétique*
		Racine born
1640	Behn born	Corneille, *Horace*
1641	Brome, *A Jovial Crew*	de Scudéry, *Ibrahim ou l'Illustre Bassa*
	Sandys, *Paraphrase Upon the Song of Solomon*	
	Evelyn begins *Diary*	
	Heywood dies	
1642	Civil War begins; theaters close	Corneille, *Cinna*
		———, *Polyeucte*
	Denham, *Cooper's Hill*	Richelieu dies
1643	Browne, *Religio Medici*	Louis XIII dies
		Corneille, *Le Menteur*
		———, *Mort de Pompée*
1644	Milton, *Areopagitica*	Corneille, *La Suite du Menteur**
		———, *Rodogune**
		Tristan, *La Morte de Sénèque*
1645	Milton, *L'Allegro; Il Penseroso*	Corneille, *Théodore, Vierge et Martyre**
1646	Browne, *Pseudodoxia Epidemica*	Corneille, *Heraclius**
1647	Fanshawe, trans. of Guarini's *Il Pastor Fido*	La Calprenède, *Cléopâtre*
1648	Herrick, *Hesperides*	Fronde, until 1653
		Godwin's *Man in the Moon* translated
		Scarron, *Virgile travesti*

YEAR	ENGLISH	FRENCH
1649	Chas I executed Dryden, "Upon the Death of the Lord Hastings"	Corneille, *Don Sanche**
1650	Hobbes, *Human Nature*	Corneille, *Andromède* Thomas Corneille, *Le Feint Astrologue*
1651	Davenant, *Gondibert* Hobbes, *Leviathan*	Corneille, *Nicomède* ———, *Pertharite** fails, Corneille retires until 1659 Scarron, *Roman Comique, pt. 1*
1652	Hall, trans. of Longinus	Pellisson, *l'Histoire de l'Académie.* . . .
1654	Orrery, *Parthenissa, pt. 1* Otway born	de Scudéry, *Clélie*
1655		Cyrano dies Chapelain, *La Pucelle* published
1656	Davenant, *Siege of Rhodes*	Thomas Corneille, *Timocrate*
1657		d'Aubignac, *La Pratique du théâtre* Cyrano, *L'Autre Monde*
1658	Cromwell dies Browne, *Hydriotaphia* Davenant, *The Cruelty of the Spaniards in Peru*	Molière returns to Paris Molière, *l'Étourdi* ———, *Le Dépit Amoureux*
1659	Dryden, "Heroique Stanzas to the Glorious Memory of Cromwell"	Corneille, *Oedipe* Molière, *Les Précieuses Ridicules*
1660	Restoration Theatrical patents granted Killigrew and Davenant Dryden, "Astraea Redux" Pepys begins *Diary*	Corneille, *Oeuvres,* containing examens and discours ———, *La Toison D'Or* Molière, *Sganarelle ou le Cocu Imaginaire*
1661	Dryden, "To His Sacred Majesty"	Mazarin dies Fouquet's fall Molière, *Dom Garcie de Navarre* ———, *L'École des Maris* ———, *Les Fâcheux*

YEAR	ENGLISH	FRENCH
1662	Butler, *Hudibras, pt. 1* Dryden, "To My Lord Chancellor"	Corneille, *Sertorius* Molière, *L'École des femmes*
1663	Dryden, *The Wild Gallant* Philips, trans. of Corneille's *Pompey*	Corneille, *La Sophonisbe* Molière, *La Critique de l'École* ———, *L'Impromptu de Versailles*
1664	Dryden, *The Rival Ladies* Dryden & Howard, *The Indian Queen* Etherege, *The Comical Revenge* Vanbrugh born	Corneille, *Othon* Molière, *Le Mariage forcé* ———, *La Princesse d'Élide* ———, *Tartuffe* Racine, *La Thébaïde* Sorbiere, *Relation d'un voyage en Angleterre*
1665	2d Dutch War (−1667) The Great Plague of London Dryden, *The Indian Emperour* Sprat, *Observations on Mons. de Sorbier's Voyage into England*	Molière, *Dom Juan* ———, *L'Amour médecin* Racine, *Alexandre le Grand*
1666	The Great Fire of London Bunyan, *Grace Abounding*	Corneille, *Agésilas* Molière, *Le Misanthrope* ———, *Le Médecin malgré lui*
1667	Swift born Dryden, *Secret Love* Dryden & Newcastle, *Sir Martin Mar-all* Dryden & Davenant, *Tempest* Dryden, *Annus Mirabilis* Milton, *Paradise Lost* Philips, trans. of Corneille's *Horace* Sprat, *History of the Royal Society*	Corneille, *Attila* Molière, *Mélicerte* ———, *L'Amour peintre* Racine, *Andromaque*
1668	Davenant dies; Dryden becomes laureate Dryden, *Essay of Dramatick Poesy*	Molière, *Amphitryon* ———, *George Dandin* ———, *L'Avare* Racine, *Les Plaideurs*

YEAR	ENGLISH	FRENCH
	———, *An Evening's Love, or The Mock Astrologer*	
1669	Pepys finishes *Diary* Dryden, *Tyrannick Love, or the Royal Martyr*	Molière, *Monsieur de Pourceaugnac* Racine, *Britannicus*
1670	Congreve born Dryden, *Conquest of Granada*, pt. *I*	Bossuet, Funeral Oration for Henriette d'Angleterre Corneille, *Tite et Bérénice* Molière, *Les Amants magnifiques* ———, *Le Bourgeois gentilhomme* Pascal, *Pensées* Racine, *Bérénice*
1671	Cibber born Dryden, *Conquest of Granada*, pt. *II* ———, *Marriage A-la-Mode* Milton, *Paradise Regained* ———, *Samson Agonistes*	Molière, *Psyché* ———, *Les Fourberies de Scapin* ———, *La Comtesse d'Escarbagnas*
1672	3d Dutch War (–1674) Addison born Steele born Dryden, *The Assignation* Wycherley, *Love in a Wood*	Racine, *Bajazet* Corneille, *Pulchérie* Molière, *Les Femmes savantes*
1673	Dryden, *Amboyna*	Molière, *Le Malade imaginaire* Molière dies Racine, *Mithridate*
1674	Dryden, *State of Innocence* (not published until 1677) Milton dies Rowe born Rymer, *Reflections on Aristotle's Treatise,* trans. of Rapin, with preface	Boileau, trans. of Longinus ———, *Le Lutrin* ———, *L'Art poétique* Corneille, *Suréna* Racine, *Iphigénie* Rapin, *Reflexions sur la Poétique d'Aristote*
1675	Dryden, *Aureng Zebe* Wycherley, *The Country Wife*	
1676	Etherege, *Man of Mode*	
1677	Behn, *The Rover*	Racine, *Phèdre*

YEAR	ENGLISH	FRENCH
	Dryden, *All for Love*	
	Lee, *The Rival Queens*	
	Rymer, *Tragedies of the Last Age Consider'd*	
	Wycherley, *The Plain Dealer*	
1678	Popish plot	de la Fayette, *Princesse de Clèves*
	Farquhar born	
	Bunyan, *Pilgrim's Progress, pt. 1*	
	Dryden, *The Kind Keeper*	
1679	Exclusion Bill	
	Dryden & Lee, *Oedipus*	
	Dryden, *Troilus & Cressida*	
1680	Butler dies	
	Rochester dies	
	Dryden, *The Spanish Fryar*	
	Dryden, et al., *Ovid's Epistles*	
1681	Charles II dissolves Parliament	Bossuet, *Discours sur l'histoire universelle*
	Dryden, *Absalom & Achitophel*	
	Lee, *Lucius Junius Brutus*	
	Tate, *Lear*	
1682	Dryden, *The Medall*	
	———, *Religio Laici*	
	———, *Macflecknoe*	
	Dryden & Lee, *The Duke of Guise*	
	Otway, *Venice Preserv'd*	
1683	Dryden, *Life of Plutarch*	
1684	Dryden, *Miscellany Poems*	Corneille dies
	Creech, trans. of Horace and Theocritus	
1685	Charles II dies, James II king	
	Monmouth's Rebellion	
	Otway dies	
	Gay born	
	Dryden, *Albion & Albanius*	
1686	Dryden, "Killigrew Ode"	
1687	Buckingham dies	Fénelon, *L'Education des Filles*

YEAR	ENGLISH	FRENCH
	Dryden, *Hind & the Panther*	
	Newton, *Principia Mathematica*	
1688	Revolution	La Bruyère, *Caractères*
	Pope born	
	Dryden loses official posts	
1689	Behn dies	Racine, *Esther*
	William III (–1702) & Mary (–1694)	
	Dryden, *Don Sebastian*	
1690	Dryden, *Amphitryon*	
	Locke, *Essay Concerning Human Understanding*	
1691	Etherege dies	Racine, *Athalie*
	Dryden, *King Arthur*	
	Langbaine, *An Account of the English Dramatick Poets*	
1692	Shadwell dies, Tate becomes laureate	
	Dryden, *Cleomenes*	
	Lee dies	
1693	Dryden, trans. of Juvenal and Persius	
	Congreve, *The Old Batchelour*	
	Rymer, *A Short View of Tragedy*	
1694	Queen Mary dies	*Dictionnaire de l'Académie*
	Congreve, *The Double Dealer*	
	Dryden, *Love Triumphant*	
	———, "To my dear Friend Mr. Congreve"	
	———, "To Sir Godfrey Kneller"	
1695	Congreve, *Love for Love*	
	Dryden, *Parallel of Poetry and Painting*	
1696	Cibber, *Love's Last Shift*	Madame de Sévigné dies
		Regnard, *Le Joueur*
1697	Congreve, *The Mourning Bride*	Regnard, *Le Distrait*

YEAR	ENGLISH	FRENCH
	Dryden, *The Works of Virgil*	
	Vanbrugh, *The Provoked Wife*	
	———, *The Relapse*	
1698	Collier, *A Short View of the Immorality and Profaneness of the English Stage*	
1699		Racine dies
		Fénelon, *Télémaque*
1700	Dryden, *Fables*	
	Dryden dies May 1	

INTRODUCTION

1. "One inoculates the public with a contingent evil to prevent or cure an essential one." *Mythologies,* trans. Annette Lavers (New York: Hill and Wang, 1972), p. 42.

2. Even the Abbé d'Aubignac, sometimes a harsh critic of Corneille's, held that Corneille was the greatest playwright since antiquity.

3. Corneille very infrequently mentions a few later critics such as Scaliger, Castelvetro, and Heinsius, and he cites five modern plays, usually to illustrate a particular form or genre that did not exist in antiquity.

4. Translations, unless otherwise noted, are mine. Substantial French passages will be placed in the notes. "On convient du nom sans convenir de la chose, et on s'accorde sur les paroles, pour contester sur leur signification . . . . Il faut que le poète traite son sujet selon le vraisemblable et le nécessaire; Aristote le dit, et tous ses interprètes répètent les mêmes mots, qui leur semblent si clairs et si intelligibles, qu'aucun d'eux n'a daigné nous dire, non plus que lui, ce que c'est que ce vraisemblance et ce nécessaire." Pierre Corneille, *Oeuvres complètes,* ed. Georges Couton, 3 vols. (Tours: Gallimard, 1980–87).

5. "Je ne puis m'empêcher de dire que cette définition ne me satisfait point."

6. "Ces termes sont si généraux, qu'ils semblent ne signifier rien."

7. "Ce sont des termes qu'il a si peu expliqués, qu'il nous laisse grand lieu de douter de ce qu'il veut dire."

8. "S'il m'est permis de dire mes conjectures sur ce qu'Aristote nous demande par là. . . ."

9. "Pour m'enhardir à changer ce terme, afin de lever la difficulté. . . ."

10. "Il répète souvent ces derniers mots, et ne les explique jamais. Je tâcherai d'y suppléer au moins mal qu'il me sera possible." The English translation of the *Discours de la Tragédie* is from the anonymously translated *Discourse on Tragedy and of the Methods of Treating it, According to Probability and Necessity,* [1660], reprinted in *Dramatic Essays of the Neoclassic Age,* ed. H. H. Adams & B. Hathaway (New York: Blom, 1965), p. 23.

11. *Monsieur Rapin's Reflections on Aristotle's Treatise of Poesie in General,* trans. Thomas Rymer, *The Whole Critical Works of Monsieur Rapin,* 2 vols. (London: 1706), 2:157. "Le vray-semblable est tout ce qui est conforme à l'opinion du public." René Rapin, *Réflexions sur la Poétique de ce Temps. . . .* [1674], ed. E. T. Dubois (Geneva: Droz, 1970), p. 39.

12. "[Le vraisemblable a] . . . la seule intention d'ôter aux regardants toutes les occasions de faire réflexion sur ce qu'ils voient et de douter de sa réalité." Antoine Adam, *L'Age Classique I: 1624–1660* (Paris: Arthaud, 1968), p. 224.

13. "Il n'y a donc que le *Vraisemblable* qui puisse raisonnablement fonder, soûtenir & terminer un Poëme Dramatique." Hédelin d'Aubignac, *La Pratique du théâtre,* 3 vols. [Amsterdam, 1715] (Geneva: Slatkine Reprint, 1971), I:67. Unless otherwise noted, translations of *La Pratique* are from *The Whole Art of the Stage,* trans. anonymous, [London, 1684], 2 vols. (New York: Benjamin Blom, 1968).

14. "Les grands sujets qui remuent fortement les passions, et en opposent l'impétuousité aux lois du devoir, ou aux tendresses du sang, doivent toujours aller au-delà du vraisemblable."

15. "Le sujet d'une belle tragédie doit n'être pas vraisemblable."

16. "But what has happened is manifestly possible: otherwise it would not have happened." Aristotle, *Poetics,* trans. S. H. Butcher (Edinburgh: MacMillan, 1927), p. 37.

17. "L'action étant vraie [historical], . . . il ne faut plus s'informer si elle est vraisemblable, étant certain que toutes les vérités sont recevables dans la poésie" (*Au Lecteur, Heraclius, Oeuvres,* 2:357).

18. "Le poète n'est pas obligé de traiter les choses comme elles se sont passées, mais comme elles ont pu, ou dû se passer, selon le vraisemblable, ou le nécessaire" (*Oeuvres,* 3:161).

19. These are usually topics about which Aristotle could have had no knowledge, such as the "humeur" of the French people, French mores and customs, and later formal developments such as tragicomedy.

20. "Ce dernier passage montre que nous ne sommes point obligés de nous écarter de la vérité, pour donner une meilleure forme aux actions de la tragédie par les ornements de la vraisemblance" (*Oeuvres,* 3:162).

21. "Si j'étais de ceux qui tiennent que la poésie a pour but de profiter aussi bien que de plaire . . . mais pour moi qui tiens avec Aristote et Horace que notre art n'a pour but que le divertissement."

22. "Une belle idée, qui n'ait jamais son effet dans la vérité" (*Oeuvres,* 3:146).

23. *Oeuvres,* 3:142–48. Corneille expands this notion of catharsis to include admiration, as well as fear, in the examen to *Nicomède.* "L'amour

qu'elle [l'admiration] nous donne pour cette vertu que nous admirons, nous imprime de la haine pour le vice contraire" (*Oeuvres*, 2:643). ("The love that [admiration] gives us for this virtue which we admire, instills us with hate for the contrary vice.")

CHAPTER ONE

1. Walter Jackson Bate ably identifies the problem, if not its true extent, in *The Burden of the Past and the English Poet* (London: Chatto & Windus, 1971). Bate identifies Dryden as the first English poet to suffer from this "burden," and he further admits the blanket importation of French neoclassicism. Yet Bate explores none of the consequences of this neoclassicism's Frenchness, the fact that it had to be imported, or the "burden" that the French writers themselves became for the English.

2. Below is a brief summary of the relative concordance of dramatic events in the two countries: Corneille's *Horace* appeared in 1640, two years before the closing of the theaters. His *Cinna*, Dryden's favorite of Corneille's plays, and, third of that great series, *Polyeucte*, appeared in 1642, the year the English theaters were closed and the same year Richelieu died; Dryden was eleven. During the interregnum of eighteen years, Corneille staged fourteen plays. Molière's *Les Précieuses Ridicules*, inspiration for so many Restoration and eighteenth-century dramas, appeared the year before the Restoration. Corneille's great edition containing his plays and the greatest body of French dramatic criticism of its age, the examens and *Trois Discours*, appeared in the same year as Charles II's return to England. For an extended chronology of the theatrical activities in France and England, see the appendix.

3. In the *Essay of Dramatick Poesy* Dryden deprecates *Polyeucte*, declaring that the play "in matters of Religion is as solemn as the long stops upon our Organs" (*Works*, 17:48). Unless otherwise stated, all quotations from Dryden's works are from the California edition, *The Works of John Dryden*, ed. Edward N. Hooker, H. T. Swedenberg, et al., 20 vols. (Berkeley: University of California Press, 1956–) and follow the pattern just given.

4. See *Works*, 13:501, 504, where the case is made that Dryden's new conclusion to *Troilus and Cressida* is influenced by Racine's *Iphigénie* (1674) and *Phèdre* (1677).

5. Ben Jonson wrote short prefaces to some of his plays, but they show little formal or tonal similarity to Dryden's (see prefaces to *Sejanus* and *Catiline*).

6. Even the form of the *Essay of Dramatick Poesy*, sometimes described

as the imitation of a Platonic or Ciceronian dialogue, does not require its origin sought so far afield. Dryden was familiar with the work of Molière, and though he could not have known the *Impromptu de Versailles,* as Watson suggests he did (Watson, 1:76), he might well have known Molière's *Critique de l'École des Femmes* (1663), a work in which Molière's previous play, *L'École des Femmes* (1662), is discussed in the round by a range of characters, each of whom brings a different critical perspective to the discussion. The defender of Molière's play, like Neander, the defender of Dryden's type of plays, is given the best arguments. I have used George Watson's *Of Dramatic Poesy and Other Critical Essays* (2 vols. [London: Dent, 1962]) for whatever of Dryden's criticism has not yet appeared in *Works*—as well as for Watson's valuable commentary on the criticism itself. Citation follows the form given above.

7. Johnson, in the *Life of Dryden,* accuses Dryden of introducing into the language unnecessary French words that, he wrongly claims, "continue only where they stood first, perpetual warnings to future innovators" (*Johnson's Lives of the Poets,* ed. J. P. Hardy, [Oxford: Oxford University Press, 1971], p. 197). Sir Walter Scott begins his chapter on Dryden's career as a dramatist by observing: "The rage for imitating the French stage, joined to the successful efforts of our author, had now carried the heroic or rhyming tragedy to its highest pitch of popularity" (*Life of Dryden* [1834], [Lincoln: University of Nebraska Press, 1963], p. 101). T. S. Eliot's *John Dryden* contains a brief but characteristically pithy discussion of Dryden's relation to the French (*John Dryden* [New York: Holliday, 1932], p. 39). Book-length studies of French influence on Restoration literary life run the gamut from the crude generalizations of Louis Charlanne's *L'Influence Française en Angleterre au XVIIe Siècle* (Paris: 1906), to Ned Bliss Allen's useful study, *The Sources of John Dryden's Comedies* (Ann Arbor: University of Michigan Press, 1935), and the superlative commentary of *Works,* now almost complete. Modern articles examine Dryden's adoption of French practice from the level of borrowed vocabulary (see Harold Brooks's "Dryden's *Aureng-Zebe:* Debts to Corneille and Racine," *RLC* 46 (1972):5–34) through his borrowing from French dramatists for his own drama, up to and including Dryden's adoption of critical practice and principle, including Dean Mace's brilliant, but in my view unsuccessful, attempt to recast the *Essay of Dramatick Poesy* as a promulgation of Cartesian psychological principles, with Lisideius as the Dryden-speaker ("Dryden's Dialogue on Drama," *JWCI* 25 [1962]:87–112).

8. George Villiers, Duke of Buckingham, et al., *The Rehearsal* [1671], *Burlesque Plays of the Eighteenth Century,* ed. Simon Trussler (London: Oxford University Press, 1969), p. 9.

9. *The Wild Gallant* (1663), Dryden's first play, and his sole effort in imitation of the Jonsonian comedy of humours, did not succeed.

10. Dryden writes in the *Defence of the Epilogue* to the *Conquest of Granada, pt. II:* "In the Age, wherein those Poets liv'd, there was less of gallantry than in ours; neither did they keep the best company of theirs. . . . I cannot find that any of them were conversant in Courts . . . greatness was not, then, so easy of access, nor conversation so free as now it is" (*Works,* 11:215–16).

11. I believe that "refined," "easy," "polished," "free" are all adjectives that denote French-type social mores; but flowing as they do through the court circles, they are easily assimilated into both the social and literary mainstream, with none of the stigma of the more obvious Gallic imports. The new, imported social (and dramatic) values are here contrasted with a set of qualities Dryden often uses to describe the last age of poetry: "*dull* and *heavy* spirits," "*stiff* forms of conversation" [emphasis added].

12. Dryden later falls back from this position as he arrogates poetic authority to himself and denies it to the court of William III. In 1692 he writes of St. Evremond: "Conversing in a manner wholly with the Court, which is not always the truest Judge, he has been unavoidably led into Mistakes, and given to some of our Coursest Poets a Reputation abroad, which they never had at home" ("A Character of St. Evremond," *Works,* 20:11).

13. See A. Nicoll, *A History of the English Drama,* 6 vols. (Cambridge: Cambridge University Press, 1952), 1:8–11 and 1:19–21, for a brief discussion of Charles II's relation to the theater; see also Colley Cibber's account in the *Apology,* chapter 4, and Robert Hume's *The Development of English Drama in the Late Seventeenth Century* (Oxford: Oxford University Press, 1976), pp. 27–28.

14. Kierkegaard said "he who is willing to work gives birth to his own father"; quoted in Harold Bloom, *Anxiety of Influence* (New York: Oxford University Press, 1973), p. 26.

15. Judith Sloman observes that Dryden's frequent comparisons of his forebears (Virgil/Ovid, Shakespeare/Jonson, Homer/Virgil) are also a means to keep from being swamped in the forebears' wake. Of the function of these comparisons Sloman writes: "The technique of comparison reveals inevitable limits in each of the figures being compared . . . and protects Dryden from the status of timid ephebe" (*Dryden: The Poetics of Translation* [Toronto: University of Toronto Press, 1985], p. 11).

16.   But if thy Præexisting Soul
                  Was form'd, at first, with Myriads more,
            It did through all the Mighty Poets roul,

> Who *Greek* or *Latine* Laurels wore,
> And was that *Sappho* last, which once it was before.
> (*Works*, 3:110)

17. *The Poems of John Dryden*, ed. James Kinsley, 4 vols. (Oxford: Oxford University Press, 1958). I have used *Poems* where *Works* remains incomplete; citations follow the form given in the text.

18. On *MacFlecknoe*'s play with notions of literary inheritance see pp. 48–49 of Earl Miner's "The Poetics of the Critical Act: Dryden's Dealings with Rivals and Predecessors," *Evidence in Literary Scholarship: Essays in Memory of James Marshall Osborn*, ed. René Wellek and Alvaro Ribeiro (Oxford: Oxford University Press, 1979), pp. 45–62.

19. "Virgil . . . has been my Master in this Poem: I have followed him every where, I know not with what success, but I am sure with diligence enough: my Images are many of them copied from him, and the rest are imitations of him" (preface to *Annus Mirabilis*, *Works* 1:55).

20. Dryden's interest in adopting his predecessors as useful fathers did not go unnoticed at the time, but it took the keen eye and sharp pen of Swift to make such an observation as the following, from *The Battle of the Books:* "[Dryden, on encountering Virgil] . . . soothed up the good *Antient*, called him *Father*, and by a large deduction of Genealogies, made it plainly appear, that they were nearly related. Then he humbly proposed an Exchange of Armor, as a lasting Mark of Hospitality between them. *Virgil* consented . . . tho' his was of Gold, and cost a hundred Beeves, the others but of rusty Iron. However, this glittering Armor became the *Modern* yet worse than his Own. Then, they agreed to exchange Horses; but when it came to the Trial, *Dryden* was afraid, and utterly unable to mount" (*A Tale of a Tub, to which is added The Battle of the Books. . . .*, ed. A. C. Guthkelch and D. Nichol Smith [Oxford: Oxford University Press, 1958], p. 247).

21. Only during the brief time of Dryden at his most Francophiliac— a time that coincided, not surprisingly, with a spate of hyper-Gallism at court—does he admit that he follows Corneille at all. See *Defence of an Essay* and the preface and prologue to *Secret Love* (both published in 1668), where Dryden admits Corneille into the ranks of his heroes, only to eject him a few months later.

22. Steven Zwicker speaks of Dryden's "false claims of historical accuracy" (p. 38) as he shows Dryden's relation to the demands of the politics of his time. Zwicker's analyses of Dryden's rhetorical strategies stand on their own as a brilliant and tough-minded approach to this material. See especially chapter 2 of *Politics and Language in Dryden's Poetry: The Arts of Disguise* (Princeton: Princeton University Press, 1984).

23. Johnson writes: "What he wishes to say he says at hazard; he cited *Gorboduc*, which he had never seen, gives a false account of Chapman's

versification, and discovers in the preface to his *Fables* that he translated the first book of the *Iliad* without knowing what was in the second" (Johnson's *Life,* 163).

24. Zwicker, *Politics and Language in Dryden's Poetry: The Arts of Disguise,* p. 26. Zwicker makes a powerful case for this type of skeptical reading, most strongly in the second chapter, which is devoted to an analysis of Dryden's rhetorical strategies of concealment.

25. ". . . our old Comedies before *Shakespeare,* which were all writ in verse of six feet, or *Alexandrin's,* such as the *French* now use" (*Essay, Works,* 17:54).

26. "To Roger, Earl of Orrery," prefixed to *The Rival Ladies* (1664), *Works,* 8:99.

27. "But of late years *Moliere,* the younger *Corneille, Quinault,* and some others, have been imitating afar off the quick turns and graces of the *English* Stage" (*Essay, Works,* 17:45).

28. Modern critics have claimed that the many errors in the *Essay of Dramatick Poesy* are due to Dryden's faulty memory, and they offer the bounty of error as proof that Dryden did not have a library by him. However, he certainly had the complete Corneille edition of 1660 (that contains *Le Cid*) by him, as he quotes verbatim from the edition (both with acknowledgment and without); having *Le Cid* on his desk did not prevent Dryden's misrepresenting, or misquoting, its content. Whether Dryden had a library by him, this instance demonstrates his lack of interest in getting things right. Of Dryden's manner of citation, Johnson writes: "His literature, though not always free from ostentation, will be commonly found either obvious, and made his own by the art of dressing it, or superficial, which by what he gives shows what he wanted, or erroneous, hastily collected, and negligently scattered" (Johnson's *Life,* 164).

29. *The Grounds of Criticism in Tragedy, Works,* 13:234. Watson observes that "the action of this comedy is spread over some three days" (Watson, 1:247).

30. Dedication of the *Æneis* (1697), *Works,* 5:331. See Watson's note, 2:247.

31. *The Author's Apology for Heroic Poetry and Poetic Licence,* prefixed to *The State of Innocence* [1677], (Watson, 1:198). Aristotle settles the dispute in chapter 26 of the *Poetics,* p. 111.

32. "*Sophocles,* says *Aristotle,* always drew men as they ought to be, that is, better than they were; another, whose name I have forgotten, drew them worse than naturally they were. *Euripides* alter'd nothing in the Character, but made them such as they were represented by History, Epique Poetry or Tradition. Of the three, the draught of *Sophocles* is most commended by *Aristotle*" (*A Parallel betwixt Painting and Poetry,*

Works, 20:70). Aristotle's actual comment on the subject reads: "Sophocles said that he drew men as they ought to be; Euripides, as they are" (*Poetics,* 101).

33. *Mélite,* Corneille's first play, was performed about 1629; Dryden was born in 1631.

34. Occasionally Dryden permits us to see the degree to which he compared himself with Corneille. In the dedicatory epistle to *The Indian Emperour,* he writes: " 'Tis an irregular piece if compar'd with many of *Corneilles,* and, if I may make a judgement of it, written with more Flame than Art" (*Works,* 9:25).

35. Speaking of Dryden's relations with his contemporaries (though not specifically the French), Earl Miner says "the writers that create a poet's alarms and arouse the liveliest limbic activity are those in one's own age rather than one's dead predecessors or as yet unborn successors" ("The Poetics of the Critical Act," p. 50).

36. Court notables such as Buckingham and Sedley translated Corneille for performances at court. See Dorothea Canfield's *Corneille and Racine in England* (New York: Columbia University Press, 1904), which shows in detail Corneille's enormous popularity at the court of Charles II. Arthur Kirsch reports that translations of Corneille were generally popular: "During the first decade of the Restoration, Pepys saw performances of the *Cid, Heraclius, Horace,* and *Pompey.*" *Dryden's Heroic Drama* (New York: Gordian Press, 1972), pp. 46–47. On seeing a performance of *Horace,* Pepys opines: "A silly Tragedy; but Lacy hath made a farce of several dances, between each act, one. But his words are but silly, and invention not extraordinary as to the dances; only some Dutchmen come out of the mouth and tail of a Hamburgh sow" (Samuel Pepys, *The Diary of Samuel Pepys,* ed. Robert Latham and William Matthews, 11 vols. [Berkeley: University of California Press, 1970–83], 9:420, 19 January 1669).

37. For a time Dryden did drift nearer to the French critical view. For critics in the provinces (outside Paris), 1674 was an annus mirabilis; it saw the publication of Boileau's *Art Poétique,* his translation of Longinus, and Rapin's *Reflexions* on Aristotle, translated almost immediately by Rymer. Dryden could not but be struck by the force of this nouvelle vague of French neoclassicism; so, after sketching out the lines of what would have been a magnificent rebuttal to Rymer and Rapin ("Heads of an Answer. . . ."), he swerved closer to the French neoclassical party than ever before.

38. "The young nobleman, very often early in his career, when aged 17, 18, 19, mounts an attack on some prominent politician. Tacitus . . . writes of the actual glory of making enemies or prosecuting feuds: 'Ipsa

inimicatarum gloria' " (Ronald Syme, "Caesar: Drama, Legend, History," *New York Review of Books*, 28 February 1985).

39. As Steven Zwicker puts it, "Dryden felt no contradiction between vendetta and literary theory" (*Politics*, p. 51).

40. This is a much more forthright reading of the *Essay* than his statement in the dedication "To the Right Honourable Charles, Lord Buckhurst," in which he claims to recount differing points of view without taking any decided position: " 'Tis true they differ'd in their opinions, as 'tis probable they would: neither do I take upon me to reconcile, but to relate them . . . without Passion or Interest" (*Works*, 17:6). At the time Dryden wrote that (1668), he had moved as close as he ever came to adopting a pro-French position, hence the disingenuous equivocation. Soon he was once more standing with Neander against the French.

41. The only other writer referred to by all four interlocutors is Caius Velleius Paterculus.

Dryden borrowed numerous critical terms from Corneille, ranging from the "examen" itself down to such minutiae as "protatic persons," almost the sole use of the term in English, according to Watson (Watson, 1:50), and certainly borrowed from Corneille; the term was rare in French as well. For a fine, if circumscribed, discussion of the extent of Dryden's borrowings from Corneille, see John M. Aden's "Dryden, Corneille, and the *Essay of Dramatick Poesy*," *RES* 6 (1955):147–56, and the commentary in *Works*. For a useful item of scholarly detective work concerning Dryden's use of the Corneille 1660 edition, see L. E. Padgett, "Dryden's Edition of Corneille," *MLN* 71 (1956).

42. Dryden often locates the action of his plays on a special day: "Heav'n seems the Empire of the East to lay / On the success of this important day" (*Aureng-Zebe* [1675], *John Dryden: Four Tragedies*, ed. L. A. Beaurline and Fredson Bowers [Chicago: University of Chicago Press, 1967], act 1, scene 1, p. 114).

"Then this is the deciding day, to fix / Great Britain's sceptre in great Arthur's hand" (*King Arthur* [1691], Scott, 8:125). I have cited those plays from the second edition of Sir Walter Scott's *The Works of John Dryden*, 18 vols. (Edinburgh, 1821) that are not available in other modern editions and that remain unpublished in *Works*; citation follows the form just given.

> *Maximin.* I will this day my Cæsar him create:
> And, Daughter, I will give him you for Wife.
> *Valerius.* O day, the best and happiest of my life!
> *Placidus.* O day, the most accurst I ever knew!
> (*Tyrannick Love, Works*, 10:126–27)

At length the time is come, when *Spain* shall be
From the long Yoke of *Moorish* Tyrants free.
   (*Conquest of Granada, pt. II, Works,* 11:105)

The concept still had enough life in it by 1731 to merit Fielding's parody in *Tragedy of Tragedies:*

Doodle. Sure, such a Day[1] as this was never seen!
   The Sun himself, on this auspicious Day,
   Shines, like a Beau in a new Birth-Day Suit:
   This down the Seams embroider'd, that the Beams.
   All Nature wears one universal Grin.
Noodle. This Day, O Mr. *Doodle,* is a Day
   Indeed, a Day we never saw before.

1. *Corneille* recommends some very remarkable Day, wherein to fix the Action of a Tragedy. This the best of our Tragical Writers have understood to mean a Day remarkable for the Serenity of the Sky, or what we generally call a fine Summer's Day: So that according to this their Exposition, the same Months are proper for Tragedy, which are proper for Pastoral. Most of our celebrated *English* Tragedies, as *Cato, Mariamne, Tamerlane,* &c. begin with their Observations on the Morning. [Fielding's note]

Tom Thumb and The Tragedy of Tragedies, ed. L. J. Morrissey (Berkeley: University of California Press, 1970), pp. 49–50.

Moreover, any seventeenth-century critic would have realized that Dryden's reference to a "memorable day" indicated his intent to observe the unity of time, a function similar to the references to the rising sun that begin so many plays of the period.

43. I rejoice to concur both with the common critic and with tradition in identifying Dryden's views with those of Neander. The uncommon critic, Dean Mace, so far as I know sole dissenter from this tradition, sees more of Dryden in Lisideius. Mace's ingenious reading is not borne out by the *Essay*'s pronounced tilt toward the English, and while investigating the influence of Cartesian psychology on Dryden's critical thought, Mace does not take into account that Dryden was a practicing playwright (as was Neander) and as such was intensely *interested* in Neander's position; Dryden's professional involvement prohibited him from acting the part of the even-handed critic making dispassionate pronouncements from the sidelines of the dramatic *agon.*

44. ". . . this incorrect Essay, written in the Country without the help of Books" ("To the Reader," *Works,* 17:7).

45. For a fuller discussion of specific borrowings, see Padgett's "Dryden's Edition of Corneille."

46. Perhaps this is not strictly true: in the examen to *Andromède* Corneille observes that the situation of the action makes the day on which the play occurs: "illustre, remarquable, et attendu" (*Oeuvres,* 2:449); however, he does not enumerate the relative virtues of such a day.

47. "C'est un grand ornement pour un poème que le choix d'un jour illustre, et attendu depuis quelque temps. Il ne s'en présente pas toujours des occasions, et dans tout ce que j'ai fait jusqu'ici vous n'en trouverez de cette nature que quatre."

48. For that matter, the examen is the sole extended examination of a play not by Dryden (with the exception of the intemperate *Notes and Observations on The Empress of Morocco*) in all of Dryden's criticism. On this he followed Corneille, all of whose critical studies only led back to his own body of dramatic work.

49. Pellisson-Fontanier, in his *Relation contenant L'Histoire de L'Academie Francoise. . . .* (Paris, 1672), says of the examen's function within the Académie: "One of the means the academicians would employ in order to achieve perfection would be the examen, as well as the correction of their own works. They would examine the subject [of the works] with severity, and the manner of treating it, the arguments, the style, the metrics, and each word in particular."

"Qu'un des moyens dont les Academiciens se serviroient pour parvenir à la perfection, seroit l'examen, & la correction de leurs propres ouvrages. Qu'on en examineroit severement le sujet, & la manière de le traiter, les argumens, le style, le nombre, & chaque mot en particulier" (*Histoire.,* 26–27).

50. D'Aubignac's examen of *Ajax* is found in *La Pratique du théâtre,* I:327–40.

51. For a judicious and brief examination of Corneille's place in the *Essay,* see Frank L. Huntley's *On Dryden's Essay of Dramatic Poesy* (Ann Arbor: University of Michigan Press, 1951), pp. 31–33.

52. The longest (*Andromède, Le Cid*) are about three thousand words; the shortest are about eight hundred. The average length is approximately one thousand to fifteen hundred words.

53. The source was Don Juan de Alarcón's *La Verdad Sospechosa* (erroneously published under the name Lope de Vega in 1630).

54. Robert Hume, *Dryden's Criticism* (Ithaca: Cornell University Press, 1970), p. 1.

55. Ben Jonson, *Works,* ed. C. H. Herford and Percy Simpson, 11 vols. (Oxford: Oxford University Press, 1925–52), 2:71.

56. In correcting Neander's error, *Works* errs itself. Neander states that after the first act the action occurs all in one house. *Works* states that "after the second act, not the first, the scene continues to be Morose's house" (17:381–82).

57. Chimène's betrothal to her father's killer is only the most infamous of Corneille's justifications-by-history of the improbable.

58. Although the final formulation sounds quite similar to Aristotle's observation that "what has happened is manifestly possible: otherwise it would not have happened" (*Poetics,* 37), Corneille's argument (and Dryden's) has a different tendency than Aristotle's: the two moderns seek a theoretically respectable way to introduce improbable elements into the drama. Hence the use of history (Jonson knew such a man; Chimène married her father's killer) to justify the representation of what would otherwise be incredible.

59. *Works,* 17:59. Dryden himself came to "say" this. See the preface to *Evening's Love:* "*Parcere personis dicere de vitiis* [to spare individuals and speak of vices] is the rule of Plays" (*Works,* 10:204–5).

60. "Variety," in Dryden's critical writings, is often used simply as a synonym for pleasure, one more instance of Dryden's loading of terms with an apparently natural or innate meaning whose true import is much more controversial.

61. This is the second instance in the *Essay* where Dryden uses old foreign words to denominate new English characters and phenomena. The first is, of course, Neander himself, the "new man" identified by an ancient word. In the tension between the antiquity of the signifier and the absolute novelty of the signified we glimpse a lexical reinscription, apparent in the partial translation, of the pressures that inform Dryden's problematical relations to his forebears.

62. I owe this reading to a remark made by Margaret Anne Doody.

63. Although English poets were vitally interested in French dramatic activity, there are few exceptions to the near-total French ignorance of English drama in the seventeenth century: the English theater was described deprecatingly by Samuel Sorbière in his *Relation d'un Voyage en Angleterre* (1664); this was replied to by Thomas Sprat in *Observations on Mons. de Sorbier's Voyage into England* (1665), some of whose arguments are appropriated by Dryden and used in *Essay of Dramatick Poesy* (see George Williamson's "The Occasion of *An Essay of Dramatic Poesy,*" in *Essential Articles for the Study of John Dryden,* ed. H. T. Swedenberg, Jr., [Hamden: Archon, 1966], pp. 65–82, and the commentary in *Works,* 17:343–46).

Regarding the general French ignorance of English literary culture:

records exist of only two volumes of Shakespeare's plays in France during the entire seventeenth century; one in the royal library, the other in the library of Superintendent Fouquet. The card referring to the 1632 folio of Shakespeare in the king's library contained the following explanation of the volume's contents: "This English poet has a fine imagination, he thinks naturally, he expresses himself with finesse; but these good qualities are obscured by the filth he mixes into his comedies." ("Ce poète anglois a l'imagination assés belle, il pense naturellement, il s'exprime avec finesse; mais ces belles qualitez sont obscurcies par les ordures qu'il mêle dans ses Comédies.") Such, J. J. Jusserand observes, is the oldest comment on Shakespeare in French (*Shakespeare en France sous l'Ancien Régime,* [Paris: Colin, 1898], pp. 137–38). Rapin in 1674 speaks tantalizingly of the English genius for tragedy, but specifies no names of authors or plays: "The *English* have more of *Genius* for *Tragedy* than other People, as well by the Spirit of their Nation which delights in Cruelty, as also by the Character of their Language which is proper for great Expressions" (*The Whole Critical Works of Monsieur Rapin,* trans. Thomas Rymer, 2 vols. [London, 1706], 2:217–18). "Les Anglois ont plus de génie pour la tragédie que les autres peuples, tant par l'esprit de leur nation que se plaist aux choses atroces que par le caractère de leur langue, qui est propre aux grandes expressions" (Rapin, 112). No English play was translated into French until Addison's *Cato* (1713). The vogue for Shakespeare in France did not begin until Voltaire's description of his dramas in the *Lettres Philosophiques* (1734), in which he is referred to as "Shakespeare, qui passait pour le Corneille des Anglais" (*Lettres Philosophiques,* ed. René Pomeau, [Paris: Flammarion, 1964], 18th letter, p. 120).

64. This comparatist approach to *All for Love* is not always inimical, as one might expect, to Dryden's play. In 1691 Gerard Langbaine charged, not with utter disapprobation, "that our Author has nearly imitated *Shakespear* is evident" (*An Account of the English Dramatick Poets* [Oxford, 1691], p. 153). In George Granville's prologue to a 1701 revival of *The Merchant of Venice,* Shakespeare's ghost is made to speak approvingly to Dryden's: "Whose stupid Souls thy Passion cannot move, / Are deaf indeed to Nature and to Love. / When thy Aegyptian weeps what Eyes are dry! / Or who can live to see thy Roman dye" (Prologue to *The Jew of Venice* [1701]; quoted in *Works,* 13:364). Sir Walter Scott opined that "perhaps, the most proper introduction to *All for Love,* may be a parallel betwixt it and Shakespeare's *Antony and Cleopatra* (Introduction, Scott, 5:287). Gosse thought the play "not merely an avowed imitation in the style of Shakespeare— it is almost an adaptation of *Antony and Cleopatra*" (*A History of Eighteenth Century Literature* [London: MacMillan, 1922], p. 45). David Nichol Smith

called *All for Love* not an imitation, but a "transmutation" (*John Dryden* [Cambridge: Cambridge University Press, 1950], p. 42). Eugene Waith finds *All for Love* "the best of Dryden's adaptations of Shakespeare," also noting that "the character of Antony is not much altered" ("Dryden and the Tradition of Serious Drama," *John Dryden*, ed. Earl Miner [Athens: Ohio University Press, 1975], p. 82). Maximilian Novak attempts "to determine what principles Dryden saw in Shakespeare which constituted a style he felt worthy of imitation" (Commentary to *All for Love*, *Works*, 13:368). James Winn concludes that at moments Dryden achieves the promised "Imitation of *Shakespeare*'s Stile" (*John Dryden and His World* [New Haven: Yale University Press, 1987], p. 299).

65. Quoted in Montague Summers, *The Restoration Theatre* [1934] (New York: Humanities Press, 1964), p. 307.

66. F. R. Leavis, "*Antony and Cleopatra* and *All for Love:* A Critical Exercise," *Scrutiny*, 5.2 (1936), p. 165.

67. Norman Suckling, "Dryden in Egypt: Reflections on *All for Love*," *Twentieth Century Interpretations of All for Love*, ed. Bruce King (New Jersey: Prentice Hall, 1968), p. 50.

68. Northrop Frye, *Anatomy of Criticism* [1957] (Princeton: Princeton University Press, 1971), p. 5.

69. See Maximilian Novak's brief account of these attempts (*Works*, 13:368–71) and his examination of what style in Shakespeare Dryden might have found worthy of imitation.

70. *The Letters of John Dryden*, ed. Charles E. Ward (Durham: Duke University Press, 1942), p. 33.

71. See Earl Miner's *Dryden's Poetry* (Bloomington: Indiana University Press, 1967), pp. 36–73, for a discussion of the essentially private quality of Dryden's treatment of the story of Antony and Cleopatra.

72. T. S. Eliot, *John Dryden* [1932] (New York: Haskell House, 1968), pp. 34–37.

73. George Saintsbury, Introduction, *Plays of John Dryden*, 2 vols. (London: Mermaid [no date]), 1:12.

74. Anonymous, *The Censure of the Rota* [1673] (New York: Garland, 1974), p. 19.

75. Anonymous, *The Tory-Poets: A Satyr* [1682], *Dryden: The Critical Heritage*, ed. James Kinsley and Helen Kinsley (New York: Barnes and Noble, 1971), p. 155.

76. Matthew Prior, "A Satyr on the Modern Translators" [1685], *The Literary Works of Matthew Prior*, ed. H. Bunker Wright and Monroe K. Spears, 2 vols. (Oxford: Oxford University Press, 1959), 1:21.

77. Martin Clifford, *Notes upon Mr. Dryden's Poems in Four Letters* [1687], *Dryden: The Critical Heritage,* p. 175.

78. "*Shakespear* . . . was the first, who to shun the pains of continual Rhyming, invented that kind of Writing, which we call Blanck Verse" ("To Roger, Earl of Orrery," prefixed to *The Rival Ladies* [1664], *Works,* 8:99).

79. Dryden, attempting to counter critics' objections to "empty arms" in the lines "At night, I will within your Curtains peep; / With empty arms embrace you while you sleep" (*Tyrannick Love, Works,* 10:146), quotes Ovid thus "vacuis amplectitur ulnis" (Preface to *Tyrannick Love, Works,* 10:113). Whereas Ovid makes no mention of emptiness, writing instead: "geminis amplectitur ulnis" (Ovid, *Metamorphoses: Books 6–10,* ed. William S. Anderson (Norman: University of Oklahoma Press, 1972), bk. 8, l. 818, p. 103).

80. In the *Author's Apology for Heroic Poetry and Poetic License* (prefixed to *The State of Innocence: an Opera* [1677]), Dryden writes: "Heroic poetry, which they [critics] contemn, has ever been esteemed, and ever will be, the greatest work of human nature: in that rank has Aristotle placed it" (Watson, 1:198).

81. The first performance of *All for Love* was ca. 12 December 1677; *Phèdre* premiered 1 January 1677 and was published the same year. Dryden would almost certainly have been able to see it in print prior to or during the composition of *All for Love.*

82. Here the reader might cite against me my own citation of Dryden's remarks against Shakespeare's poetic style. To this I would answer that there is every evidence that Dryden meant what he said about Shakespeare's style, as he does not imitate it, and every evidence that he did not mean what he said in writing about the French, as he constantly imitates them.

83. William Frost's "*Aureng-Zebe* in Context: Dryden, Shakespeare, Milton, and Racine" (*JEGP* 54 [1975]:26–49) sketches out parallels of plot between *Aureng-Zebe* and *Mithridate* and suggests the general importance of Dryden's unacknowledged connection to Racine.

84. Jean Racine, *Britannicus,* trans. C. H. Sisson (Oxford: Oxford University Press, 1987), p. 37.

Si vous daigniez, Seigneur, rappeler la mémoire

Des vertus d'Octavie, indignes de ce prix,

Et de son chaste amour vainqueur de vos mépris;

Surtout si de Junie évitant la présence,

Vous condamniez vos yeux à quelques jours d'absence:

Croyez-moi, quelque amour qui semble vous charmer,
On n'aime point, Seigneur, si l'on ne veut aimer.
Jean Racine, *Britannicus, Théâtre et Poésies,* ed. Raymond Picard (Tours: Gallimard, 1950), act 3, scene 1, p. 419.

85. Others have made this observation. See Dorothy Burrows's dissertation, "The Relation of Dryden's Serious Plays and Dramatic Criticism to Contemporary French Literature" (Urbana: University of Illinois, 1933), pp. 254–58, for a fine discussion of the parallels between the two plays; see also *Works,* 13:380. Robert W. McHenry's "Betrayal and Love in *All for Love* and *Bérénice*" (*SEL* 31 [1991]:445–61) argues that *All for Love*'s most salient debt to Racine's *Bérénice* is the play's treatment of the theme of betrayal.

86. By means of printing passages from both plays that show a pattern of loose imitation, Dorothy Burrows makes a strong case for some of the language of *All for Love* being borrowed from, or at least inspired by, the language of *Bérénice.* See Burrows, pp. 255–58.

87. "Il n'y a que le vraisemblable qui touche dans la tragédie. Et quelle vraisemblance y a-t-il qu'il arrive en un jour une multitude de choses qui pourraient à peine arriver en plusieurs semaines? Il y en a qui pensent que cette simplicité est une marque de peu d'invention. Ils ne songent pas qu'au contraire *toute l'invention consiste à faire quelque chose de rien*" [emphasis added].

88. *Arcas.* Il l'attend à l'autel pour la sacrifier.
Achille. Lui!
Clytemnestre. Sa fille!
Iphigénie.　　　　Mon père!
Eriphile.　　　　　　　　O ciel! quelle nouvelle!

　　　　　　　　　　　　　　(*Théâtre,* 705)

Arcas. He waits at the altar to sacrifice her.
Achille. Him!
Clytemnestre. His daughter!
Iphigénie.　　　　My father!
Eriphile.　　　　　　　　Oh heaven! What news!

89. See Leavis, pp. 158–69.

90. See Kenneth Muir's "The Imagery of *All for Love,*" *Twentieth Century Interpretations of All for Love,* ed. Bruce King, pp. 32–42, for a discussion of the degree to which Dryden borrowed images from Shakespeare. Muir, apparently of the school that considers Dryden beholden to Shakespeare for much that is good in *All for Love,* often sees evidence of borrowing where I do not.

CHAPTER TWO

1. "The vices and virtues of Augustan poetry are the vices and virtues of buccaneering millionaires" writes Margaret Anne Doody in *The Daring Muse* (Cambridge: Cambridge University Press, 1985), p. 18. She observes that the "Augustan Age" coincides with England's "first great age of imperialism" (p. 15).

2. Earl Miner says of Dryden's vision: "English imperialism of the next two centuries has been envisioned and its ideals provided" ("Forms and Motives of Narrative Poetry," *John Dryden,* ed. Earl Miner [Athens: Ohio University Press, 1975], p. 245). Steven Zwicker reads this vision much as he reads the rest of the poem: as a secularizing of biblical typology. See *Dryden's Political Poetry* (Providence: Brown University Press, 1972), pp. 78–83.

3. I include *Marriage A-la-Mode* in this list because one of the several types of battles described therein is the battle between the English and French languages and dramatic forms, waged in the person of Melantha, who is accorded a comically rueful victory in "Sicilian" society.

4. *The Enchanted Isle* was written in collaboration with Davenant; *All for Love,* as I argue in chapter 1, purports to imitate Shakespeare's style, but does not.

5. Horace, Ovid, Petronius, Tacitus, Pliny the Younger, Statius, and Terence are each cited once. Virgil is cited ten times.

6. Steven Zwicker argues that Dryden associates himself with Virgil "because Virgil is the poet of accurate representation"; that is, by this choice Dryden strengthens his claim to historicity. In my view our readings are complementary. See *Politics and Language in Dryden's Poetry,* pp. 40–41.

7. "John Dryden [acted out], in his position as poet laureate and historiographer royal, the roles of Augustus' great propagandists, Virgil and Horace. If Pope could say that Virgil's *Aeneid* was as much a 'party piece' as Dryden's *Absalom and Achitophel,* it was because he was accurately gauging the way both poets responded to the will of their masters" (Maximillian Novak, "Shaping the Augustan Myth: John Dryden and the Politics of Restoration Augustanism," *Greene Centennial Studies: Essays Presented to Donald Greene in the Centennial Year of the University of Southern California,* ed. Paul J. Korshin and Robert R. Allen [Charlottesville: University Press of Virginia, 1984], p. 9).

8. The image of cannons breaking over water seems to have preoccupied Dryden at this time; the *Essay of Dramatick Poesy* and *Annus Mirabilis* both begin with battles, the one for the realm of poetry, the other,

for the realm of trade. It is interesting that even in the New World, the conquerors should announce themselves with an image reminiscent of battles being fought closer to home, for commodities of greater immediate relevance: trade and poetic form.

9. A rare exception to this is the portrayal of the Dutch in *Amboyna* (1673), written during the Third Dutch War, which had begun in 1672. Dryden claims, and the play bears him out, that the play was hurriedly written as propaganda. The Dutch are depicted as freebooting proto-capitalists, devoid of all sentiment but avarice, with the exception of the young Haman, who expresses his desires for Ysabinda by raping her, thus triggering the catastrophe of the play. Written in the heat of war (and in the heat of a few weeks, according to Dryden), it is not one of Dryden's greater plays—although the creation of homo economicus in a state of nature is a feat of imagination worthy of our admiration and study.

10. Anne Barbeau Gardiner, in her thoughtful and quirky book *The Intellectual Design of John Dryden's Heroic Plays* (New Haven: Yale University Press, 1970), argues that the Indians brought the disaster of the Conquest on themselves by their political disunity. The racking scene, she insists, "should not be overemphasized." See pp. 81–83.

11. But for the Indian priest's later plea to reveal the treasure's location, we might read Montezuma's speech solely as a cunning transposition of native wealth in which what the priest will never have is the "gold" of Montezuma's subjectivity.

12. These terms resemble those Dryden uses in his pre-1688 criticism to describe himself, his works, and what is best in English poetry.

13. I owe this observation, and some of my thinking on the representation of foreign cultures, to Edward Said's *Orientalism* (New York: Vintage, 1979).

14. An interesting aside is that the racking scene proved especially engaging to one of the play's most distinguished eighteenth-century readers, Voltaire, who in a notebook translated (and embellished) Montezuma's skeptical speech from this scene, and besides discussing the scene in *Essai sur les moeurs* (in which the torture scene is passed off as authentic history), he used the scene (though of course narrated) in *Alzire* (1736), a play written along the same lines as *The Indian Emperour*. See T. W. Russell's *Voltaire, Dryden, & Heroic Tragedy* (New York: Columbia University Press, 1946), pp. 66–85. Voltaire's free translation of Montezuma's speech (p. 73) begins: "cessez de nous vanter vos faibles avantages, nous avons comme vous nos martirs et nos sages" ("cease bragging to us of your feeble advantages; like you we have our martyrs and sages"). Russell proves that Dryden was Voltaire's favorite English dramatist; at the age

of seventy Voltaire quoted Dryden copiously, years after having read any of his works and in the *Siècle de Louis XIV* (quoted in Russell, p. 81) had this to say of him: "aucun poëte de sa nation n'égale, et qu'aucun ancien n'a surpassé" ("no poet of his nation equals him, and no ancient poet surpassed him").

15. See N. B. Allen's *The Sources of John Dryden's Comedies* (New York: Gordian Press, 1967), pp. 156–70, as well as Allen's much more sympathetic treatment in "The Sources of Dryden's *Mock Astrologer,*" *PQ* 36 (1957):453–64; and *Works,* 10:434–43. Allen's earlier discussion of *An Evening's Love,* though competent, is marred by the belief that the play isn't very good, a belief that further study seems to have altered.

16. Langbaine has this to say of *An Evening's Love: "Evening's Love,* or *The Mock Astrologer,* a Comedy acted at the Theatre-Royal by His Majesties Servants, printed in quarto *Lond.* 1671. and dedicated to his Grace *William* Duke of *Newcastle.* This Play is in a manner wholly stollen from the *French,* being patcht up from *Corneille's Le Feint Astrologue; Molliere's Depit amoureux,* and his *Les Precieuses Ridicules;* and *Quinault's L'Amant Indiscret:* not to mention little Hints borrow'd from *Shakespear, Petronius Arbiter* &c. The main Plot of this Play is built on that of *Corneille's,* or rather *Calderon's* Play call'd *El Astrologo fingido"* (163).

17. Pierre Corneille writes: "I would grant very freely that whatever we make happen in a single city could have the unity of place. It's not that I would want the theater to represent this whole city—that would be a bit too vast—but only two or three particular places shut in by its walls' enclosure" ("J'accorderais très volontiers que ce qu'on ferait passer en une seule ville aurait l'unité de lieu. Ce n'est pas que je voulusse que le théâtre représentât cette ville toute entière, cela serait en peu trop vaste, mais seulement deux ou trois lieux particuliers, enfermés dans l'enclos de ses murailles") (*Discours des Trois Unités, Oeuvres,* 3:188).

18. Dryden also adapted *Sir Martin Mar-all* (1667) and *Amphitryon* (1690) from Molière's *l'Étourdi* (1658) and *Amphitryon* (1668), his *Oedipus* (1679) from Corneille's (1659), and the serious plot of *Marriage A-la-Mode* (1671) from George and Madeleine de Scudéry's *Le Grand Cyrus* (1649–53).

19. See chapter 1 for a discussion of Dryden's misquotation of Corneille's desideratum.

20. A time used before in Thomas Porter's *The Carnival* (1664) and later in Aphra Behn's *Rover* (1677).

21. In the *Defence of the Epilogue* Dryden ascribes the refinement of the entire age "to the Court: and, in it, particularly to the King; whose example gives a law to it" (*Works,* 11:216).

22. Dryden lifts and translates whole speeches and scenes from Molière, Quinault, and Thomas Corneille, and inserts them verbatim and near-verbatim into *An Evening's Love.* See *Works,* 10:437–41 for some parallel passages showing nearly verbatim translations from French to English. For an attempt to demonstrate that Dryden borrowed from the Spanish, see Angel Capellan's "John Dryden's Indebtedness to Pedro Calderón de la Barca in *An Evening's Love or The Mock Astrologer,*" *RLC* 49 (1975):572–89.

23. Ralph Cohen feels Dryden's modes of reception of anterior poets might form the basis for a more sophisticated view of poetic inheritance: "Dryden's view of imitations of models implied a concept of intertextuality as more than a mere verbal enterprise, and it may prove more valuable to us than our own purely linguistic view of intertextuality" (Phillip Harth, Alan Fisher, and Ralph Cohen, *New Homage to John Dryden* [Los Angeles: Clark Memorial Library, 1983], p. 85).

24. Dryden says he himself read *Romeo and Juliet* in Cinthio's Italian. As George Watson points out, the *Hecatommithi* was indeed a source for *Othello,* but not for *Romeo and Juliet.* See Watson, 1:154.

25. Although the *Oxford English Dictionary* credits Dryden with the first English use of "spirituel" in *Marriage A-la-Mode* (1671), the speech that follows in the text dates from three years earlier. The earliest use the *OED* gives of "spiritual" (spelled with an *a*) to mean "clever, smart, witty" occurs in 1791.

26. I would translate the French:

Magdelon. Quick, come and set us up the counsellor of the graces.

Marotte. By my faith, I don't know what stupidity that is; you have to speak christian if you want me to understand you.

Cathos. Bring us the mirror, know-nothing that you are. And take care not to dirty it by the communication of your image.

Molière, *Oeuvres Complètes,* ed. Georges Couton, 2 vols. (Bruges: Gallimard, 1971).

27. Perhaps it contains some points of contact with the kind of imported French Dryden so often said he despised and so often used himself. See the *Defence of the Epilogue, Works,* 11:211, for Dryden's assault upon a vocabulary he elsewhere favors.

28. Leslie Howard Martin makes a clear case for the nonlinguistic ("ubiquitary") elements of Melantha's character deriving, at least in part, from a character named Berisa in Madeleine de Scudéry's *Grand Cyrus.* See "The Source and Originality of Dryden's Melantha," *PQ* 552 (1973):746–53.

29. Here is what Melantha will give for a good word:

Melantha. [practicing her "postures for the day"] How does that laugh become my face?

Philotis. Sovereignly well, Madam.

Melantha. Sovereignly! Let me die, that's not amiss. That word shall not be yours; I'll invent it, and bring it up my self: my new Point Gorget shall be yours upon't: not a word of the word, I charge you.

Philotis. I am dumb, Madam.

Melantha. That glance, how sutes it with my face?

[*Looking in the Glass again.*

Philotis. 'Tis so *languissant.*

Melantha. Languissant! that word shall be mine too, and my last *Indian-*Gown thine for't.

That sigh? [*Looks again.*

Philotis. 'Twill make many a man sigh, Madam. 'Tis a meer *Incendiary.*

Melantha. Take my Guimp Petticoat for that truth. If thou hast more of these phrases, let me die but I could give away all my Wardrobe, and go naked for 'em.

(*Works,* 11:264–65)

For a fine discussion of Melantha's "decadence of language," see J. Douglas Canfield's *Word as Bond in English Literature from the Middle Ages to the Restoration* (Philadelphia: University of Pennsylvania Press, 1989), pp. 74–76.

30. To examine the phenomenon of self-plundering would be to develop the notion of poetic imperialism in quite another direction, but that Dryden did take from himself as well as from others has long been observed. Below is an attestation by Dryden's contemporary, Martin Clifford, from his *Notes upon Mr. Dryden's Poems in Four Letters* (1687): "You are therefore a strange unconscionable Thief, that art not content to steal from others, but do'st rob thy poor wretched Self too" (*Dryden: The Critical Heritage,* p. 178).

31. Allen substantiates Langbaine's charge that the serious plot is from the story of "Sesostris and Timareta," of *Tome* 6, Livre 2, of *Le Grand Cyrus.* See *Sources,* p. 112.

32. An example of bad, or unacceptable, borrowing that hinges on an in-joke is Dryden's hidden complaint about being borrowed from himself. Doralice refers to her creator: "A friend of mine, who makes Songs sometimes, came lately out of the West, and vow'd he was so put out of count'nance with a Song of his; for at the first Countrey-Gentleman's he visited, he saw three Tailors cross-leg'd upon the Table in the Hall, who were tearing out as loud as ever they could sing, —*After the pangs of a desperate Lover, &c.* and all that day he heard nothing else, but the

Daughters of the house and the Maids, humming it over in every corner, and the Father whistling it" (*Works,* 11:262). The friend, of course, is Dryden himself; the song, which was a hit in the provinces, is from *An Evening's Love.*

33. See E. A. Horsman's fine discussion of Dryden's innovations of French (and Horsman's correction of the following remark of Johnson's) in "Dryden's French Borrowings," *RES* 1 (1950):346–51.

34. Horsman lists some of Dryden's French borrowings that have become standard English: a propos, balette, dupe, embarrass, mal a propos, brunette, coquette, incontestable, billets doux, double entendre, eclaircissement, mal a droitly, minouet, foible, naiveté, panchant, ridicule, spirituelle, tendre, nom de guerre, fatigue, carte blanche, console. And, as Horsman observes, "these are a tiny minority of the total number of French words he uses." See "Borrowings," pp. 346–47.

35. Dryden himself came to refer to the English language in these terms; after 1688 he frequently refers to the English language as "barbarous."

CHAPTER THREE

1. See Michael McKeon's *Politics and Poetry in Restoration England: The Case of Dryden's Annus Mirabilis* (Cambridge: Harvard University Press, 1975) for a sophisticated treatment of the connections between poetry and ideology; Steven Zwicker's *Politics and Language in Dryden's Poetry: The Arts of Disguise* (Princeton: Princeton University Press, 1984) and Alan Roper's *Dryden's Poetic Kingdoms* (New York: Barnes and Noble, 1965) are indispensable studies of the subtle and often misleading ways in which Dryden's poetry can speak of contemporary figures, the events in which those figures participate, and the causes behind these events.

2. Judith Sloman, *Dryden: The Poetics of Translation* (Toronto: University of Toronto Press, 1985); Cederic Reverand, *Dryden's Final Poetic Mode* (Philadelphia: University of Pennsylvania Press, 1988); David Bywaters, *Dryden in Revolutionary England* (Berkeley: University of California Press, 1991); and James Winn, *John Dryden and His World* (New Haven: Yale University Press, 1987).

3. See Jean Hagstrum's fine chapter, "John Dryden: Sensual, Heroic, and 'Pathetic' Love," in *Sex and Sensibility from Milton to Mozart* (Chicago: University of Chicago Press, 1980), pp. 50–71. I regret that James Anderson Winn's *"When Beauty Fires the Blood": Love and the Arts in the Age of Dryden* (Ann Arbor: University of Michigan Press, 1992) came to

my hands too late to do anything but mention it as a work that appears to have made a permanent contribution to the discussion.

4. Sandra M. Gilbert and Susan Gubar, *The Madwoman in the Attic: The Woman Writer and the Nineteenth-Century Imagination* (New Haven: Yale University Press, 1979), p. 1.

5. Samuel Butler, "Satyr Upon Plagiaries," *Satires and Miscellaneous Poetry and Prose,* ed. René Lamar (Cambridge: Cambridge University Press, 1928), p. 64.

6. "Timon," *The Complete Poems of John Wilmot, Earl of Rochester,* ed. David Vieth (New Haven: Yale University Press, 1968), p. 66.

7. Aphra Behn, Epilogue to *Sir Patient Fancy, The Works of Aphra Behn* [1915], ed. Montague Summers, 6 vols. (New York: Phaeton Press, 1967), 4:116.

8. Anne Carson, *Eros the Bittersweet: An Essay* (Princeton: Princeton University Press, 1986), p. 30.

9. In *Using Biography* (Cambridge: Harvard University Press, 1984), William Empson proposes an ingenious explanation for Dryden's simultaneous concealments and revelations, based on the couplet's formal characteristics: "The heroic couplet is perhaps a narrow instrument, but his [Dryden's] mastery of it is so great that it betrays feelings he had meant to conceal—or else, its merit is that even while expressing one part of his mind forcibly it expresses contrasted feelings which he is only pretending to conceal" (p. 111).

10. Several have noticed this parallel. Judith Sloman notes: "To some extent Cleomenes seems to represent Dryden's own idealized self" (45). See her generally fine discussions of the late plays, pp. 37–46; see also Winn, 452.

11. See my discussion of *The Indian Emperour* in chapter 2.

12. Transsexuality seems to have been on Dryden's mind at this time. He refers to both Tiresias and Ceneus (another transsexual) as he considers the marriage of an unidentified friend. He writes to John Dennis: "Jupiter and Juno, as the Poets tell us, made Tiresias their Umpire, in a certain Merry Dispute, which fell out in Heav'n betwixt them. Tiresias you know had been of both sexes, and therefore was a Proper Judge. . . . Virgil says of Ceneus, Nunc Vir nunc Faemina Ceneus / Rursus & in veteram fato revoluta figuram" (*Letters,* 74). John D. Tatter's dissertation, "The Androgynous Spirit in the Heroic Plays and Tragedies of John Dryden" (Athens: Ohio University, 1984), examines androgynous qualities in the heroes and heroines of Dryden's drama.

13. As for the Poet of this present night,

Though now he claims in you an Husband's right,
He will not hinder you of fresh delight.
He, like a Seaman, seldom will appear;
And means to trouble home but thrice a year:
That only time from your Gallants he'll borrow;
Be kind to day, and Cuckold him to morrow.
(Prologue to *An Evening's Love, Works,* 10:215).

14. Earl Miner, "The Poetics of the Critical Act: Dryden's Dealings with Rivals and Predecessors," *Evidence in Literary Scholarship: Essays in Memory of James Marshall Osborn,* ed. René Wellek and Alvaro Ribeiro (Oxford: Oxford University Press, 1979), p. 55.

15. The allusion to Virgil was pointed out to me by my colleague (and editor of Virgil) Brian Wilkie.

16. Terry Castle's "Lab'ring Bards: Birth *Topoi* and English Poetics: 1660–1820" (*JEGP* 1979, 193–208) charges Dryden with being the first of the "neoclassical" poets to turn against traditional organicist notions of "giving birth" to poetry; she cites *MacFlecknoe* as proof of an antiorganic bias that persisted throughout the eighteenth century (197–98). Her essay raises important questions relating to eighteenth-century poetics; it does not, however, consider Dryden's late, specifically intertextual notion of organicist poetics, in which the poet explicitly feminizes his poetic persona and unites with a male poet of the past to conceive and bear a poetic birth parented by both living and dead poets.

17. J. Douglas Canfield,"*Regulus* and *Cleomenes* and 1688: From Royalism to Self-Reliance," *ECL* 1988 (3): 67–75, p. 74.

18. The preface to *An Evening's Love* (*Works,* 10:208) contains Dryden's discussion of the apportionment of reward and punishment in comedies.

19. Dryden claims to have gone to some trouble to make his poetic booty "his." He describes the inadequacy of simple conquest and the subsequent degree of reworking in the epilogue to *An Evening's Love,* reporting his own speech in the third person: "But should he all the pains and charges count / Of taking 'em [French plays], the bill so high wou'd mount, / That, like Prize goods, which through the Office come, / He could have had 'em much more cheap at home" (*Works,* 10:314).

APPENDIX

1. The appendix is compiled from chronologies appearing in the following works: Antoine Adam, *L'Age Classique I: 1624–1660* (Paris: B. Arthaud, 1968), pp. 342–55; Anonymous, *Annals of English Litera-*

ture (Oxford: Clarendon Press, 1936); Richard Brome, *A Jovial Crew,* ed. Ann Haaker (Lincoln: University of Nebraska Press, 1968), pp. 134–44; Pierre Corneille, *Oeuvres complètes,* ed. Georges Couton, 3 vols. (Gallimard: Tours, 1980–87), 1:il–lxxiii; *John Dryden,* ed. Earl Miner (Athens: Ohio University Press, 1975), pp. xiii–xxvi; Molière, *Oeuvres complètes,* ed. Georges Couton, 2 vols. (Gallimard: Bruges, 1971), 1:xxxix–lix; Jean Racine, *Oeuvres complètes,* ed. Raymond Picard, 2 vols. (Gallimard: Tours, 1950), 1:xvii–xx.

cot of imperialism,
pp. 75 ff.

RES   700 wds   Nov. 1994